PUBLIC ETHICS AND GOVERNANCE: STANDARDS AND PRACTICES IN COMPARATIVE PERSPECTIVE

RESEARCH IN PUBLIC POLICY ANALYSIS AND MANAGEMENT

Series Editor: Lawrence R. Jones

Volumes 1–9:	Research in Public Policy Analysis and Management
Volume 10:	Public Management: Institutional Renewal for the Twenty-First Century – By Lawrence R. Jones and Fred Thompson
Volumes 11A & 11B:	Learning from International Public Management Reform – Edited by Lawrence R. Jones, James Guthrie and Peter Steane
Volume 12:	The Transformative Power of Dialogue – Nancy C. Roberts
Volume 13:	Strategies for Public Management Reform – Edited by Lawrence R. Jones, Kuno Schedler and Riccardo Mussari

RESEARCH IN PUBLIC POLICY ANALYSIS AND MANAGEMENT
VOLUME 14

PUBLIC ETHICS AND GOVERNANCE: STANDARDS AND PRACTICES IN COMPARATIVE PERSPECTIVE

EDITED BY

DENIS SAINT-MARTIN

Université de Montréal, Montréal, Canada

and

FRED THOMPSON

Willamette University, Salem, OR, USA

ELSEVIER
JAI

Amsterdam – Boston – Heidelberg – London – New York – Oxford
Paris – San Diego – San Francisco – Singapore – Sydney – Tokyo

JAI Press is an imprint of Elsevier

JAI Press is an imprint of Elsevier
The Boulevard, Langford Lane, Kidlington, Oxford OX5 1GB, UK
Radarweg 29, PO Box 211, 1000 AE Amsterdam, The Netherlands
525 B Street, Suite 1900, San Diego, CA 92101-4495, USA

First edition 2006

Copyright © 2006 Elsevier Ltd. All rights reserved

No part of this publication may be reproduced, stored in a retrieval system
or transmitted in any form or by any means electronic, mechanical, photocopying,
recording or otherwise without the prior written permission of the publisher

Permissions may be sought directly from Elsevier's Science & Technology Rights
Department in Oxford, UK: phone (+44) (0) 1865 843830; fax (+44) (0) 1865 853333;
email: permissions@elsevier.com. Alternatively you can submit your request online by
visiting the Elsevier web site at http://elsevier.com/locate/permissions, and selecting
Obtaining permission to use Elsevier material

Notice
No responsibility is assumed by the publisher for any injury and/or damage to persons
or property as a matter of products liability, negligence or otherwise, or from any use
or operation of any methods, products, instructions or ideas contained in the material
herein. Because of rapid advances in the medical sciences, in particular, independent
verification of diagnoses and drug dosages should be made

British Library Cataloguing in Publication Data
A catalogue record for this book is available from the British Library

ISBN-13: 978-0-7623-1226-9
ISBN-10: 0-7623-1226-2
ISSN: 0732-1317 (Series)

For information on all JAI Press publications
visit our website at books.elsevier.com

Printed and bound in the Netherlands

06 07 08 09 10 10 9 8 7 6 5 4 3 2 1

Working together to grow
libraries in developing countries

www.elsevier.com | www.bookaid.org | www.sabre.org

ELSEVIER   BOOK AID International   Sabre Foundation

Library
University of Texas
at San Antonio

CONTENTS

LIST OF CONTRIBUTORS   *vii*

INTRODUCTION
   Fred Thompson   *1*

PATH DEPENDENCE AND SELF-REINFORCING PROCESSES IN THE REGULATION OF ETHICS IN POLITICS: TOWARD A FRAMEWORK FOR COMPARATIVE ANALYSIS
   Denis Saint-Martin   *5*

THE ETHICS ERUPTION: SOURCES AND CATALYSTS
   Robert Williams   *29*

CODES OF CONDUCT FOR PUBLIC OFFICIALS IN EUROPE: COMMON LABEL, DIVERGENT PURPOSES
   David Hine   *43*

POLITICAL ETHICS AND RESPONSIBLE GOVERNMENT
   Andrew Potter   *71*

COMPARING SYSTEMS OF ETHICS REGULATION
   Oonagh Gay   *93*

CANADA'S UPSIDE-DOWN WORLD OF PUBLIC-SECTOR ETHICS
   Andrew Stark   *109*

THE COSTS AND BENEFITS OF ETHICS LAWS
B. A. Rosenson   *135*

THE EFFECTS OF LEGISLATIVE ETHICS LAW: AN INSTITUTIONAL PERSPECTIVE
Alan Rosenthal   *155*

MANAGERIAL LEADERSHIP AND THE ETHICAL IMPORTANCE OF LEGACY
J. Patrick Dobel   *179*

PROFESSIONAL ETHICS FOR POLITICIANS?
John Uhr   *207*

ETHICAL POLITICAL CONDUCT AND FIDELITY TO THE DEMOCRATIC ETHOS
Colin M. Macleod   *227*

GOVERNING PLURALISM
Andrew Sabl   *243*

ETHICAL REASONING, EPISTEMOLOGY, AND ADMINISTRATIVE INQUIRY
James W. Myers and Fred Thompson   *257*

SUBJECT INDEX   *283*

LIST OF CONTRIBUTORS

J. Patrick Dobel	University of Washington, WA, USA
Oonagh Gay	House of Commons Library, London, UK
David Hine	University of Oxford, Oxford, UK
Colin M. Macleod	University of Victoria, BC, Canada
James W. Myers	Chemeketa Community College, OR, USA
Andrew Potter	Centre de Recherche en Éthique, Université de Montréal, Montréal, QC, Canada
B. A. Rosenson	University of Florida, FL, USA
Alan Rosenthal	Rutgers University, NJ, USA
Andrew Sabl	University of California, Los Angeles, CA, USA
Denis Saint-Martin	Université de Montréal, Montréal, QC, Canada
Andrew Stark	University of Toronto, Toronto, Canada
Fred Thompson	Willamette University, OR, USA
John Uhr	Australian National University, Canberra, Australia
Robert Williams	University of Durham, Durham, UK

INTRODUCTION

Fred Thompson

One of the strengths of this symposium is its focus. All of the articles in this volume concentrate on economically developed nations, with stable polities, traditions of popular government, legal systems grounded in common law, and relatively low levels of corruption. Moreover, they all deal with countries that to a greater or lesser degree have embraced the so-called New Public Management, which implies a degree of skepticism about the governance arrangements grounded in bureaucratic norms derived from the *Rechtsstaat* tradition. Finally, and perhaps most importantly, they all deal with countries, which, as Denis Saint-Martin explains in his introductory essay, are increasingly distressed about the ethics of public officials despite a paucity of lapses on their part. This makes the case comparisons reported in the symposium especially telling: there is enough variance to be informative, not enough to overdetermine the findings. Consequently, what holds for one case may reasonably be presumed to apply to all.

Denis Saint-Martin, Fulbright Scholar at Harvard and an Associate Professor at Université de Montréal, where he is a professor of political science, asks why concerns over the erosion of public trust has led to the elaboration of formal standards and independent regulatory agencies to enforce them in some of these countries and not in others. He concludes that path dependence explains most of the variance. However, he hints that ethics regulation aimed at preventing the standard conflict-of-interest problems that arise wherever the public sector is large, contracting, purchasing, outsourcing, and public–private partnerships are extensive, government regulation of business has major economic and commercial impacts, individuals move across the private/public sector boundary with relative ease, and parties need funding from private sources, even if effective, would not restore public confidence in politics. The articles that follow, which look regulatory mechanisms, tend to confirm Saint-Martin's surmise.

Robert Williams, professor of politics, University of Durham, explores the political aspects of public ethics as well as the macro or global sources of ethics discontent in an attempt to understand the heightened level of concern about political ethics in recent decades. He seeks to identify the sources of this heightened concern. He attributes much of the problem to the conflict between partisanship, on the one hand, and expectations of decency and civility, on the other.

Oxford's David Hine examines codes of conduct for public officials in five West European countries: the UK, France, Germany, Italy, and Spain. He concludes that introducing common codes across such widely differing administrative cultures, particularly if all they would do is codify values that are widely shared in practice, makes very little sense. Andrew Potter concludes much the same for conflict of interest regulation in Canada.

Oonagh Gay, Andrew Stark, and Beth A. Rosenson focus on formal ethics regulation and its efficacy. All three are skeptics; Gay and Stark conclude, however, that the parliamentary ethics regimes might be well advised to emulate the American model. Rosenson puts paid to that notion, effectively arguing that the costs of American ethics regulation outweigh its benefits – too many butterflies are caught in its net and no elephants.

Alan Rosenthal of the Eagleton Institute of Politics, Rutgers University, is especially skeptical of the effects of ethics laws enacted by state legislatures. There is no evidence that they reduce corruption. They haven't restored public confidence, but have discouraged legislator recruitment and retention. The most that can be said on their behalf is that they placate the media and place mutual limits on partisan attack, thereby permitting the legislature to concentrate on useful work. Even there the evidence is mixed.

The remaining articles look beyond regulatory mechanisms look to the problem of promoting behaviors and building institutions that are worthy of trust. J. Patrick Dobel implicitly accepts the dominant academic approach to applied ethics. This approach combines virtue ethics, with its emphasis on character formation, and moral reasoning, with its emphasis on individual decisions. When these approaches are brought together, what emerges is a view of ethical governance and leadership as good individuals trying to make good ethical judgments. This view leads to an emphasis on training, standards and procedures, and, ultimately, regulation. However, Dobel proposes a reformulation of what it means to make good ethical judgments to stress constructing sustainable legacies.

In contrast, the next two participants in this symposium, John Uhr and Colin M. Macleod, emphasize that governance is a social process, which implies that, in this context, applied ethical reasoning should comprehend the objective of establishing and sustaining ongoing relationships between individuals with diverse values, tastes, and needs. Uhr argues that ethical governance means attending to the relational aftermath of complex decisions – the ways in which decisions and their execution affect and sustain social relationships. Macleod argues that governance is concerned with mechanism and process, which implies that the applied ethical reasoning in this context must not only confront certain stock issues: desirability, practicality, workability, freedom from greater evils, and best-available alternative, but must also lead to widespread participation in decision-making processes. Viewed in this way, ethical governing means a respectful discourse involving the participation of all legitimate viewpoints. Absent a renewed commitment to this democratic ethos, he concludes that politics will remain a spectator sport, dominated by "sleazeball tactics and shrinking soundbites."

Andrew Sabl of UCLA's Department of Public Policy discusses the ethical consequences of the diffusion of political power and authority from state to nonstate actors. He claims that with the increased power of civil society or NGOs come more stringent political responsibilities. The sources of these responsibilities resemble those of classic political duties – ordinary moral obligations, Weber's ethic of responsibility, and responsibilities attaching to democratic relationships – but their form differs across roles, tracking the different forms of politician–citizen relationships. NGO politicians should adopt, and be held to, a stringent role ethic as the least bad substitute for the accountability mechanisms of classic state-based politics.

Finally, James W. Myers and I explore the notion that practical reasoning is a social process, and its corollary, that policy argumentation ought to be firmly grounded in an appropriate social epistemology. What we find is a fundamental, unresolved tension at the heart of all theories of social inquiry. While this approach still seems far more useful for understanding and advancing a collectivity's capacity to create value by doing things cooperatively than traditional moral reasoning, with its emphasis on individual decisions, it, too, is ultimately inconclusive.

ACKNOWLEDGEMENTS

This book is the product of a fruitful collaboration between American, Australian, Canadian and European scholars that began in Montreal in 2004 at the workshop on 'Governance and Political Ethics'.

We would like to thank everybody who participated in the workshop. Special thanks are due to the Honourable Stéphane Dion, Minister of the Environment in the Canadian government and to Dennis F. Thompson, Harvard University, for their role as discussants. Their stimulating comments helped to improve the quality of the contributions.

Denis Saint-Martin acknowledges support from the Fulbright Foundation for Educational Exchange, and from the Canada Research Chair in Citizenship and Governance (Jane Jenson chairholder) and the Canada Research Chair in Ethics and Political Philosophy (Daniel Weinstock chairholder).

PATH DEPENDENCE AND SELF-REINFORCING PROCESSES IN THE REGULATION OF ETHICS IN POLITICS: TOWARD A FRAMEWORK FOR COMPARATIVE ANALYSIS

Denis Saint-Martin

ABSTRACT

Concerns over the erosion of public trust have led British and Canadian parliamentarians to introduce some form of independent element in their arrangements for regulating political ethics, while legislators in the U.S. are refusing to make similar changes even if they also face severe problems of declining confidence in politics. To explain these differences, this chapter shows how ethics regulation processes are self-reinforcing over time, leading to more rules enforced through self-regulation mechanisms or to path-shifting changes where legislatures, hoping to break the ethics inflationary cycle, opt for a more depoliticized form of ethics regulation.

In most countries, the constitution assigns the legislature the responsibility for disciplining its own members. Rules of conduct for members of parliament or the U.S. Congress are generally enforced through a system of self-regulation. Yet, countries like Canada and Britain have recently adopted measures allowing, for the first time, the involvement of outsiders in their system of ethics regulation, making it less internal and more external. The move toward a more external form of ethics regulation is designed to enhance public trust and confidence in the procedures that parliament uses to discipline its members. It is intended to depoliticize the process of ethics regulation. The goal is to mitigate the perception that MPs face an inherent and inescapable conflict of interest when they sit in judgment of fellow MPs. Yet, even if the maxim that no one should be the judge in his own cause has great moral power and seems difficult to oppose, both the U.S. Congress and the Australian Parliament are still sticking to their traditional system of self-regulation and refusing to follow Britain and Canada in creating a more independent or more depoliticized form of ethics regulation. How can we explain these differences? This is the key question I seek to answer in this chapter. The goal is to explore the fruitfulness of historical-institutionalist approaches, and of path dependence in particular, to address why in some countries concerns over the erosion of public trust led legislatures to introduce some form of independent element in their arrangements for regulating political ethics, while legislators in other countries are refusing to make similar changes even if they also face severe problems of declining confidence in politics.

The chapter is divided into four sections. The first is a brief overview of the different models that exist for regulating political ethics. The second is about theory. It introduces an approach that stresses the interplay between formal institutions and policy feedback, pointing out how policies function as institutions, imposing on actors' norms and rules, and conveying, through their design, subtle messages to citizens (Ingram & Schneider, 1993), which subsequently reshape politics itself. In the third section I discuss the notion of path dependence and suggest how it can be recast in a less deterministic way so that it can explain both institutional continuity and change. The last section presents a framework that could be used in future research for explaining variation in how legislatures discipline their members.

VARIETIES OF ETHICS REGULATION REGIMES

Most systems of ethics regulation fall along a spectrum that has pure self-regulation at one end and wholly external regulation at the other, with some form of co-regulation in the middle. But as Dennis Thompson (1995) argues, any process of self-regulation – which has traditionally been the norm for all legislatures – raises suspicion. It creates what he calls an institutional conflict of interest. As he writes, "Members judging members raises reasonable doubts about the independence, fairness, and accountability of the process" (Thompson, 1995, p. 131). In seeking to address these reasonable doubts, a growing number of national and subnational jurisdictions have been moving, in the past few years, toward systems that includes some external form of ethics regulation (Carney, 1998). This is because, as one British politician argues, traditional systems of self-regulation are now discredited. They can no longer command public confidence (Committee on Standards in Public Life, 2002, p. 8).

Three diverging approaches to institutionalizing codes of conduct are apparent in comparable democracies. One approach involves enshrining ethics rules in some sort of legislative framework through, for example, establishing by legislation a body that is external to, and independent from, the legislature. Such a body administers the rules, oversees the conduct of the members of the legislature, and reports to the legislature. This is the model in place in the Canadian provinces and in the federal Parliament with the recent adoption of Bill C-4. The Standards in Public Office Commission in Ireland is also based on this model.

The second approach is to establish within the legislature a body that oversees the conduct of members. This may take the form of a parliamentary committee working in collaboration with an independent parliamentary commissioner, established under standing orders or a resolution of the house. This is the co-regulation approach (which involves a certain element of independence in the presence of the parliamentary commissioner for standards) that Britain has adopted following the 1995 Nolan recommendations.

The third option is that followed in the U.S. Congress and in the Australian Parliament. In this approach, discipline is internal to the legislature and based upon a detailed set of rules and guidelines as in the U.S., or traditions and standing orders as in Australia. Each chamber has its own ethics committee (or Members' Interests Committee, as this is called in Australia), and each committee provides interpretative and advisory rulings and can investigate allegations of improper conduct and impose sanctions.

If "self-regulation appears to have little credibility with the public," as one comparative study on legislative ethics concluded (Brien, 1998, p. 16), and if the trend toward what Mackenzie (2002, p. 5) calls always "more ethics" is driven by the erosion of public confidence in politics, one would expect that countries facing a problem of decline in public trust would have all converged toward systems of ethics regulation that includes at least some form of external or independent involvement. But this is not the case. There is no indication that the standards of conduct that the American or Australian public expects of politicians has risen less significantly than in Canada or Britain. Yet, in the two former countries, politicians are still sticking to their traditional system of self-regulation and have resisted for years attempts at introducing any form of outside involvement in the regulation of legislative ethics.

In much the same way, the widely held belief that ethics reform is a scandal-driven process has difficulties accounting for the differences between, for instance, Britain and the U.S. In the British case, the cash for questions scandal in the early 1990s (Ridley & Doig, 1995) led to Parliament accepting, albeit belatedly, the need for an independent element in the investigative part of the ethics regulation process. But although there also were numerous ethics wars and scandals taking place in the U.S. Congress during the Gingrich era in the 1990s (Tolchin & Tolchin, 2001), this did not lead to the same outcome as in Britain. Why? I argue in the next section that formal institutions and policy feedback from previous political choices are most important.

HISTORICAL INSTITUTIONALISM AND THE REGULATION OF POLITICAL ETHICS

There is a growing body of research in political science – often grouped under the name of historical-institutionalist analysis – emphasizing how relatively stable, routinized arrangements structure political behavior (Thelen, 1999). Most of the work on political ethics is reflective of analytical strategies that tend to treat policy (ethics regulation) as the result of various social and political forces. But in this research I take a different approach, arguing not only that politics creates policies, but that policies also remake politics. This suggests that ethics regulation is not purely a product of what has variously been described as the "politics of trust" or the "politics of ethics" (Mackenzie, 2002, p. 53), but rather that ethics regulation also produces the politics of trust.

Formal Political Institutions

In discussing the impact of formal institutions – or constitutional arrangements – on the regulation of political ethics, at least two dimensions need to be distinguished. First, the constitutional principle of legislative autonomy means that the legislature has sole responsibility for disciplining its own members. For instance, both Westminster and the U.S. Congress have tenaciously and consistently resisted any suggestion that the conduct of their members should be subject to the authority of any external body or person. In the American case, Article 1, Sec. 5 of the U.S. Constitution of 1789 holds that each house may punish, including expelling, its members. In the British case, Article 9 of the Bill of Rights of 1689 suggests that it is not possible for outside bodies to call into question the actions of MPs in Parliament (Williams, 2002). For more than 300 years, the House of Commons has maintained that its decisions, including those on the disciplining of its members, cannot be challenged in the courts.

> Self-regulation has a constitutional importance because the House is sovereign. In order to fufill its responsibilities as a sovereign institution, Parliament must have the freedom of privilege so that it is protected from outside interference. (Committee on Standards in Public Life, 2002, p. 9)

In all parliamentary systems based on the Westminster model, the role of parliamentary privilege is considered essential to maintain the constitutional doctrine of separation of powers and the principle of free speech by the representatives of the people. Parliamentary privilege gives the legislature its authority for creating and controlling its own ethics regulation machinery. For instance, in Canada, the recent adoption of a bill to create an independent ethics commissioner to regulate parliamentary ethics has been denounced by some as a possible encroachment on the principle of legislative autonomy. A number of parliamentarians object to having their actions overseen by an ethics officer based in law, fearing that this could allow the courts to interfere in their business. They prefer a nonstatutory model (as in Britain) where the parliamentary commissioner for standards was established by a simple resolution of the House.

> Parliament [they say] is an institution that should remain the sole manager of its discipline ... The issue of court revision is something that is of great concern. Judges should not be involved in the disciplining of parliamentarians. Otherwise, you mix up the two systems. (Francoli, 2003, p. 4)

The point here is that despite the fact that politicians may be invoking ancient constitutional authority for defending their traditional system of self-regulation, there have been some changes, as the British and Canadian cases indicate. They may not be radical changes, but they nevertheless imply an important departure from practices that have very deep historical roots. The fact that these changes have taken place in parliamentary systems points to a second dimension of formal institutions that needs to be underlined: the concentration of power. Analysts interested in explaining policy change have often argued that because the concentration of political authority lowers the number of veto points, governments operating in parliamentary systems have a much greater capacity to pursue significant policy shifts (Bonoli, 2000). As long as the governing party or parties has a majority, legislation can be passed even over heated opposition. By contrast, the American system of checks and balances can often lead to deadlock or inaction. Party discipline is much weaker in the U.S. Congress. There are, moreover, many veto points in the legislative process at which opponents can effectively block policy changes (Weaver & Rockman, 1993).

As a basic account of the concentration versus the dispersion of power and its impact on policy outcome (change or no change) this is rather convincing. It is helpful to understand the differences between Britain and Canada on the one hand, and the U.S. on the other – but not between Australia and the two other parliamentary systems. The presence or absence of some independent element in the ethics regulation process is not simply a matter of formal institutions. The U.S. Congress may be resisting calls for a more independent form of ethics regulation, but this is not simply because it has a separation of powers system. After all, there are in the U.S. more than 30 state legislatures with similar institutional arrangements that have independent ethics commissions. Australia may well have formal political institutions that would make the creation of an independent ethics commissioner a relatively easy task, but it has been constantly rejecting such suggestions over the past years (McKeown, 2003). Formal institutions may facilitate or impede policy change, but they are insufficient to explain why political actors are more likely to follow one particular trajectory of policy development rather than another. Formal institutions may frustrate reformers who are seeking changes but do not explain why they are pursuing them. This is more a matter of actors' interest and preferences which, I argue below, are profoundly shaped by previous policy choices.

Policy Feedback and Political Change

The idea of policy feedback stresses how past policy decisions influence subsequent political developments and struggles (Mettler, 2002; Pierson, 1993). It focuses on the ways in which the specific design choices made by preceding policymakers feedback into contemporary politics, thus constraining the options that are before the political actors of the present.

Research on policy feedback suggests that public policies, once they are adopted, have feedback effects in at least two ways. First, policy design has resource effects – how the resources and incentives that policies provide shape patterns of behavior. Second, policy design has interpretative effects – how policies convey meanings and information to citizens. What does the research on political ethics have to say about the presence of these two types of effects?

Arguments about the resource effect of policies stress how new policies, and the efforts to implement them, often lead to the creation of new institutions, thereby expanding state capacities and affecting the goals and strategies of groups seeking to promote or frustrate the further extension of that line of policymaking (Skocpol, 1992, p. 58). This is an aspect that critics of ethics regulation in the U.S. have already highlighted, arguing that "the expansion of ethics regulations and enforcement agencies and personnel [has led to growing] public controversy over the ethical behavior of public officials" (Mackenzie, 2002, p. 112). In much the same way, Thompson claims that escalating concerns about ethics is

> a product of overly zealous reformers who believe corruption is rampant and that the only way to stop it is by enacting more rules and bringing more charges. The problem, the critics say, is not political corruption but those who seek to eliminate it. The "ethics police," a new breed of activists who devote their careers to fighting corruption, have produced a "culture of mistrust" that has made the difficult job of governing that much harder. (Thompson, 1995, p. 4)

While not himself a critic of ethics regulation, Thompson nevertheless recognizes that this argument has some validity and that

> public concern about ethics in Congress is generated by ethics reformers themselves [but in the end he argues that] the demand for ethics regulation has grown beyond anything the ethics police could have instigated on their own. It is a *manifestation of a public mood.* (Thompson, 1995, p. 4, my emphasis)

This position, which basically argues that the demand for ethics regulation comes from society, is in sharp contrast with the idea that the most noteworthy thing about "the politics of ethics was *the absence of any identifiable public demand*" (Mackenzie, 2002, p. 53, again, my emphasis). This is a position also shared by Ginsberg and Shefter in their *Politics by Other Means* (1990). As the two authors write, the

> heightened level of public concern with governmental misconduct [as well as] the issue of government ethics [are] closely linked to struggles for political power in the United States. In the aftermath of Watergate, institutions were established and processes created to investigate allegations of unethical conduct on the part of public figures. Increasingly, political forces have sought to make use of these mechanisms to discredit their

opponents ... The creation of these processes, *more than changes in the public's moral standards*, explains why public officials are increasingly being charged with unethical violations. (Ginsberg & Shefter, 1994, p. 7, still my emphasis)

Ginsberg and Shefter argue that because of party decline and the declining significance of the electoral arena, ethics rules have become a form of "politics by other means ... [and are] weapons of institutional combat" (1994, p. 1). As competition in the electoral arena has declined, the significance of other forms of political combat has increased. This view is clearly one that emphasizes how ethics rules shape politics by providing resources and incentives that influence the strategies and activities of social or politically active groups.

Public policies have feedback effects also in terms of the meaning and information they convey to political and social actors. Such effects not only provide information to policymakers but also to citizens and the public in general. The idea is that the content of public policy (policy design) affects citizens' orientation by sending messages about the value of the group or groups that are the target of policy (Ingram & Schneider, 1993). Policies generate cues that help social actors to interpret the world around them. As discussed earlier, self-regulation is generally the primary mechanism for enforcing ethics standards in political life. In opting for this particular type of arrangements – of policy design – most politicians probably believe that they are defending the constitution: that they are upholding the principle of legislative autonomy that allows the representative of the people in parliament (or the U.S. Congress) to be free of outside interference (Committee on Standards in Public Life, 2002, p. 7). This is, for instance, what the parliamentary leader of the Labour government argued in the House of Commons when he said that "the refusal of the House to accept any external authority over its proceedings is a fundamental principle of British parliamentary democracy" (cited in Williams, 2002, p. 615). But self-regulation, as a type of policy design, may well be sending another message to the public, one that self-regulation is "self-serving and anachronistic" (Williams, 2002, p. 612); that it favors a system of "quiet collusion" (Tolchin & Tolchin, 2001, p. 9), or as Thompson (1995, p. 135) argues, that it conveys the idea that legislators are in a basic "institutional conflict of interest [because self-regulation] is not observing the principle that one should not judge in one's own cause." In much the same way, the fact that the instruments generally used for regulating political ethics are often nonstatutory also creates the impression that the rules of conduct that legislators apply to themselves are malleable and can be easily manipulated because they lack the authoritative or coercive character of the law.

In addition, ethics regulations are very often born in scandals. The "rules are written hastily and with punitive intent, and they usually embody laundry lists of prohibitions to eliminate the most recent scandalous actions" (Dobel, 1993, p. 161). They generally focus on conflict-of-interest definitions and the attempt to insulate public office holders from the influence of money, family, or business (Stark, 2000). They try to demarcate public and private life by limiting the giving and receiving of gifts and the use of public resources for gain or for personal use. More recently, they have attempted to solve the revolving-door syndrome by constraining the post-employment possibilities of public officials.

In *Policy Design for Democracy*, Schneider and Ingram (1997, p. 102) argue that public policies always involve the social construction of target populations that separate the "deservings" from the "undeservings." Based on this distinction, they develop a typology of four different kinds of possible policy targets: the advantaged (who are powerful and positively constructed); the contenders (powerful, but constructed as undeserving or greedy); the dependents (positively constructed as good people, but relatively needy or helpless and who have no political power); and the deviants (who also have no power and are negatively constructed as undeserving, violent, mean, and so forth). Politicians are, obviously, the group targeted by ethics regulations. In Schneider and Ingram's typology politicians, as a target group, are part of the contenders category, which includes "privileged and elite groups that appear to be abusing power" (1997, p. 117). This, they recognize, constitutes a negatively constructed image of politicians.

Looking at the message that rules intended to regulate the conduct of politicians send to the public, Dobel writes that

> generally, the tone conveys a clear lack of trust and respect for public officials. The code reduces ethics to a negative prohibition on monetary and personal gain from private service, and enumerates long lists of minutia that now become ethics violations. (Dobel, 1993, p. 161)

Rosenthal (1996, p. 10) similarly points out how the legislative ethics reforms of the 1970s have "directed public attention towards examples of legislative corruption, in part by expanding prohibited activities and introducing far greater complexity into legislative life."

Between the public and the messages sent by public policies, there is the media. Some have argued that ethics rules also have feedback effects on what the media do (e.g., Sabato, 1991). Ethics rules, in seeking to reduce conflict-of-interest situations, break down barriers between private and public life, thus making personal aspects such as friendships, family, and business interests subject to public scrutiny and judgement. Most ethics rules or codes are built around reporting and disclosure requirements, which make it possible for the media to identify hidden conflicts of interest by linking actions to revealed private interests. The failure to disclose properly or fully also becomes a violation of the rules, and the disclosure forms become important information for the media. Dobel notes that

> disclosure forms are a mother load for investigative reporting. Given the information on disclosure forms and the way ethics codes extend culpability to family members or to friendship patterns, the opportunity to uncover wrongdoing or verify patterns suggestive of wrongdoing invites media intervention. In addition, the simple failure to report information adequately and in great detail now becomes a publicized "violation" in the press. (Dobel, 1993, p. 162)

In *Scandal Proof*, Mackenzie also suggests that more ethics rules have produced more media investigations. "The public," he argues, "only knows what it hears and sees and reads. And all those receptors are filled almost constantly with stories that, far from suggesting high levels of public integrity, too often suggest just the opposite" (Mackenzie, 2002, p. 112).

Policy Feedback and the Regulation of Ethics in Politics

Arguments about policy feedback are broadly persuasive. As the preceding section indicates, there are various signs in existing research suggesting that ethics rules have both resource and interpretative effects on the strategies of politicians, parties, bureaucrats (e.g., the ethics police), the media, and the public. But before going further, it is important to recast some aspects of the policy feedback approach to make it more relevant for the study of ethics regulation.

Undoubtedly, Paul Pierson (1994) has been one of the foremost theorists of policy feedback since the publication of his book *Dismantling the Welfare States?* In fact, most of the research in political science using the policy feedback approach is to be found in welfare state studies (Esping–Andersen, 1999; Pierson, 2002). While this research has been extremely innovative, its usefulness for the type of questions I want to explore in this research is not without limit. First, the policies that seek to enforce standards of conduct in public life are very different from social policies. To use Lowi's (1972) typology, the policies on which this study focuses are regulatory and not primarily redistributive as social policies are. This is not to deny that there is no regulatory dimension involved in redistributive policies (or vice versa). Rather, the point is that each type of policy, at least in the case of ethics regulation, involves different types of actors. For instance, in looking at the interpretative effects of policy feedback, Pierson focused primarily on those interest groups receiving some form of direct benefit from social policy, such as the Association of American Retired People (AARP) in the case of the U.S. Pierson showed that New Right leaders failed to achieve their goals of significantly reducing the welfare state. This, he argued, was mainly due to the power of pluralistic interests attached to various social programs. Pierson's work very much focused on the sources of resistance to change as he discovered that little change had occurred in British and American social policies despite the political will of Thatcher and Reagan.

But in the case of ethics regulation, the social or the interest groups' side of the equation is much less visible than in the case of social policies. No group in society derives direct material benefits from the regulation of political ethics. In Pierson's work, those like the pensioners, who received an essentially positive message (constructed as deserving people who worked hard all their lives) from the policies of the postwar welfare state, mobilized energetically against retrenchment, and the outcome was no change or only minor change. But to the extent that members of the public are affected by ethics regulation, the message they receive seems to be a negative one, which portrays politicians as people who are often tempted to abuse power. Taking their cues from the informational content of ethics rules, citizens may either become actively engaged in advocacy groups such as Common Cause in the U.S. and Democracy Watch in Canada. Or they can, more simply, express themselves through public opinion polls indicating that they have less confidence in politics. But in the two scenarios, citizens, or public opinion more generally, are likely to act as a force for change regarding ethics regulation, whereas in Pierson's work they were more a force that limited change.

In fact, in Pierson's analysis those pushing for changes were the New Right leaders elected in the 1980s who sought to dismantle the welfare state. But in the case of ethics regulation, the situation seems to be the reverse: politicians, rather than citizens or interest groups, are often those who are more forcefully opposing changes.[1] To put it simply, if the AARP in the U.S. represented in Pierson's work the entrenched interests blocking change, in the case of ethics regulation this role is more likely to be played by politicians themselves than by groups in civil society.

Finally, while Pierson used the policy feedback approach to explain the absence of change in welfare state restructuring (his dependent variable), in this study the phenomenon to be accounted for is also the presence of change. The basic point of departure for each of the four countries included in this study is that rules of conduct for members of parliament or the U.S.

Congress have always been enforced through a system of self-regulation and peer review. But as already indicated, both Britain and Canada have recently departed from this system by introducing some form of external involvement, while Australia and the U.S., despite growing pressures, have made no such change. Why?

PATH DEPENDENCE AND POLICY LOCK-IN

Research focusing on policy feedback (i.e., how past policies shape later developments) is increasingly asking such questions about institutional change and stability by using the notion of path dependence (Hall & Soskice, 2001; Pierson, 2002). At its weakest, path dependence is little more than the observation that history matters to current outcome. It means "that what happened at an earlier point in time will affect the possible outcomes of a sequence of events occurring at a later point in time" (Sewell, 1996, pp. 262–263). The stronger claim is that once a country or region has started down a certain path, it is likely to stay on it in the future. In other words, initial choices are not easily reversed, and the path cannot be left without large costs. This notion of path dependence refers to those particular sequences which have self-reinforcing properties. It highlights how preceding steps in a particular direction induce further movement in that same direction, thereby making the possibility of switching to some other previously credible alternative more difficult. This, Pierson suggests, happens because of increasing returns:

> In an increasing returns process, the probability of further steps along the same path increases with each move down that path. This is because the *relative* benefits of the current activity compared with other possible options increase over time. (Pierson, 2000, p. 252)

What does this imply for the type of questions this study seeks to explore? The steady adoption of more ethics rules (more either in terms of number or in terms of their stringency and detail) is the trajectory or direction that policymakers have taken, especially since the Watergate scandal, in seeking to restore trust in public life. The regulation of political ethics seems to constitute a clear case of policy lock-in, with self-reinforcing processes that are making it difficult for political actors to switch to another alternative – for instance, to what Mackenzie (2002, p. 163) calls "ethics deregulation" – even when they may be aware that the path on which they are is not really producing efficient outcomes (e.g., that more ethics rules, at least when they are managed through self-regulation, may not help to build more public trust).

Self-Reinforcing Processes in the Regulation of Political Ethics

Policy becomes locked-in to a given path because of increasing returns processes. What can these processes be in the case of ethics regulation? What are the relative benefits of ethics reform? First, arguments in support of ethics regulation suggest that tighter rules and a more transparent ethics process can increase public confidence in politics. Since citizen confidence can never be too strong in a healthy democracy, politicians have no realistic alternative. They must constantly try to improve the ethics process (Thompson, 1995, p. 177). Second, and as a corollary, it is politically difficult to be against ethics in a democracy. "Ethics regulation," writes one observer, "has been the motherhood issue of recent times – too politically costly to oppose" (Mackenzie, 2002, p. 5) even when the direct benefits are uncertain. Third, as the work of Ginsberg and Shefter (1990, p. 1) suggests, ethics rules are often used as "weapons of institutional combat." They are resources that politicians can easily mobilize to attack and discredit their opponents. Fourth, ethics rules are often born in political scandals. In such a context, politicians are more interested in the short-term than in the long-term effects of their actions. Political actors will tend to act rapidly and adopt new rules to ensure that the scandal that gave rise to the crisis in the first place will not happen again. In this sense, ethics rules provide what Eldeman (1967) calls symbolic reassurance. As rules, they "reassure the public that the ethics problem has been solved because a rule stands on the books" (Dobel, 1993, p. 161). But often, the rules are "toothless" (Rosenson, 2000, p. 220). They are politically not costly to adopt because their implementation is weak to the extent that they have always been (until recently) enforced through systems of self-regulation and peer review.

As a result of these increasing returns processes, path dependency theory tells us that policies and institutions should persist over time. In other words, politicians should keep on adopting more ethics rules because: (a) this is the proper thing to do in a democracy; (b) it is politically difficult to be against more ethics; (c) because ethics rules provide easily accessible resources for political combats; (d) they also provide symbolic reassurance against misconduct; and (e) they are cheap to adopt because enforcement is weak. Consequently, one should not expect any major change in the regulation of political ethics. This should be a sector that is highly change resistant.

Combined together, a, b, c, d, and e should act as positive feedbacks, or as self-reinforcing processes, that are effectively locking in ethics regulation to a particular policy trajectory (e.g., self-regulation) from which it becomes extremely difficult to depart. In short, the regulation of political ethics clearly exhibits the processes of increasing returns at the heart of path-dependence theory. But one of the goals of this research is to explain the changes that have taken place in the regulation of political ethics. The cases of Canada and Britain, where some independent (or external) element has recently been introduced in the ethics regulatory process, indicate that this does not necessarily constitute an instance of policy lock-in. Initially, all legislatures in the democratic world were (and most still are) on the path of self-regulation in terms of the mechanisms and processes used for disciplining their own members. This is the basic point of departure. But Britain and Canada have recently deviated from that initial path, while Australia and the U.S. have not. How can this be explained?

Political Authority and the Correction of Path Inefficiencies

Path-dependence accounts have often been accused of excessive determinism, unable to account for variance in the dependent variable they seek to explain (Saint-Martin, 2002). If path-dependent mechanisms work the way leading theorists suggest, it is difficult to know why institutions and policies ever change at all. In a recent critique, Stewart Wood (2002, p. 373) argues that one way out of this excessive determinism is not to claim that "there is only one possible route after a momentous initial turn," but to suggest rather "that certain moves are ruled out by past events in a sequence." Viewed in this less deterministic way, "path-dependence becomes capable of accommodating change as well as continuity, by delineating the limits within which change can occur and identifying the factors that both mitigate against change and influence its direction" (Wood, 2002, p. 373).

This, Wood suggests, can best be done by questioning the issue of path inefficiencies. According to Pierson and others, because of increasing returns processes, inefficient institutions and policies tend to persist over time. In the economic world, where market competition provides effective selection mechanisms, inefficiencies may be more easily corrected. However, Pierson argues, in the political world such corrections are especially difficult (2000, p. 261). Inefficient political outcomes are not always selected out because of their inefficiency (in part because it is difficult to know what inefficient political outcomes are). Also, political actors, because of the logic of electoral politics, tend to have short-time horizons that reduce the incentive to tackle inefficiencies, particularly when the payoff to doing so is diffused or delayed.

It is true that selection mechanisms do not operate to privilege more over less efficient policies in the realm of politics. Inefficient outcomes may have long lives. But inefficiencies do have costs for actors, and the fact that these may persist or even accumulate as further steps down a given path are taken can serve to magnify their impact. At some point (a "tipping point," as Wood (2002, p. 373) calls it), we should expect actors to seek policy change to correct an inefficiency. However, rectifying inefficiencies need not necessarily imply wholesale overthrow of a policy. Inefficiencies can be corrected through modifications to existing practice that fall in between continuation of the status quo and complete policy shifts. This, I hypothesize, is precisely what happens in Britain and Canada. In these two cases, the introduction of some independent element in the ethics regulation process was partly designed to address what Thompson (1995, p. 147) calls the "deficiencies of self-regulation." But these changes do not necessarily constitute a radical departure from the initial policy path of self-regulation. In Canada, as in the British case (Kaye, 2002), critiques have been raised against the insufficient degree of independence of the ethics regulation system that Bill C-4 creates (Saint-Martin, 2003). Critics in the two countries want more independence because they think that the initial decision to depoliticize the regulation of ethics did not go far enough. Even if the two countries may no longer have a system of "pure self-regulation," as this has been called (Committee on Standards in Public Life, 2002, p. 10), and even if some changes did take place, the regulation of political ethics nevertheless remains path dependent. What distinguishes a path-dependent process is that it is self-reinforcing: the probability of one outcome rather than another increases with each step down the path after an initial event. The fact that some degree of independence may have been introduced (even if small) means that ethics regulation in Britain and Canada is likely in the future to focus increasingly around that issue, and that the political costs of exit – of trying to switch to the previous system of pure self-regulation – will rise over time.

What the British and Canadian cases suggest is that politics is not only something that makes the identification of policy inefficiencies difficult. Recall Pierson's position that in politics, inefficient policies have long lives. The complexity and ambiguity of political life may well favor institutional inertia and continuity. But it is also the authoritative nature of politics that offers opportunities for changes of direction. As Wood argues, "the *concentration of political authority* in political contexts means that the interests of the few may dictate the fate of policies that apply to all" (2002, p. 374, my emphasis).

The key theoretical point here is that when the costs of the perceived inefficiency of certain policy trajectories are concentrated among those that have access to policymaking powers or to significant political resources, changes in policy are always possible. This suggests a more modest claim for the effects of path-dependence processes. There is no reason why the murkiness of politics should always compel policy continuity.

LOOKING AHEAD

Using the research on policy feedback, I have argued that ethics regulation should be conceived as an independent variable. This hypothesis is schematically described in Fig. 1.

Inevitably, diagrams such as this have a static, ahistorical quality. Let me underline, therefore, that I take from the policy feedback approach the fundamental insight that policies need to be studied over time; that once enacted, policies restructure subsequent political processes. Public policies, in the form of ethics rules, have both resource and interpretative effects. In terms of resources, ethics rules can be seen as weapons of institutional combat that politicians and parties can use to discredit their opponents. This, in turn, may lead to more ethics investigations and increases publicity and public controversy about the ethical behavior of public officials. It creates, in the words of John B. Thompson (2000, p. 106), the impression that "political scandal is more prevalent today." Ethics rules also convey meanings to citizens regarding the standards of conduct they can legitimately expect from those in public life. In this process the media plays a key role. The more ethics rules are used as weapons in partisan struggles, the more likely the air will be filled with news about political ethics. This in turn will affect the level of citizen confidence in politics, leading either to active mobilization (Democracy Watch, Common Cause, etc.) or to more passive expressions of disenchantment toward politics.

As path-dependence theory suggests, all these processes are self-reinforcing over time, leading to at least two types of scenarios. In the first instance, they can lead to more rules that are still enforced through self-regulation mechanisms, as in the U.S., for instance (the no-change scenario). Malbin explains how this path-dependent dynamic works in the case of the U.S. Congress. New ethics rules always bring

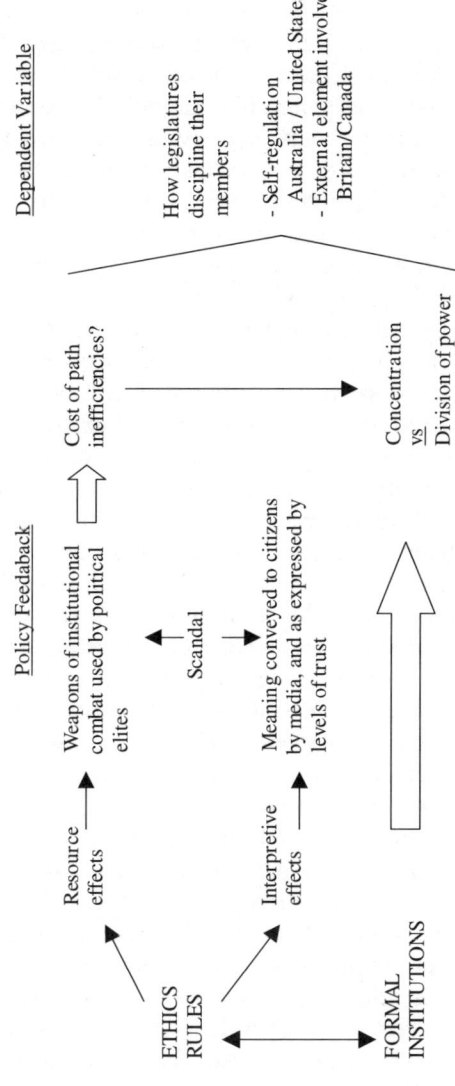

Fig. 1. Policy Feedback and Formal Institutions in the Regulation of Political Ethics.

a broader range of behavior subject to official review. In this way, the new standards themselves have become catalysts for bringing attention to situations that once might have been accepted without question. This attention, in turn, creates pressure for still more changes in the formal rules and standards. (Malbin, 1994, p. 1155)

But path dependence can lead to a different outcome (e.g., the change scenario). If we take the cases of Britain and Canada we can see, following the discussion on path inefficiencies, that at some point, when the feedback of previous policy choices start to create negative effects – when they produce diminishing returns – actors will seek to change policy to correct the inefficiency. Again, the key point here is that when the costs of the perceived inefficiency of certain policy paths are concentrated among those that have access to policymaking powers, changes are always possible. Notice that at this stage of the causal chain of reasoning illustrated in Fig. 1, the relevant factor leading to variation in the dependent variable points toward formal political institutions (i.e., concentration versus dispersion of powers). Formal institutions need to be studied together with policy feedback. But the question of whether legislatures are opting for an internal or external form of ethics regulation process is not simply a product of formal institutions. The fact that formal political arrangements facilitate or impede change is not what shape actors' views and policy preferences. This is primarily a matter of policy feedback, of previous experiences with similar policy decisions. Reformers and activists in Democracy Watch Canada do not want more ethics rules because they think that such rules are more likely to be enacted in a parliamentary rather than in a congressional system. In much the same way, even if a concentration of powers system allows for more radical policy shift, MPs, either in Canada or Britain, do not seem to appreciate ethics rules more than their American counterparts in the U.S. Congress. Finally, the last element in Fig. 1 is the dependent variable, which broadly refers to the way legislatures discipline the conduct of their members. As we have seen, this is something that varies along a continuum, which has pure self-regulation at one end and external regulation at the other, with some form of co-regulation in the middle.

It is important to make clear that countries where legislatures have opted for some form of external involvement in the ethics regulation process have not necessarily raised the ethics bar to a new or superior level of moral standards. Research at the state level in the U.S. suggests that independent ethics commissions are often underfunded and understaffed because they have no real allies to defend their interests, and many enemies (Rosenson, 2003). The key point is that opting for a more independent form of enforcement mechanism depoliticizes (at least to some extent) the regulation of ethics. The cost of opting for such a strategy is that political actors no longer fully control the ethics regulation process. There is a strong element of risk and uncertainty that does not exist in the pure self-regulation path. But the potential benefit of deviating from this original path is that it may become more difficult for ethics rules to be used as tools of partisan combat when an external element is involved in the enforcement process. Part of the self-reinforcing aspect of ethics regulation is largely caused by the use of ethics rules as weapons of political combat. It is when ethics rules are used as weapons in power struggles that the ethics bar rises. The objective is to discredit opponents by raising ethical standards to higher levels. And as the ethics bar rises, the likelihood that behavior will not meet expectations probably becomes stronger, thus leading to more public distrust and to yet more rules. One way to break this cycle – to somehow exit from that particular policy path – might be to depoliticize ethics regulation by introducing some form of external element into the process. But if the cost of the inefficiencies created by the use of ethics rules as tools of partisan combat are dispersed, as in the U.S. Congress, then change is less likely to occur. In contrast, in Britain and Canada the costs of using ethics rules as political weapons are likely to have been felt more strongly among members of the governing majority. In the British and Canadian systems of government, the use of ethics rules as weapons of political combat primarily serves to discredit the government. But since government controls the legislature – and even if many MPs may not like the idea of no longer having their system of self-regulation – changes in the ethics process then become highly possible. For the government, depoliticizing some portions of the ethics regulation process may provide a partial way of pulling the rug out from under the feet of its political opponents.

But in the U.S. Congress, the absence of change is not only a matter of formal institutions. The cost of using ethics rules as weapons of political combat may well be diffused as a result of the division of power system, but the sources of policy continuity are also path dependent because of increasing returns processes. In that case, the sources of policy continuity are endogenous to ethics rules themselves because politicians see some relative benefits in continuing to use them. Increasing returns processes (e.g., the five factors discussed earlier) engender a status quo bias by influencing the interests and preferences of actors in ways that incline them to support a particular course of policy development. This dynamic leads to the same outcome (i.e., absence of change) but is different from the one where policy stability is the result of constitutional obstacles that make reforms difficult. Whereas increasing returns arguments work through their effect on actors' interests and preferences, formal institutions laden with multiple veto points and separated powers may make reform difficult, but they do so by frustrating reformers rather than by influencing their policy preferences.

The Importance of Timing

As for the case of Australia, the available evidence suggests a dynamic different in many ways from the three other countries. Like the U.S., Australia has a system of pure self-regulation. But unlike the U.S., it has what Atkinson and Mancuso (1992) call an etiquette approach for regulating political ethics. Rules governing standards of behavior in the Australian Parliament are uncodified; there is no single, coherent blueprint for ethical conduct (Preston, 2001). In Australia, there is no ethics code as in Britain, as well as no statutory ethics parliamentary officer such as the one recently established in Canada by Bill C-4. If ethics regulation regimes can be broadly divided between those relying on a rules-based versus an etiquette approach, the U.S. and Australia would, respectively, be the most and least rules-based regimes, with Britain and Canada somewhere in the middle, both using a mix of the two approaches. But in the three cases that have a parliamentary form of government – where the etiquette approach has long been dominant – there is a common trend toward using a more rules-based approach to ethics (Atkinson & Mancuso, 1992). This trend, however, seems to be the least developed in the Australian case (Brien, 1998).

In contrast to Australia (which can be described as a latecomer), of the four cases studied here the U.S. has, by far, the more mature system of ethics regulation. In the U.S., the decision to adopt a more rules-based approach to ethics was made when the House and the Senate each adopted its own code of ethics in the 1960s. It was the initial decision made in the 1960s to formalize ethics that subsequently led to the use of ethics rules as weapons of political combat. And as argued earlier, it is precisely this kind of politicization that produces self-reinforcing processes in ethics regulation. As path-dependence theorists argue, sequencing is critical: earlier events sometimes matter more than later ones, and thus different sequences may produce different outcomes. Compared to the other cases, timing in the U.S. is different because Congress was among the first legislatures in the world to formalize ethics in the 1960s, and from the beginning politicians have always maintained that self-regulation was the most efficient means to enforce standards of conduct in the legislative sphere. Compared to their British and Canadian counterparts, American legislators have gone much further down the path of managing ethics rules through self-regulatory mechanisms. One key hypothesis is that how far one has gone down a given policy path is critical for delimiting reform options. Reform is likely to be more difficult when a country has traveled far down a given policy path.

NOTES

1. This is because they think they will lose power when, for instance, they agree to have some form of outside involvement in the ethics regulation process, or because the type of disclosure and the opening to scrutiny of personal and family matters that ethics rules generally require is resented by officials and considered a form of harassment (Dobel 1993, p. 162). A recent illustration of this is the rebellion by MPs in Ottawa against the disclosure requirement for the financial affairs of parliamentarians' spouses and dependents called for in the code of conduct proposed by Oliver and Miliken (Liberal Backbenchers don't like ethics proposals, 2002).

REFERENCES

Atkinson, M., & Mancuso, M. (1992). Edicts and etiquette: Regulating conflict of interest in Congress and the House of Commons. *Corruption and Reform*, 7, 1–18.
Bonoli, G. (2000). *The politics of pension reform*. New York: Cambridge University Press.
Brien, A. (1998). *A code of conduct for parliamentarians?* London: Parliament of Australia, Department of the Parliament Library (Research Paper 2, 1998–1999).
Carney, G. (1998). *Conflict of interest: Legislators, ministers and public officials*. (Study Prepared for Transparency International). Retrieved from http://www.transparency.org/working_papers/carney/.
Committee on Standards in Public Life. (2002). *Standards of conduct in the House of Commons*. London: UK Parliament (Eighth Report, Cm. 5663).
Dobel, J. P. (1993). The realpolitik of ethics codes: An implementation approach to public ethics. In: G. H. Frederickson (Ed.), *Ethics and public administration* (pp. 158–176). New York: M.E. Sharpe.
Eldeman, M. (1967). *The politics of symbols*. Bloomington: Indiana University Press.
Esping-Andersen, G. (1999). *The social foundations of post-industrial economies*. New York: Oxford University Press.
Francoli, P. (2003). PM ethics bill headed for roadblock. *Ottawa Hill Times*, May 26, p. 4.
Ginsberg, B., & Shefter, M. (1990). *Politics by other means: The declining importance of elections in America*. New York: Basic Books.
Hall, P. A., & Soskice, D. (2001). *Varieties of capitalism*. New York: Oxford University Press.
Ingram, H., & Schneider, A. (1993). Constructing citizenship: The subtle messages of policy design. In: H. Ingram & S. Rathgeb Smith (Eds), *Public policy for democracy* (pp. 68–98). Washington, DC: Brookings.
Kaye, R. (2002). Regulating legislators. Paper presented at the British Political Science Association Conference, Manchester, UK (April).

Liberal backbenchers don't like ethics proposals. (2002). CBC News, October 2. Retrieved from http://www.cbc.ca/stories/2002/10/02/ethics_libs021002.

Lowi, T. J. (1972). Four systems of policy, politics, and choice. *Public Administration Review, 32*, 298–310.

Mackenzie, C. G. (2002). *Scandal proof: Do ethics laws make government ethical?* Washington, DC: Brookings.

Malbin, M. J. (1994). Legislative ethics. In: J. H. Silbey (Ed.), *Encyclopedia of the American legislative system* (Vol. II, pp. 1155–1170). New York: Charles Scribner's Sons.

McKeown, D. (2003). Codes of conduct in Australia and some overseas parliaments. E-brief, Parliament of Australia (December). Retrieved from http://www.aph.gov.au/library/intguide/POL/CodeConduct.htm.

Mettler, S. (2002). Bringing the state back in to civic engagement: Policy feedback effects of the G.I. Bill for World War II veterans. *American Political Science Review, 96*, 351–365.

Pierson, P. (1993). When effect becomes cause: Policy feedback and political change. *World Politics, 45*, 595–628.

Pierson, P. (1994). *Dismantling the welfare state?* Cambridge, UK: Cambridge University Press.

Pierson, P. (2000). Increasing returns, path dependence, and the study of politics. *American Political Science Review, 94*, 251–267.

Pierson, P. (Ed.) (2002). *The new politics of the welfare state*. New York: Oxford University Press.

Preston, N. (2001). Codifying ethical conduct for Australian parliamentarians 1990–99. *Australian Journal of Political Science, 36*, 45–59.

Ridley, F. F., & Doig, A. (1995). *Sleaze: Politicians, private interests and public reaction*. Oxford, UK: Oxford University Press.

Rosenson, B.A. (2000). Legislative ethics regulation in the American states: Explaining conflict of interest legislation, 1954–1996. Doctoral dissertation, Massachussetts Institute of Technology, Cambridge.

Rosenson, B. A. (2003). Against their apparent self-interest: The authorization of independent state legislative ethics commissions, 1973–96. *State Politics and Policy Quarterly, 3*, 42–65.

Rosenthal, A. (1996). *Drawing the line: Legislative ethics in the states*. New York: Twentieth Century Fund.

Sabato, L. (1991). *Feeding frenzy: How attack journalism has transformed American politics*. New York: The Free Press.

Saint-Martin, D. (2002). Apprentissage social et changement institutionnel. *Politique et Sociétés, 21*(3), 41–67.

Saint-Martin, D. (2003). Should the federal ethics counsellor become an independent officer of parliament? *Canadian Public Policy, 39*, 197–212.

Schneider, A. L., & Ingram, H. (1997). *Policy design for democracy*. Lawrence: University Press of Kansas.

Sewell, W. H. (1996). Historical events as transformations of structures. *Theory and Society, 25*, 641–681.

Skocpol, T. (1992). *Protecting soldiers and mothers*. Cambridge, MA: Harvard University Press.

Stark, A. (2000). *Conflict of interest in American public life*. Cambridge, MA: Harvard University Press.

Thelen, K. (1999). Historical institutionalism in comparative politics. *Annual Review of Political Science, 2*, 369–404.

Thompson, D. F. (1995). *Ethics in Congress*. Washington, DC: Brookings.
Thompson, J. B. (2000). *Political scandal: Power and visibility in the media age*. Cambridge, UK: Cambridge University Press.
Tolchin, M., & Tolchin, S. (2001). *Glass houses: Congressional ethics and the politics of venom*. Boulder, CO: Westview Press.
Weaver, R. K., & Rockman, B. (Eds) (1993). *Do institutions matter?* Washington, DC: Brookings.
Williams, R. (2002). Conduct unbecoming: The regulation of legislative ethics in Britain and the United States. *Parliamentary Affairs*, 55, 611–625.
Wood, S. (2002). Labour market regime under threat? Source of continuity in Germany, Britain and Sweden. In: P. Pierson (Ed.), *The new politics of the welfare state* (pp. 368–409). New York: Oxford University Press.

THE ETHICS ERUPTION: SOURCES AND CATALYSTS

Robert Williams

ABSTRACT

The chapter is divided into two broad sections. The first addresses macro or global sources of ethics discontent. This will discuss concern about political ethics in the broad context of complex processes such as globalization, development, liberalization, and democratization. These are clearly huge subjects and there is no space to do justice to their complexities, but the aim here is to identify some key aspects, which have particularly important implications for increasing concern about political ethics. The second section is concerned with exploring the political aspects of public ethics through a consideration of political scandal, because scandals are often cited as the source of unease about ethical standards in public life and as the catalysts for institutional reform.

It is difficult to locate the precise moment when concerns about political ethics began to increase, and different countries, different institutions, and different parts of the world may have different starting points (Heywood, 1997). It is also difficult to specify whether levels of concern increased steadily to their present pitch or whether concern has been subject to violent fluctuations with sudden, dramatic increases in concern followed by periods of quietude. It is equally difficult to assess how much concern is home grown and how much is the product of spillover or diffusion from neighboring states or distant institutions.

Marking formal political responses to concern about political ethics is a little easier because we can point to particular official reports, new laws or codes, and the creation of new public bodies such as the ethics committees created in the U.S. Congress in the 1960s. But in some political contexts there may be action on political ethics, which cannot be traced to expressions of concern in a particular locality. Here the concern and the response may be exogenous to the area where the alleged ethical transgressions are occurring. This is most obviously the case where less-developed countries interact with developed ones or with international financial institutions. It can also be extended to situations where medium-income states are trying to join particular international clubs such as NATO or the European Union, where the doorkeepers require certain standards from prospective new members and express concern about current ethical abuses in applicant states.

Measuring levels of discontent is also fraught with difficulty. It is sometimes as deceptively straightforward as opinion poll or focus group responses to direct questions about political ethics. It could also be expressed in terms of some more generalized disillusionment or disengagement from politics and public life. Recently, there has been an upsurge of academic and wider interest in the issue of trust in institutions and in political figures or, more specifically, in the decline of trust (O'Neill, 2002). Tangible, even dramatic events, such as demonstrations, riots, and other forms of protest can also be interpreted as reflecting very high levels of concern about the ethics of the political elite. In the extreme case, revolutions or coup d' états may occur, and widespread and intense discontent about the conduct of leaders or the ruling party may be offered as an explanation for political upheaval and transformation. Thus, the timing and level of rising concerns about political ethics, as well as the political responses such escalating concerns elicit, need to be further explored.

It is a commonplace to observe that, because of globalization, the world is a smaller place than it used to be. Technology transfer, the electronic movement of data, images and news, the liberalization of world trade, the economic reach of transnational companies, the mobility of people and capital, and improving educational and income levels have all played some part in ensuring that autarchy and isolation are no longer viable options. The era of closed societies and economies has almost passed and, just as island status no longer offers protection from military or economic invasion, so too ethical boundaries are permeated by exogenous influences, ideas, and fears.

When the political ethics of leaders cause such intense levels of public concern that they threaten economic and political stability, the efforts of global capitalism to promote trade and protect investments helps spread the concern beyond national boundaries. The concerns of market democracies are to spread good practice, by which is normally meant current Western practice – or perhaps it should be current Western theories of best practice. In this way, companies in less-developed countries can aspire to the new standards of ethical business conduct and good corporate governance.

It is the declared intention of major international players such as the World Bank and the International Monetary Fund to use their considerable leverage to ensure that their concerns about political ethics in recipient countries are not only heard, but also responded to by way of substantive reforms. Where the ethical standards of political elites are perceived as obstacles to growth and development, as undermining public trust and political institutions, and generally impairing the ability of recipient states to repay debts to private leaders, donors, and international financial institutions, something has to be done (Mauro, 1995).

The particular aspect of the aid regime employed to address public ethics is known as *political conditionality* (Sorensen, 1993), which is an extension and development of the economic conditionality associated with structural adjustment programs in the 1980s (Caufield, 1996). The international finance institutions (IFIs) were, as essentially economic institutions, slow and reluctant to learn the primacy of the political, but once grasped, in 1989, this form of conditionality has been used as a carrot and stick to attempt to ensure compliance with Western best practice in political ethics. Such pressure may also be exercised irrespective of whether or not there has been any local expression of concern about the ethical standards and practices of the indigenous political elite.

The timing of this expression of intense ethical concern on behalf of the IFIs was intimately connected to the implosion of the Soviet Union, the end of the cold war and the rise of unipolar global politics (Naim, 1995). Put crudely, while the cold war was the first priority, Western concerns about political ethics in less-developed countries were often subordinated to the greater cause of resisting and overwhelming 'the evil empire' of communism. In consequence, concerns about flagrant conflicts of interest in various African, South American, Asian, and, on occasions, European states were muted or suppressed altogether. The World Bank's first articulation of political conditionality came in 1989 (World Bank, 1989) and, as such, raised the ethics bar not only for the less-developed countries of the Third World but also, by implication, for countries like Italy, where the necessity to sustain the anti-communist coalition disappeared with the consequent unravelling of the post-war political settlement and the exposure of the dirty hands of Italian political and business life.

One of the rhetorical devices used in relations with both less-developed and former communist countries was to wave the banner of transparency. What was termed *glasnost* in the last days of the Soviet Union, and what has become the mantra of IFIs, is openness and transparency. With transparency would come accountability, and once publics were able to see, witness, and discover the ethical transgressions of their leaders, they could call them to account. What was once hidden and only rumored and suspected could now be revealed to substantiate and inflame public concerns about political ethics.

Increased expressions of concern about unethical conduct do not necessitate any discernible or measurable increase in such conduct. Indeed, it is difficult to see how any claim of a quantitative kind in relation to unethical conduct could be demonstrated other than by reference to perception surveys (similar to Transparency International's Corruption Perception Index) which are open to a variety of methodological objections.

It is, of course, slightly more difficult to preach political conditionality overseas through the rhetoric of good governance (World Bank, 1992) when it becomes increasingly obvious that there is trouble at home. Crudely expressed, there seems to have been a belief, in the U.K. at any rate, that political ethics improve over time with political and economic development. This leads to the common neocolonial assessment that once newly independent former colonies were equipped with British ethical standards and practices then, as they matured, they would absorb the ethical traits of the British Civil Service, whose ethical standards were and are beyond reproach. The intricacies and implications of political scandal are examined later, but suffice to say at this point that a spate of scandals in Europe and North America from the 1970s onward indicated that ethical problems could not be located in some transitional phase of development or dismissed as a variety of growing pains that would disappear as countries reached economic and political maturity (Williams, 1999).

IFIs and donor countries are global sources of ethical concern because they are convinced that the ethical standards of political elites in recipient countries are a major obstacle to the successful implementation of economic and political development programs. The new concern over political ethics has encouraged IFIs to identify democracy as a cure for unethical conduct, to argue that it is a necessary condition for good governance, and to stipulate it as a prerequisite for further financial support (Abrahamsen, 2000).

How do publics around the globe learn about the state of political ethics, and what information do they receive? How are ethical problems specified, and how do publics learn what the likely remedies are? The answers, in one form or another, involve the media, and some comments on particular aspects of media development which have contributed to escalating ethical concerns are appropriate.

Perceptions of political ethics have been influenced by technology, by the growth of media markets and media conglomerates, and by comment on 24/7 news coverage. But some features in the development of journalism in recent decades merit particular attention. First, the relationship of journalists to politicians has profoundly changed, and the change is of a character, which encourages an escalation of ethics concerns.

A review of the development of media and politics in the U.S. reveals that, in periods characterized by intense concerns over political ethics, journalists and editors have played prominent parts in investigating, reporting, alleging, and possibly inventing claims of unethical conduct by politicians. During the Gilded Age in the 19th century, newspapers frequently made allegations about the propriety of leading political figures. De Tocqueville lamented the tendency of journalists to assail the character of individuals, to track them into their private life and disclose all their weaknesses and vices (Summers, 2000). What made this period distinctive was that newspapers were overtly partisan, so much so that one observer has claimed that "partisanship was a public and ubiquitous phenomenon that defined the very essence of nineteenth century American journalism" (Kaplan, 2002, p. 1).

But, in the transition to the 20th century and the Progressive Era, the press refashioned its ways of shaping public discussions. In particular, partisanship declined as newspapers found commercial alternatives to party funding. Some argue that the change in newspapers and journals reflected a decline in public attachments to parties and thus, as party ties to voters declined, so did the partisanship of newspapers – and so editors and journalists could seek a new form of independence in reporting on political affairs generally, and political ethics in particular. Such trends coincided with the efforts of journalists to establish themselves as an autonomous profession, and university schools of journalism, codes of ethics for journalists, and even the founding of the National Press Club signified that journalists were now important, respectable people whose judgment deserved public and political attention (Wiebe, 1967).

The new breed of journalists were concerned with making news, and forcing issues onto political agendas, rather than simply reporting events. Journalists labeled *muckrakers* by Theodore Roosevelt accepted the label as a badge of honor. The muckrakers discovered and exposed unethical conduct, but their discoveries were on par with Captain Renault's shock on being told there was gambling at Rick's Bar in *Casablanca*. What had been discussed in Washington by political and elite circles now became public knowledge. There was nothing very new about the reports of political misconduct but "national magazines helped turn local concerns about political ethics into national concerns" (Scheirov, 1994, p. 203).

From the 1920s onward the influence of journalists like Walter Lippman grew, and some journalists sought recognition and began to be treated as experts whose independence was beyond question and who saw their role as gatherers, interpreters, and disseminators of political information. As the claim to objectivity was asserted, the wilder allegations of political misconduct disappeared and, aside from the occasional scandal such as the Teapot Dome, the press had little to say about political ethics for several decades after the First World War. The claim of serious journalists to be authoritative required them to seek high-level political information from politicians, and their links to government and politics began to strengthen and multiply. Journalist organizations such as the National Press Club helped institutionalize these political ties.

But while the benefits of proximity to decision makers were obvious, it came with a condition of reticence. If journalists were to earn and retain the confidence of their well-placed political sources, they would have to protect them from some of their own follies. Getting to know senior politicians socially as well as professionally carries with it some responsibility to protect confidences and exercise prudent discretion about what the public is told about the conduct of their political leaders. Entrance to the exclusive political club brought greater status to certain journalists, but this could only be sustained or enhanced by observing club rules.

This comfortable and mutually supportive relationship between journalists and politicians has eroded of late, but while it lasted those journalists with privileged access at the highest political levels were the stars of their profession and commanded respect and deference from their peers and the public. But times have changed, and while reporters once gained status by dining out with politicians, they now win prizes by feasting *on* them. The reasons for the change in the role and attitudes of the media are complex, but one observer cites Watergate and the Vietnam War as contributors to the decline of trust between media and politicians, with the latter exposing the journalistic dangers of believing and reporting political briefings (Sabato, 2000). No doubt many other factors were in play, including the increasing diversity and commercialization of the media, but whatever the reasons, the comfortable and exclusive relationship senior politicians enjoyed with senior journalists broke down.

Sabato offers a telling metaphor: the transformation of the press from lapdog to watchdog, and ultimately to junkyard dog during the 20th century. If the metaphor is apposite, the media's attitude toward politicians and their unethical conduct has evolved from co-conspirators preventing information from reaching the public, to watchful skeptics unlikely to accept political rectitude at face value, to cynics concerned with headlines and sales and mindful of the market for revelations of wrongdoing by the political elite. A former editor of Britain's premier Sunday broadsheet advised any journalist listening to a politician to ask themselves, "Why is this bastard lying to me?" (Mulgan, 2004). Those under attack from cynical, commercial journalism complain of the ethical deficit at the core of the information society, but the question is who do the public believe and who should they believe? Opinion polls suggest that politicians and journalists are classed among the least trustworthy groups, even if they have not quite fallen to the trust levels of realtors and used car dealers.

Politicians, then, are likely to respond to stories of their unethical conduct by blaming the messengers. Their problem is that there are more messengers than ever before and, with the growth of the Internet, there are few gatekeepers able to decide whose opinions are valid. Whereas prominent journalists once enjoyed authoritative status, there are no Lippmans or Cronkites in the 21st century, because they have been replaced in the public mind with the likes of Matt Drudge and Rush Limbaugh. The journalist as an expert insider armed with official information has given way to the fearless outsider ready to broadcast any scurrilous gossip or rumor about the ethics of the political elite. Rumor combines with allegation and encounters new gossip, which all help set off a feeding frenzy in the media and, in such a hostile environment, concerns about political ethics are likely to increase.

It may be that the U.S. is an exception to a general rule about the connections between the media, politics, and concerns over political ethics. It may also be true that, as in so many other cultural fields, the U.S. is pointing the way for other countries. Certainly in the U.K., politicians experience a constant barrage of criticism and personal attack, and the strenuous claims of any politician to be telling the truth is more often derided than accepted. Political denials of unethical conduct are greeted with the response first attributed to Mandy Rice-Davies, a witness giving evidence in the Profumo scandal: "He would say that, wouldn't he?" It seems at least plausible to consider that changes in the forms, structures, and attitudes of the media are of potential global significance, and have implications for the levels of public concern about political ethics wherever an independent media exists.

Although unethical conduct may be no more prevalent than it used to be, the more frequent allegations of misconduct are likely to cause greater public concern, and denials by politicians are less likely to be believed. Thus far, this chapter has identified the global export of ethics concerns by IFIs and other Western bodies, the global spread of new forms of journalistic practice facilitated by political trauma, commercialization, and changing technology as key sources of the ethics eruption. But if these are key sources of escalating concerns about political ethics, what are the mechanisms and catalysts that have helped generate this growing concern?

There are a number of possible responses to this question, but one catalyst in particular, political scandal, seems to have had a great influence on concerns about political ethics in the U.S. and perhaps more widely.

SCANDALS AS A CATALYST

Political scandal appears to cause an ethical reaction in both those whose conduct is questioned and in the minds of those who observe and consume scandals. Theorizing about political scandal is still at a rudimentary stage, and Thompson's (2001) work remains the only substantial attempt to formulate a general causal theory. Thompson is a social and media theorist who sees political scandal arising from changes in the media which lead to a personalized projection of political image. The result, crudely summarized, is that politicians present more of themselves to the public, and this condition of *mediated publicness* becomes both a resource of and a threat to political power.

Politicians, having exposed themselves, can never retreat into privacy. Thus, for example, once politicians have agreed to disclose personal details of their health or finances, they cannot later insist on privacy and any attempt to withhold or conceal such information can become the basis of a political scandal. Another good example of the problems mediated publicness can generate is the British royal family. In the 1970s it decided to make public aspects of their personal lives which had hitherto been hidden from public gaze. But, while this helped produce a surge in popular support for royalty, this publicness was later to cause intense embarrassment and even humiliation to royals, as their various personal and financial difficulties were exposed to public ridicule.

There are, however, some problems with Thompson's analysis, both in its timings of media development and in its indexation of personal exposure to media development. Most obviously, it denies that politicians have choices in how they are presented or, indeed, whether certain aspects are presented. Also, it is the political aspects of political scandal which are so important, and which Thompson underestimates.

An important idea offered by Markovits and Silverstein (1988) is that accounts of political scandal need to integrate "the exercise of, and struggle for political power" (p. 4). But their own approach is a formal, legal-institutional approach which is confined to notions of political due process. They exclude scandals involving politicians, which do not involve abuse of procedural limitations in pursuit of political power. But the point surely is that sexual, financial, and other scandals bearing on political and personal reputation can have just as serious political effects and reactions from the public as their more restricted definition of political scandal.

We need a broader conception of politics to capture the generation of political scandal and its influence on political ethics. The most important element in this is the extent of political contestation. In a political scandal, it is notable that everything is contested and nothing is accepted. It is partly because so much is contested that attempts are made to find an authoritative resolution. This, in turn, has given rise to what Garment (1992) called a scandal generating *machine*. This is an apparatus of various official investigating organizations and committees, notably the Office of the Independent Counsel, but including the auditing arms of federal agencies and also congressional committees. Every major political scandal of the past 30 years or so has contributed to developing this machine.

Thus, the U.S. has developed a scandal-investigating machine of great size and resources. Garment's main focus, though, is not on the political use of this machine. The use of the machine is regulated by rules designed to minimize the appearance of improper tampering – in effect, to remove human control of the machinery – and this combination has helped to bring massive, costly, and time-consuming investigative procedures to bear on the basis of often very narrowly founded suspicions of unethical conduct. In the case of the Clinton presidency, it appears that once the initial allegations of improper conduct relating to the Whitewater land deal had gained media and political traction, the scandal-investigating machine kept finding new allegations of unethical conduct for him to address (Rozell & Wilcox, 2000).

After Watergate, the political architecture of the American state significantly changed in ways likely to ensure that potential ethical misconduct would be subject to both formal inquiries and greater publicity. The appointment of a special prosecutor, or later, independent counsel, provoked headlines – as did congressional committee hearings and the appointment of grand juries. In the post-Watergate culture even traditional law enforcement agencies got into the process of testing political ethics, e.g., the FBI's sting operation, known as Abscam, where members of Congress were offered bribes by FBI agents posing as Arab sheikhs (Williams, 1998).

The collective impact of the various elements of the scandal-investigating machine was to ensure that political conduct was more closely monitored than ever before. Together with the more aggressive, intrusive media, the scandal machine ensured that political ethics were very publicly examined. Those who ignored the changed scandal climate, e.g., Robert Packwood and, arguably, Bill Clinton, were likely to find their conduct under close professional and public scrutiny. Unethical conduct, which was once seen as a privilege of belonging to a political club and largely ignored, if not formally condoned – such as improper use of the franking privilege, breaches of employment and earnings rules, and sexual harassment – now became serious ethical matters and ended the careers of senior politicians.

An interesting feature of the Clinton scandals is the way that some forms of misconduct were recast in order to shift them firmly into the political and legal arena. This is, of course, another feature of political contestation. Hence, where one party concedes a private, moral failing by admitting marital infidelity, Clinton's opponents sought to frame the ethical and legal questions in terms of perjury and obstruction of justice. As Brock (2002) and others have suggested, it seems that Clinton was set up in his testimony in the Paula Jones case because the independent counsel already had knowledge of the Lewinsky relationship.

Ginsberg and Shefter (1999) have argued that political scandal is a form of politics by other means, and this accords with the stress I have laid elsewhere on partisanship and the escalation of ethics wars (Williams, 1998), where the tension of partisan forces in the separated institutions acts as the power driving this escalation. The escalation of allegations and counter-allegations reached such heights in the U.S. Congress as to prompt the creation of an Ethics Reform Task Force in 1997 (Williams, 2002), and encouraged the House of Representatives to approve unanimously a frequently extended moratorium on the filing of new ethics complaints. The origins of the ethics wars in the House can partly be found in the decades of Democrat control, which ended in 1994, and the associated Republican perception that the

Democrats had displayed blatant political arrogance, partisanship, and corruption. A series of ethics complaints were made against Speaker Jim Wright, who was forced to resign in 1989. The subsequent Republican victory reshaped the political and ethical landscape, and it was predictable that the Democrats would seek revenge and try to regain their position by any means available. The intensification of the ethics wars was making it hard to find members willing to serve on the Committee on Standards of Official Conduct, and a truce was called in the form of the task force.

The ethics wars in the House invited parallel with the discourse of nuclear warfare strategy with its language of first strike, overwhelming retribution, escalation, and mutually assured destruction. Speaker Wright's farewell speech warned his colleagues of the dangers of mindless cannibalism and those, like Newt Gingrich, who had been among the first to raise the ethics sword for partisan advantage, were soon damaged by it.

Reforming ethics regulations in legislatures with a view to preventing ethics eruptions is fraught with difficulty. There is a notorious lack of institutional leadership in the U.S. Congress, and members are more concerned with what their constituents think of them and less concerned about what they think of the ethics of their legislative colleagues. It has long been recognized that many legislators run "for Congress by running against Congress" (Fenno, 1978, p. 167), and explain poor institutional performance in terms of the failings of their colleagues. Thus, other legislators' ethics are questionable, and the blame for the failure to reform the ethics process can also be placed on the shoulders of other legislators.

Scandals over political ethics in Britain have never matched the drama of Watergate or the impeachment of Clinton, but they have prompted some reform. Interestingly, such reforms of ethics regulations have rarely occurred when one party has an effective majority. Ethics appears only to stand a chance of getting on the British political agenda when party government has weakened and the executive loosens its control over the political process. One conclusion that could be drawn from this is that governments in Britain are indifferent to the claim that public trust and confidence in political ethics can only be restored by tightening up the regulatory regime and by ending the conflict of interest inherent in self-regulation.

Another way of looking at this issue is by stressing the political. The political aspect of political scandal is important because it influences the motivations of the parties involved, their ideological frame, the processes by which the scandal is resolved, and the consequences that ensue. The media, in their new attack style, pursue political scandals in search of the smoking gun – the incontrovertible proof that unethical, scandalous, transgressive behavior occurred on the part of a political figure. The phrase was used first by Representative Barber Conable in reaction to an Oval Office tape during the Watergate scandal (Safire, 1993). This pursuit assumes that a particular set of facts will resolve any doubt about ethical misconduct and, very occasionally, it does. But most of the time politics shapes the meanings attached to actions and events. Whatever the facts, those engaged in the pursuit or the defense of alleged political scandal will attempt to shift the scenery and bring to bear background norms that cast the facts in the most damaging or the most favorable light.

In the case of the Clinton scandals, the infamous stain on the dress proved not to be the decisive smoking gun necessary to bring down the president. The Starr Report and the Republican enemies of the Clintons interpreted the evidence against him in accordance with a particular political frame. This politicization then provided grounds for further contestation by the Clintons and their Democrat supporters, who then posed questions about the motives of their accusers and made claims of a vast right wing conspiracy. The final stage of the drama was the impeachment process, whose political character was most obviously revealed by the almost entirely partisan way the Senate voted.

CONCLUSION

This chapter has been both ambitious and selective in addressing the question of what has prompted escalating concerns about political ethics. Much of the literature on political ethics focuses on the experience of Western democracies, and it is a useful corrective to make some observations about the extent to which rising concerns about political ethics are a global phenomenon. For reasons of space, less attention has been given to the local, domestic sources of ethics concerns in any particular country or region of the Third World. But the argument has been made that much of the concern about ethics is generated in the West by IFIs, and their financial leverage has, through political conditionality, placed ethics concerns and their reduction at the top of the political agenda from Addis Ababa to Zanzibar.

The other main source of rising ethics concerns identified in this chapter is the evolving forms, commercialization and attitude of the mass media which, especially in the West, makes the political ethics of the ruling elite a major topic of critical media discussion. Good news is no news, and little attention is paid to identifying good practice or celebrating political figures who act with great integrity. Rather, the emphasis has become essentially negative and cynical. Sober, serious journalism has, in part, given way to sensationalist scandal hunting. And the new media forms, especially the Internet, have given mainstream media a never-ending source of allegation, rumor, and innuendo.

But the blaming-the-messenger approach does not allow for the ways in which politicians have acted as catalysts in this process. There is evidence that partisan advantage and individual ambition have encouraged a generation of politicians to go negative, and use accusations of unethical conduct as a political weapon of first resort. This negativity is seen in campaigning and in conduct within political institutions, and both are exacerbated by the ways in which they are reported and publicized by the media. Those in government see no political percentage or advantage in taking political ethics seriously, and thus reform of any sort is difficult to effect. Readers, listeners, viewers, and surfers absorb this negativity and, while there is some evidence that they can distinguish the entertainment function from the political information function (Zaller, 1998; Owen, 2000), the accumulated effect is to escalate concerns about political ethics.

We know more now than we have ever known about the conduct of our political masters. Accountability and transparency regimes are the norm in public life, and yet there appears to be a culture of suspicion and cynicism about politicians and their motives. One problem is how to distinguish "rumour from report, fact from fiction, reliable source from disinformant, truth-teller from deceiver" (O'Neill, 2002, pp. 63–64). Unqualified confidence in both the media and in politicians is understandably rare when we have no means of assessing the veracity of what they tell us. In Britain, the press were critical of Parliament's tradition of ethics self-regulation during the years of Conservative sleaze in the 1990s, and called for more effective, independent regulation in order to restore public confidence in political ethics. But the same press does not apply the same remedy to themselves and have vigorously opposed independent regulation, and their concern for restoring public confidence in editorial and journalistic ethics remains muted.

Ethics eruptions, like volcanic ones, are probably impossible to prevent and difficult to predict. The ethical seismograph has recently registered more audible disquiet about political ethics, but we have limited means of assessing where we are on any political equivalent of the Richter scale. An intensification of political scandals can be likened to a sort of ethical lava flow, and while we wait for the big one, we go about our daily business and wonder whether the rumblings are ominous or simply political hot air.

REFERENCES

Abrahamsen, R. (2000). *Disciplining democracy*. London: Zed Books.
Brock, D. (2002). *Blinded by the right*. New York: Crown Publishers.
Caufield, C. (1996). *Masters of illusion: The World Bank and the powers of nations*. New York: Henry Holt and Co. Inc.
Fenno, R. F. (1978). *Home style: House members in the districts*. New York: Little Brown.
Garment, S. (1992). *Scandal: The culture of mistrust in American politics* (Updated ed.). New York: Anchor Books.
Ginsberg, B., & Shefter, M. (1999). *Politics by other means* (Rev. ed.). New York: W.W. Norton.
Heywood, P. (1997). Political corruption: Problems and perspectives. *Political Studies, 45*, 417–435.
Kaplan, R. L. (2002). *Politics and the American Press: The rise of objectivity, 1865–1920*. Cambridge, UK: Cambridge University Press.
Markovits, A. S., & Silverstein, M. (Eds) (1988). *The politics of scandal: Power and process in liberal democracies*. New York: Holmes and Meier.
Mauro, P. (1995). Corruption and growth. *Quarterly Journal of Economics, 110*, 681–712.
Mulgan, G. (2004, May 7). The media's lies poison our system. *Guardian*. Retrieved August 12, 2005, from http://www.guardian.co.uk/commentary/story/0,3604,1211423,00.html
Naim, M. (1995). The corruption eruption. *Brown Journal of World Affairs, 2*, 245–261.
O'Neill, O. (2002). *A question of trust*. Cambridge, UK: Cambridge University Press.
Owen, D. (2000). Popular politics and the Clinton/Lewinsky affair: The implications for leadership. *Political Psychology, 21*, 161–177.
Rozell, M. J., & Wilcox, C. (2000). *The Clinton scandal and the future of American politics*. Washington, DC: Georgetown University Press.
Sabato, L. J. (2000). *Feeding frenzy: Attack journalism and American politics* (Rev. ed.). Baltimore, MD: Lanahan Publishers.
Safire, W. (1993). *Safire's new political dictionary*. New York: Random House.
Scheirov, M. (1994). *The dream of a new social order: Popular magazines in America, 1893–1914*. New York: Columbia University Press.
Sorensen, G. (Ed.) (1993). *Political conditionality*. London: Frank Cass.
Summers, J. H. (2000). What happened to sex scandals?. *Journal of American History, 87*, 825–854.
Thompson, J. B. (2001). *Political scandal: Power and visibility in the media age*. Cambridge, UK: Polity Press.
Wiebe, R. (1967). *The search for order, 1877–1920*. New York: Hill and Wang.
Williams, R. (1998). *Political scandals in the USA*. Chicago: Fitzroy Dearborn.
Williams, R. (Ed.) (1999). *The politics of corruption: Vol. 1, Explaining corruption*. Cheltenham, UK: Edward Elgar.
Williams, R. (2002). Conduct unbecoming: The regulation of legislative ethics in Britain and the United States. *Parliamentary Affairs, 55*, 611–625.
World Bank (1989). *Sub-Saharan Africa: From crisis to sustainable development*. Washington, DC: The World Bank.
World Bank (1992). *Governance and development*. Washington, DC: The World Bank.
Zaller, J. R. (1998). Monica Lewinsky's contribution to political science. *PS: Political Science and Politics, 31*, 182–189.

CODES OF CONDUCT FOR PUBLIC OFFICIALS IN EUROPE: COMMON LABEL, DIVERGENT PURPOSES ☆

David Hine

ABSTRACT

Codes of conduct have been adopted very broadly on both sides of the Atlantic in the last two decades. They have been introduced for both elected representatives and appointed officials. Though the accountability mechanisms vary, elected politicians prefer self-policing and enforcement. For appointed officials who carry out specialized functions with exposure to particular, clearly identifiable, ethical risks, where the need for public trust and confidence is great, it is important but also relatively straightforward to develop codes of practice. For generalist public servants, the situation is different. The range of ethical risk to which civil servants are exposed is broader. It is less easy to be specific about the risks involved.

☆ Research for this article was supported by the Economic and Social Research Council (Future Governance Programme: Lessons from Public Policy), Grant no. L216252003: *Standards in Public Life in Western Europe*.

Public Ethics and Governance: Standards and Practices in Comparative Perspective
Research in Public Policy Analysis and Management, Volume 14, 43–69
Copyright © 2006 by Elsevier Ltd.
All rights of reproduction in any form reserved
ISSN: 0732-1317/doi:10.1016/S0732-1317(05)14004-4

This chapter examines codes of conduct for public officials in various west European countries that have either introduced them or considered doing so: the UK, France, Germany, and Italy. Its aim is to understand differences between the codes that exist, and why some countries have abjured them, and through this to gain a better comparative understanding of the cultural context in which ethics management takes place in Western Europe. It is part of a wider comparative study of ethics management policies in these countries, and in the European Commission, the aim of which is to understand how much countries linked by geography and EU membership have learned, or could learn, from each other, and whether their approaches have converged over time. Given the great range of categories of officials – elected and appointed, national and local – what is reported here covers only appointed public officials (broadly, members of the national civil service). The explanation advanced is that ethics management outcomes in this area are a product of the administrative and legal culture, the particular ethical problems that get public attention at moments of critical importance when the system is under pressure, and the capacity for corporate self-defense of the target officeholders. The emphasis here, then, is on comparing public-policy response to ethical problems, not on the extent of these problems or their underlying causes. The risk factors potentially leading to corruption in Western Europe seem to vary in intensity, but are not unfamiliar in general public ethics debates. They are mainly variants of fairly standard conflict-of-interest problems posed where, as in most of Europe's welfare states, the public sector is large, contracting, purchasing, outsourcing, and public/private partnerships are extensive, regulation has major economic and commercial impacts, individuals can and do move backwards and forwards across the private/public sector boundary with relative ease, and parties need funding from private sources. There are, of course, major differences in perceptions of levels of corruption in the five countries of the study-perceptions being about the only comparative measure, given the unavailability of detailed comparable data on prosecutions, and the difficulty of interpreting prosecution data in any case. For what it is worth, taking the widely quoted Transparency Corruption Perceptions Index, the UK stands highest (for probity), followed by Germany, then Spain and France, and then Italy. The differences are quite significant, with the UK ranking at 8.7 out of 10, Germany at 7.7, France and Spain at 6.9, and Italy at 5.3. The UK ranks 11th in the global rating (equal with Canada); Italy 35th (equal with Kuwait).[1] These widely reported rankings have been fairly stable over time.

CODES AND THEIR PROBLEMS

In the public sphere, codes of conduct are a small but seemingly important part of an ethics infrastructure. It is difficult to conceive of liberal-democratic public life operating without some clarificatory understandings not only of procedural norms by which choices are aggregated, policies implemented, and rules enforced, but also of ethical values guiding individual behavior. The criminal law seems inadequate to do this on its own, however necessary its presence is to punish corruption when it happens. Ethical values seem important collectively, as legitimizing devices, sustaining belief in orderly and principled governance, and individually, motivating action that is socially valuable and possibly inflicting reputational damage on miscreants. The notion of public-service values – disinterested service, respect for the rule of law, fairness and equity of treatment, professional commitment – requires at least an unwritten code. However, once written down, significant problems arise.

Codes of ethics without sanction for misconduct raise the question of why officials actively seeking or passively tempted to act corruptly should change their behavior because of the existence of a code that has no sanctions. If the moral reward of doing the right thing is not sufficient to stop someone acting corruptly, why would the existence of a code do so? One either knows and values ethically correct behavior, or one does not. If one does not – if the individual has no moral instincts, and no psychic return of any kind from ethical behavior – it is difficult to see how it can be taught, and how codes without any sanctions will help.

One answer might be that in reality few individuals have no moral sense, but many have underdeveloped ones. Without guidance they may fail to recognize that their judgments in some ethical areas are defective; though if so, the deployment of a code of ethics requires effective ethical training and support. Second, it is clear that in practice in the public sphere, and even more in the private sphere where many of the same issues arise, there exist several gray areas where, even to someone concerned to act correctly, the right course of action is not self-evident. The efficiency costs of rigorous enforcement of appearance standards are an example, as are the problems defining the limits to corporate and organizational hospitality – extensively practiced in the modern world, even in the public sector. Third, organizational sociology suggests that values can be imparted throughout an organization, and individuals can internalize its values, so that what starts as social conditioning and emulation for acceptance may eventually turn into something which is practically indistinguishable from a developed ethical awareness, as long as the values are clearly and regularly signaled.

Nevertheless, the problem remains that individuals will vary in their susceptibility to these processes, leaving significant areas of risk for sanctionless codes. The risk will be all the greater in poorly run organizations with low morale and low efficiency. The relationship between efficiency and ethics is a complicated one, but it is evident that where staff are under pressure because of inadequate resources, poor training, and complex procedures (including procedures put in place to safeguard ethics), there will be trade-offs between ethics and efficiency (or at least immediate results) which will confuse the moral environment and significantly impair the diffusion of values.

It is for these reasons that codes of ethics frequently turn into codes of conduct with some form of sanction behind them. Immediately, however, a second set of questions arises. If a code of conduct is not hard law, what is it? What is the nature of the sanctions it imposes? What is its relationship to the stronger sanctions of criminal law? Administrative law and regulation can generally be written and changed more readily than hard law. It is less threatening, and while this can be a defect it can also be desirable when what is being sought is active compliance rather than passive obedience. Bringing the sanctions of criminal law into the workplace of a public organization (which obviously happens implicitly even in the UK through the Prevention of Corruption Acts, and very explicitly through the sections in most continental criminal codes that deal with public officials) is nevertheless inhibiting to a climate of trust and cooperation. Reprimand, loss of promotion, or even loss of a job or pension are not desirable, but all are probably a lot less worrying than personal liability for organizational financial loss, a hefty fine, or prison. It is precisely for these reasons that conditions-of-service rules are developed, enforceable in extremis in civil or administrative law (and when enforceable, as much to protect employee as employer), but for the most part worked out through less formal internal rules concerning discipline, confidentiality, organizational loyalty, honesty, and commitment, as well, of course, as pay and promotion – issues which, for the most part, cannot be dealt with by criminal law.

The real difficulty, as these latter considerations come to require more explicit elucidation in a more complex public-sector environment, is found when fitting them into the existing legal framework and each country's historical tradition. It is not easy to do so in a way that does not threaten and alienate the target groups on whom the codes are to be imposed, nor, as we shall see, is it always the case that what is contained in the code addresses long-term needs and not the concerns of the moment. First, insofar as codes involve some additional degree of normative guidance, supervision, and even formal control of the conduct and performance of officeholders beyond the normal systems of election (for elected officeholders), conditions of service and/or employment contract (for appointed public servants), and criminal, civil, and administrative law for them all, then codes in general may encounter some considerable resistance from those they are imposed on.

Elected officeholders have two standard sets of reasons for resisting tight normative controls. The first is the elective accountability relationship: elected officeholders can argue that they are accountable in a more fundamental way than any permanent, appointed officeholder to voters who can throw them out if they disapprove of their behavior. The second is the competitive nature of the struggle for office, and the potential for instrumental use of the sanctions that may back codes of conduct, and at the limit the potential to use it for the purposes of political persecution (the fundamental rationale for systems of immunity). We do not need to look far to realize the limits of these arguments. The elective accountability relationship is a very blunt and crude mechanism for controlling behavior, and at the local level it may be entirely useless. And the use of immunities, and the appeal to the merits of self-regulation as a substitute for external umpiring, is endlessly exposed to the risk of manipulation by unholy alliances and blocking coalitions of mutual interest, particularly in the era of grand coalitions and cartel parties.

Appointed officeholders cannot marshal these political arguments (at least, not so easily), but they can argue that codes of conduct introduce an ambiguity in the employment relationship, especially that which applies to public servants whose employment relationship is in some respects – particularly in the traditional context of European administrative and constitutional law – a special one in which the public servant commits to a career of public service, with a particular set of ideals and values behind it, abjures other career opportunities and even some social rights, including in some contexts the right to collective bargaining or withdrawal of labor, in return for long-term tenure and guaranteed conditions in retirement. If that ideal type is less easy to recognize today than in the past, it is precisely the consequences of the move toward the privatization of employment contracts in the public service across Europe (albeit at different rates) that provides a potentially strong motive among public employees to be suspicious of codes as separate and free-standing normative controls.

Codes of conduct introduce new and potentially ambiguous criteria of performance judgment. Insofar as they deal with issues that are not encapsulated in hard law, they introduce considerations into the employment relationship that expose public servants to controls and sanctions by either political masters or public managers that are, at the least, risky. Many aspects of codes of conduct – commitment, effort, diligence, relationships with superiors, processes of financial responsibility, the questioning of the probity or legality of work colleagues and especially superiors, relationships with elected political officeholders, relationships with the public and with outside interests in contexts where that relationship is a necessary part of the work of the office – are fraught with complexities. It is true that civil servants also have good reason to be thankful for codes of conduct, insofar as they clarify potential elements of ambiguity in some of the above situations, and in this sense offer protection, not potential exposure. But codes of conduct can also appear to move the performance goal posts about alarmingly, particularly if they are linked either directly or indirectly to contracts of employment and conditions of service, and generate uncertainty about judgments that may be brought to bear about behavior that is not defined as illegal and may not damage performance efficiency.

Indeed, it is precisely in circumstances of public-service reform of the type seen in recent years that codes of conduct are susceptible to misunderstanding between managers and public servants. For public managers and politicians, the introduction of market elements, performance incentives, devolved budgets, and outsourcing provide a new form of risk and exposure in the public service. Allocative economic efficiency supports such measures, but where public money and public accountability are also involved there is an ever-present risk of controversy over impropriety and conflict of interest that mostly does not arise in private commercial contracts. Codes offer a precautionary protective device. Insofar as they show that public-sector managers have established the limits of acceptable behavior, they demonstrate awareness of risk. If they actually modify behavior, so much the better, because then the remedy is real and not just cosmetic. But for officials it is precisely in the context of public-sector reform that codes of conduct, or at least some elements of them, can seem most threatening. If they are simply codes of ethical guidance, with no further effects beyond the reinforcement of self-policing norms for individuals, that is one thing. But if by adding to performance criteria they add to the pressures on public servants at the very moment at which more is expected of them in terms of productivity, performance, innovation, and responsibility, that is quite another. We may, therefore, expect some significant differences in the fate of the debate on codes of conduct, depending on the strength of public-service unions and the state of employment relationships.

Administrative Tradition

A second consideration is the legal and administrative culture in which codes are called upon to operate. Four of the five countries in this study have systems which share, in varying degrees, an adherence to Roman law traditions that, through common exposure to the Napoleonic code and the adherence to the legal values and traditions of the *etat de droit*, have developed heavily codified and internally differentiated systems of constitutional, administrative, criminal, and civil law. They are not, by any means, all the same today. The paradigm case of this is generally thought to be France, since of the four it has been the least affected by variance stemming from decentralization and has the longest and most strongly developed philosophy of public service and the unitary state. The UK has a different tradition, and this has affected legislation, on one hand, on corruption in the public sphere, which is subject to the common-law offense of bribery and three fairly archaic statutes which are widely seen as in need of overhaul, and on the other, on legislation on the civil service in general, which is heavily influenced by a tradition in which public authorities are treated in the common law as much closer to private citizens than in the continental tradition.

The complexities and ambiguities examined above concerning the status of a code of conduct as a potential addition to administrative law appear, as we shall see, to pose greater potential difficulties in countries with a Roman law tradition than in the UK. The political/constitutional status and conditions of service of civil servants under the Roman law tradition have historically been defined with much greater precision than in the UK, and in some, albeit fairly minimal respects, codes of conduct have long existed, in the shape of the ubiquitous rights and obligations clauses (brief though they have traditionally been), in the *statut général de la fontion publique* (and its German, Italian, and Spanish equivalents), even if, as contractual conditions of service, they rarely seem to have been seen by civil service managers or by civil servants themselves as real ethical guides. Moreover, the law on corruption of public servants (both elected and appointed) has generally been accorded a special and frequently detailed section inside the criminal law. Finally, administrative law itself generally regulates at least some aspects of conditions of service. In short, in this ideal type, there is not perceived to be a great deal of room for additional, soft-law status prescriptions on how civil servants ought to behave without the risk of appearing to weaken some of the existing statute laws, and without raising difficult questions about how some aspects of the code might interlink with harder law.

The UK could be said to stand at the other end of this paradigm. Very few words have ever been put into hard law regarding either ethical behavior or the role and status of civil servants. That is not to argue that in the UK their role and status is unclear (on the contrary, it may be said that in the UK, the distinction between civil servants and politicians is at least in some respects a good deal clearer than in most continental regimes), but this does not depend on formal law. The UK to this day lacks a formal law governing the status of the civil service. One has been proposed by both the Select Committee on Public Administration (2003–04) and the Committee on Standards in Public Life (*Ninth Report*, 2003), and the current government has undertaken to find parliamentary space for it, though it has so far failed to do so (United Kingdom Committee on Standards in Public Life, 2003; United Kingdom House of Commons Public Administration, 2003–04). The relatively clear boundary between the two has historically depended on a series of iterations semi-officially enshrined as conventions (the Northcote Trevelyn Report of 1854 [which recommended a short definitional law, no more than a few clauses, still absent 150 years later], the treasury circulars of 1919 and 1920, the Tomlin Report of 1931, Warren Fisher's evidence to the Public Accounts Committee in 1936, the 1985 Armstrong Memorandum). It is also found in easily alterable administrative decisions linked to what were originally called pay and conditions, nowadays incorporated into the Civil Service Management Code (CSMC). The law on corruption, contained in the common-law offense of bribery and the three Prevention of Corruption Acts of 1889, 1906, and 1916, is best described as in a state of advanced calcification.[2]

Between these two ends of the Anglo-French spectrum stand two cases – Germany and Italy – which, while derivations of the codified public-law tradition, have represented higher degrees of decentralization and subnational legislative authority than France. Germany relies more than the others on administrative coordination, and has a more flexible use of administrative regulation in its legal order, the effects of which are considered below. Spain has a system which, despite the impact of asymmetrical decentralization, continues to reflect very faithfully the characteristics of the French Roman law tradition.

The Content of Codes

The two variables above are likely to help determine how easy a matter it is to introduce a code of conduct, and what its status is when introduced. But there is also the matter of its content. Thus far, we have tended to proceed on the assumption that codes of conduct have the same general purpose, and more or less the same content. In fact, this is far from being the case. There are some striking differences. A code may be a statement of the quasi-constitutional status of the relevant reference group (for example, civil servants or members of the judiciary). It may be a very general statement of the ethical climate in which the public service should operate. It may be a guide to more detailed ethical behavior applying to the whole of the public service or to particular categories (for example, regulators, judges, or the police). Or, it may contain general statements of what the public can expect in its interactions with the public service. None of these categories is necessarily incompatible with any of the others, but what is actually selected for inclusion is susceptible to variation, and the explanation for what is actually selected seems to be a combination of what is possible (given the sorts of constraints imposed by the considerations discussed above) and what is current and pressing on the political agenda. The latter is not an easy variable to pin down. To write a narrative of the circumstances in which codes are introduced, and to arrive at definitive judgments about what the actors concluded was both necessary and possible, requires a good deal more space than is available in this article. Here, it is only possible to outline the bare bones of this narrative and some simple associated explanations. In summary, what we shall find is that the UK, Germany, and Italy have all adopted what look like codes of conduct for public officials, and all three have developed codes in at least some other areas of public service – national legislatures, subnational government, and other public agencies, especially in the legal and regulatory fields. France and Spain have been more reluctant to do so for public officials, relying much more on hard law, though France has a wide range of *codes deontologiques* performing a related role. We also find, however, that even for the three which have introduced general public-service codes of conduct, both the content and the apparent use to which the codes have been put are subject to some considerable variation.

THE UNITED KINGDOM

The most striking feature of the UK's Civil Service Code is that while at first sight it might seem to be a code of conduct, its real focus is on the constitutional status of civil servants. The code contains relatively little about the personal propriety of public officials, or about conflicts of interest, postemployment, or personal gain from office. Of its 13 paragraphs, only three (paragraphs 6–8, covered in eight lines) deal with this type of issue. All the others cover matters of concern that had arisen somewhat haphazardly in the years preceding the code's appearance in 1996, affecting constitutional relationships between civil servants and ministers: confidentiality, accountability to ministers, service exclusively to the government of the day, impartiality, abstinence from political activity, confidentiality in the use of information acquired in public employment and, in the last three paragraphs, the rules of behavior governing situations in which the civil servant believes he or she is being asked to perform acts which may involve illegality, maladministration, or a breach of constitutional convention.

What they add up to is a formal statement of the traditional British set of principles: that civil servants are there to serve ministers in a role of reinforced neutrality, that they must give honest and objective advice, and that the public interest is defined by the government of the day. Civil servants may not appointment themselves as guardians of some other definition of national interest, making use of information or strategic position to further that interest against ministers or Parliament, and in the case of policy which they believe is improper, illegal, involves maladministration, or runs against a fundamental issue of conscience, after a series of internal reporting procedures up to the civil service commissioners has been exhausted, it reaffirms that it is the duty of the civil servant to resign – and to maintain a duty of confidentiality even after they have left Crown employment. This seems to have been very much what Parliament, and particularly the then treasury and Civil Service Select Committee, the civil service commissioners, the Cabinet Office, and indeed the Committee on Standards in Public Life, had seen themselves as doing: reiterating and reaffirming in clearer, but still inherently nonstatutory language, principles that (as they saw it) were in danger of being misunderstood by the actors, particularly in the context of controversies generated by a range of cases which, taken together, did not constitute evidence of anything approaching systemic levels of corruption, but were seen as putting at risk public confidence in the probity of officeholders, and obfuscating some basic understandings on which the British system operates.

This becomes understandable when the context in which the code was introduced is recalled. That context was a somewhat unfocused debate about small-scale parliamentary corruption, which, when tacked on to other miscellaneous concerns floating in public debate at the time, led a tired and divided government to attempt what governments are often tempted to do in such situations: pass the problem over to a committee of apparently authoritative individuals with a general brief to think about the problems broadly, to take some time to do so, and above all to restore public confidence. As far as the role of public officials was concerned, this was the agenda of the Committee on Standards in Public Life, and it was very much also the approach to the civil service taken by the treasury and Civil Service Select Committee. Neither appeared to believe there was systemic corruption across the public service, or that there was a wholesale need to take a wholly new approach. The committee reported that it had heard of a range of concerns from witnesses, especially about the possibility of postemployment offering inducements to corruption among civil servants, and that it had some concerns about planning in local government, but in the presence of hearsay evidence, and indeed not being empowered to investigate particular cases, it did not conclude that there were fundamental problems, though it recommended some tightening of the rules concerning postemployment (United Kingdom Committee on Standards in Public Life, 1995). Its first report, moreover – the only one to precede the appearance of the Civil Service Code – was extremely wide ranging and covered a number of issues, of which the behavior of public officials was not the most important. The result was a focus – as far as the latter issues were concerned – very largely on the one issue that was very current: the question of ministers and civil servants. On this the committee came down in favor of a restatement of traditional relationships, followed by the treasury and Civil Service Committee, and this became the approach taken by the civil service commissioners when the code was issued on January 1, 1996.[3]

The result was that the Civil Service Code emerged in the form in which it has essentially remained in the intervening eight years: a document light on conventional ethical guidance, and comparatively long on constitutional relationships. Its status as an ethical guide is further placed in question by the ambiguity of its formal role. It has been incorporated into all staff conditions of service as an annex, and all departments and agencies must, in further defining any standards of conduct they require of staff, ensure that the rules set down for staff fully reflect the code. Whether that would mean, as regards either the issues of personal ethics or relationships with ministers, that the code is somehow justiciable, is unclear. The civil service commissioners have been assigned the task of reporting regularly on their role as final court of appeal in any cases in which civil servants believe they are being asked to do things which, on the grounds listed above, they believe are wrong, but the commissioners report that in essence the number of cases is negligible and also a belief that familiarity with the code across the service is low. The Committee on Standards in Public Life, in both its Fourth and Ninth Reports, also took this view and recommended that the civil service take steps to ensure greater familiarity with the code. Of course, the presence or absence of formal cases emerging under the code does not prove it is not having a real effect. It may be providing a framework in which both ministers and civil servants understand relationships more clearly, and it may indeed provide some form of ethical guidance to civil servants, though if so, it provides only the most general context and little practical help, even in comparison with the CSMC.

The CSMC is, however, a further example of the light-touch approach adopted in the UK toward ethical regulation. On the face of it, in regard to conduct and discipline, it appears to contain a good deal more than the Civil Service Code, consisting of five sections running to 26 pages.[4] However, like the latter, the management code is, on close examination, quite light on defining standards of personal ethical behavior except in one area (postemployment) and indeed remains quite detailed on the political and constitutional status of the civil service. The principles of conduct are very briefly stated: a four-point paragraph, the first two points of which are a further restatement of political impartiality, confidentiality of official information, and obedience to ministerial decisions (i.e., they too are about constitutional relationships); the third regarding the general avoidance of conflicts of interest; and the fourth a two-line ban on gifts, hospitality, or benefits which might be seen to compromise judgment or integrity. Then follow some further general principles on the reporting of relevant business interests; staff may not engage in any contracts directly or indirectly with their own department or agency, nor can agency property be sold to staff who may have special knowledge about these assets or have been involved in preparation of the sale. In terms of practical advice, however – the identification of risk situations, advice to civil servants on how those situations arise, what to do when they loom, advice to managers about measures to take to limit risks, etc. – neither the Civil Service Code nor the CSMC has much to offer.

The one area of real concern seems clearly to be postemployment, where the explicitly stated concern is the appearance standard: the concern to counter any possible suspicion that an appointment might involve reciprocity of favors between the new employer and the former civil servant. Here the rules are set out in extensive detail and in discursive fashion.[5] Procedures and criteria are described, as are the categories of civil servants who must submit themselves to the scrutiny of the Advisory Committee on Business Appointments during the two-year period following departure from the civil service. There is also, unique among all aspects of ethical regulation in the UK civil service, a routine for making staff regularly aware of the rules. Nevertheless, the CSMC is at pains to make clear that "it is in the public interest that people with experience of public administration should be able to move into business and other bodies. ... [and that] most applications submitted under the rules are approved without condition" (United Kingdom CSMC, 1996: Sec. 4.3, Annex A).

In the UK case, therefore, we find in the Civil Service Code, taken together with the CSMC (the latter a document in contractual but nonstatutory form), documents that do address some aspects of the ethical behavior of public officials and present few problems of compatibility with existing legislation. The code is, however, a document that is heavily weighted in the direction of political and constitutional relationships. There is, moreover, little evidence that UK civil service staff associations have had any difficulty with the Civil Service Code, even in the area where its provisions regarding whistle-blowing seem inadequately protective of the rights of employees under the 1999 Public Interest Disclosure Act. Indeed, staff associations are reported as having been in favor of actually incorporating the Civil Service Code into law as a civil service act, appearing to welcome the clarification of civil service/politician relationships which the code was designed to deliver (United Kingdom Committee on Standards in Public Life, 1995).

FRANCE

The French case, and in practice the Spanish case[6] (since the reasoning and approach there appears to have mirrored what has occurred in France), reflect the enduring pull of the administrative law tradition. French authorities have not been reluctant to try to deal with political corruption, and the range of new legislation on multiple fronts since the mid-1980s is unparalleled elsewhere in Western Europe. Historically, moreover, France resorted to what are termed *codes deolontologiques* on a very broad front to regulate professions and particular areas of the public service. Several of these go back many decades, and certainly to much earlier than the last 10–15 years. But they have a form of formal legal backing which makes them very different from the soft-law codes of conduct developed more recently, and take their cue from an approach to public-service management which stands at the opposite end of the spectrum from that in the UK.

In France, authorities have constructed a series of systematic and regularly updated codifications of the legal framework surrounding particular types of public activity, and have also inserted into the criminal code provisions regarding the corruption of public officials which are much more precise and explicit than anything stemming from the various corrupt practices acts in the United Kingdom. In particular, Articles 432–435 of the *Code Penal* lay down a series of specific and precise penalties for particular acts of misconduct (of which, the central one is the *delit d'ingerence* – obtaining undue advantage) applying to a wide range of public officeholders, both appointed and elected, including not only MPs and elected local councilors and public civil servants, but also members of the police, judiciary, and public enterprise. For public officials, since 1946 this has been backed up by a wide-ranging, public-service statute (*statut général de la fontion publique*) which defines, first, the nature of the civil service (today technically divided into three groups[7]), second, its relationship to the elected political class, and third, general conditions of service, including the rights and obligations of civil servants. Beyond this, for many areas of public activity, the law has been codified into a series of specific codes covering areas like customs, labor, building and housing, public health, commerce, etc., where (inter alia because these codes cover many aspects of the sectors) the work of public officials is subject to a range of proscriptions, the breaking of which subjects them to fines and potentially incarceration. Sometimes this is directly applied, sometimes by cross-reference to the criminal code. These, it should be added, are additional to the professional codes of conduct governing groups such as doctors, dentists, lawyers, etc., who happen to work in the public sector and who are thus subject to both forms of regulation. Finally, there is the case law of the *Conseil d'Etat*. The *conseil* has, over many decades, developed an extensive set of additional rules known as *principes généraux du droit* (see Aubin, 2001, pp. 16–25).

The characteristics of the French system are its comprehensiveness, its formality, its reliance on hard law and sanctions, and its long-standing quality. It is a system in which distrust of public officials, both elected and appointed, could be said to have been institutionalized in gradually more comprehensive fashion for nearly two centuries, and in which the corpus of formal public (and criminal) law has been seen as the main vehicle by which ethics is policed. An ethics commissioner from Mars, on a policy-learning mission to Western Europe and unfamiliar with the concept of political culture, would certainly conclude that France was the best policed system on the subcontinent. The reality, of course, is somewhat different. France is a society where economy and government have been bound up in special ways that have created a cross-fertilization of personnel between the public sector and the economy (the system of *pantouflage*) which has characteristics widely thought to expose public life to very high ethical risks compared to systems where boundaries are better maintained. Something similar may be said of the influence exercised by the political class over the judicial system (see, inter alia, Piastra, 2000; Ferstenberg, 1998). This is not an argument which can be developed here, however, since this article is not concerned primarily with the adequacy of ethical systems in the face of particular types of problems, or indeed whether the formal rules function properly (on both of which there may be considerable doubt in relation to France), but rather on how the system is set up, what assumptions it rests on, and what this means for innovations such as codes of conduct.[8] What is relevant here, however, is the impact of the extensive and enduring debate, which the widespread incidence of political corruption has occasioned in France, on assumptions about how to deal with the threat of corruption among public servants. In the last 15 years, France has been through a formidable range of corruption cases involving a large number of prominent political leaders on both sides of the principal political divide.[9] There have also been a large number of cases involving officials who have been prosecuted for having moved from the public-service to the private-sector concerns which they previously regulated, which have been frequent, bitter, and highly politicized. That process has been paralleled by a similar one at the local level in which, not infrequently, an incoming administration, opening up the books of its predecessor, has enthusiastically denounced its political opponents to the judicial system for corruption, mainly in purchasing and contracting.

The consequence has been that it has been extremely difficult for authorities to take the route taken in the UK, of minimal legislative intervention and of an essentially voluntary code of conduct – projected outward for public consumption and reassurance as much as inward to public servants. This approach would have been greeted by a good deal of public skepticism, and would almost certainly have encountered vociferous skepticism from the opposition of the day. The activism shown by French authorities has thus been far higher than that in the UK if judged by regulatory action: as early as 1983 there was a major overhaul of the general public service law, and the criminal code's articles on corruption of public officials have been revised on several occasions since 1990 – initially in response to the cases inside France, and later in preparation for transnational initiatives from the Council of Europe, the EU, and the Organisation for Economic Cooperation and Development (OECD). On each occasion when new legislation was being prepared, there was also consideration given, both by Parliament and by special investigative commissions, to the introduction of a separate code of conduct for public officials. This was particularly true in the years from 1990 to 1995, when a series of new measures was introduced imposing stiffer penalties against public officials who exploit their office to show favor to private-sector actors and then move to work for the latter. Legal rules were tightened in a series of stages, and three new ethics commissions – one for central government officials, one for local government, and one for the hospital sector – were established to regulate applications from former public officials wanting to move to the private sector. All through this process, however, and right down to the most recent changes to the criminal code in 1999–2000, the strong preference was to avoid supplementing the formal process with a nonstatutory code of conduct. In fact, a common code had been considered by the so-called Bouchery Commission, set up by the then Prime Minister Pierre Beregovoy, in April 1992. The commission issued a series of interim discussion points for departmental feedback, among which was a proposal for a common code of conduct to be drafted by the Ministry for the Public Service, the details of which would be supplemented where appropriate by individual departments. On this basis, and in fact before the final report of the Bouchery Commission (1992), the ministry initiated a series of discussions on the content of such a code. Departments were invited to make amendments, though it appears that the ensuing responses, and fears that the text would be either too vague or inadequate in relation to the detailed functions of each department, stalled the whole process. In the meantime, the new legislation emanating from other aspects of the Bouchery report was very quickly turned into law: (*loi n° 93–122, 29/1/1993 relative à la prévention de la corruption et à la transparence de la vie économique et des procédures publiques*).[10] The law determined only that working parties would be established to give further consideration to a common agreement on postemployment issues – leading to the previously mentioned ethics commissions. The proposal for a more general code was abandoned, with some individual directorates in the Finance Ministry (customs, taxes) and the Ministry of Supply (where contracting issues were significant) drafting individual ethical codes related to departmental operations.[11]

Given the volume of legislation already on the statute books, and the detail in which it existed, it is certainly difficult to see what would have been added by a code of conduct without that code becoming unreadably long. But the most fundamental reason seems to be that no one – not the authorities, the public-service unions, or the other agencies with either operational or strategic oversight responsibility for ethics management – believed that codes of conduct would add anything, at least in the French context. In an environment in which the black-letter law interpreting the compatibility of activities while in post with subsequent employment was already extensive, staff associations were circumspect about adding soft law and hence an added element of uncertainty to potential future corruption prosecutions, and have appeared to prefer the certainty and safeguards generated by a strictly legal approach (for a discussion, see OECD, 2003). The *Service central de prévention de la corruption* (SCPC), the *Direction générale des Renseignements généraux* (RG), the *Direction centrale de la police judiciaire*, and the *Office central de répression de la grande délinquance financière* (OCRGDF), which together constitute the entire formidable galaxy of 16 central agencies with responsibility for anti-corruption strategy in France, have all declared themselves to be opposed to the introduction of a soft-law code of conduct for the public service on the grounds that it would confuse ethics management and might well undermine existing legislation.

GERMANY

The status and the manner of the German code of conduct for civil servants and other public officials stands in marked contrast to the British Civil Service Code. Its content does not involve a definition, let alone a reworking, of any issue of status or constitutional relationship, and it has not had the political visibility of the UK code. It is embedded in administrative procedure, and while aimed ultimately at individuals, it is also, and just as much, a guide to anti-corruption management procedures for individual agencies. In this sense, it is an administrative tool, but precisely because of that, it is worked out in extensive practical detail. In the UK case, the one area where administrative practice is laid out in detail is postemployment. In the German case, a wide range of areas is described, driven by an overarching philosophy of risk identification and risk management.

For most of its life, the German Federal Republic relied for ethics management on mechanisms derived from the traditional hierarchy of constitutional law, criminal law, the civil service law (both the federal civil service act and the civil service statutes of the individual states), and federal disciplinary rules governing breach of official duty. This begins at the point of entry to the service when the public servant swears an oath of allegiance to a constitution which, through Articles 1 and 3, and especially clause 5 of Article 33, sets out basic ethical principles on which public service is to be based. Curiously, for a system that shows such continuity of tradition from Roman law, through the German civil code of 1900, to the modern *Rechtsstaat*, clause 5, which refers to traditional principles of the civil service, it in some respects relies on an uncodifed convention, since statements of these principles are only to be found in commentary, not in original law. However, while these basic principles guide civil servants in understanding the duties and privileges of public service in a general way, the real weight of ethical control was traditionally carried out in coercive fashion through criminal law (in the German case through paragraphs 331 to 334 of the German criminal code), and through the 1957 framework legislation for the federal civil service. The latter laid down a series of obligations in relation to appropriate behavior, limitations on secondary income, and situations of possible conflict of interest. Corruption, moreover, was interpreted in the criminal law quite widely, with appearance standards being applied as well as those regarding a completed act of bribery, so that just the acceptance of a bribe, irrespective of its impact on the public official's behavior, may be considered evidence of corruption. This led to a high degree of specificity in the definition of gifts in Article 70 of the *Bundesbeamtengesetz*.

Consequently, until the late 1990s, Germany, like France, saw no need for a nonlaw-based approach to ethics management in the civil service, and while a number of political scandals in the 1980s and 1990s raised the profile of corruption as a political issue, the handling of these did not generate the same sort of generalized response as in the UK, nor was their extent anything as far reaching and as politicized as in France. The interparty debate over political corruption was muted, for reasons that reflect the deep-seated practice of cross-party consensus on constitutional issues in postwar Germany, and the political class in general preferred to hand the issues over to the courts and to limit political debate to particular instances of wrongdoing. The notion that there were systemic issues, which ought to be handled in a politically visible but nonpartisan way through anything akin to the Committee on Standards in Public Life, was widely seen as both unrealistic and incompatible with the legal traditions applying in the German system.

However, German approaches to ethics management were affected by other developments in the 1990s. While the legal framework in Germany, and the high degree of administrative decentralization generated by German federalism, left the system much less affected by the New Public Management (NPM) revolution than in Anglo-Saxon countries, it was not totally unaffected. Germany had its own debate about the implications for ethics management, and had its own concerns about the scope for political corruption that some aspects of NPM could create. Germany was also subject to the same range of transnational initiatives that started in this period and that affected other European countries: the OECD anti-bribery convention making the bribery of foreign officials by German nationals a criminal offense prosecutable in Germany, the EU Bribery Act (implementing the protocol to the Convention on the Protection of the European Communities' Financial Interests), and the Council of Europe's Group of States Against

Corruption (GRECO) process. All these generated a growing concern to address corruption issues, as did the significant rise in corruption cases handled by the police and prosecutorial authorities during the course of the decade (up from 258 in 1994 to 1,034 in 1999), with rises particularly notable in the area of public-procurement contracts and health-service contracts (Council of Europe/Group of States Against Corruption, 2002).

The consequence was that in 1998 Germany did adopt what it described as a code of conduct for federal civil servants and other public officials, embedded in the context of a set of administrative guidelines issued under the authority of Article 86 of the Basic Law. The code was presented as a mechanism "to make employees aware of dangerous situations, in which they can unintentionally be drawn into corruption ... to motivate employees to fulfill their duty and obey the law ... and to increase awareness of corruption." It consists, first, of a set of nine fairly simply stated precepts directly addressed to individual civil servants, each elaborated by a three- or four-paragraph explanation of how to behave in particular situations; second, of a further set of guidelines for unit and agency managers, again running to several pages and detailing risk situations and best-practice measures; and third, at the top level, of a further set of practical principles of more general applicability.

The focus, throughout the document, which runs to some 7,000 words, is on measures to combat corruption and on the identification of situations of risk. It addresses a wide range of practical issues including: best-practice procedures on the internal transparency of decision making, the development of decisional audits (the so-called four- or six-eyes principle), the rotation of staff, internal financial audit procedures, behavior in situations with the potential to generate corruption opportunities, the obligation of heads of service to inform a public prosecutor's office when corruption is reported by subordinates and suspicions are confirmed, dealing with offers of gifts, sponsorship, and the establishment of special anti-corruption units at the agency level.

What is striking about this process is, first, its separation from the legal framework. There is no question, in the German context, of the code of conduct, either for individual officials, or for agency managers, forming part of a contract of employment or formal disciplinary regulations. In this sense, despite the formalism of traditional German approaches to ethics management, the code is actually closer to a mechanism for internal self-discipline than, for example, the British code, which at least in principle is part of the contract of employment. The code is intensely practical: of all the attempts to define corruption and deal with it in criminal and administrative law and codes of conduct across the countries of the study, the German code, and its associated administrative guide, gets far closer than any other to defining ways in which public officials can identify risk situations and avoid exposing themselves to them. Finally, the code has been followed up at regular intervals since its first appearance. Contact points have been set up for dissemination across the federal civil service, there is a regular reporting process on implementation, and there have been three evaluation exercises by the federal government since 1998.

ITALY

The Italian code of conduct for public servants was first promulgated in 1994, making it one of the earliest generalized codes of conduct for civil servants in Western Europe. Its early arrival coincided with, and certainly owed its origin to, an unusual window of opportunity. The corruption scandals known collectively as *tangentopoli* had broken over the political system starting in the aftermath of the 1992 general election. By spring 1993, a referendum on electoral reform, and the issuing of *avvisi di garanzie* (notification of criminal investigation proceedings) against over 200 members of Parliament brought the collapse of the Amato government. In the absence of a workable majority, a caretaker government under former Central Bank Governor Carlo Azeglio Ciampi was created, consisting largely of technocrats. Briefly, they enjoyed wide freedom to introduce a range of measures, which in other circumstances might have been bitterly contested by the parliamentary patrons of public-sector groups. Thus it was that the Ministry for the Public Service fell temporarily into the hands of Italy's leading academic expert on administrative law and long-standing proponent of radical public-service reform, Professor Sabino Cassese, who rapidly set about implementing his long-nourished dreams on a number of fronts.

Tangentopoli was mainly a set of scandals related to party funding, involving systemic corruption of contract awards and grants of permits. Private businesses paid public officials an illicit levy, proportional to the value of the contract or permit. Although heavy political control of the administration permitted funds to be diverted in this way, it could not be achieved without wholesale cooperation by public officials through a variety of incentives and side payments. The administrative apparatus was therefore as important a target for reformers as parties and politicians. Public service reform was, however, as in the case of the European Commission, a sphere of policy where efficiency and ethics were almost inseparable, and for many analytically indistinguishable. Ethical failures stemmed from a range of difficulties including arcane and complex structures and procedures, often introduced originally to safeguard probity; an unwillingness of senior managers to take responsibility for the soundness and value-for-money of expenditure plans and programs, but rather to take refuge in legal formalism; the inappropriateness and ineffectiveness of audit and control mechanisms; the absence of efficiency incentives and career-management systems; and so on.

In 1993–1994, none of this would have been sufficient to move the process of public-service reform (deadlocked for years) without the window of opportunity provided by the nature of the recently installed government. The political vacuum of 1993 offered an opportunity for something which, by Italian standards, was years ahead of its time: the introduction of a code of conduct, simultaneously with a new statute governing contracts of employment, that the public-service unions found difficult to oppose in the face of a government with formidable, if temporary, moral authority, and little in the way of the normal opposition in Parliament that protected public-service workers. The result was a brief but intense period of activity during 1993–1994, during which the ministry seized the opportunity to set up a commission, report, and introduce – by ministerial decree (i.e., without formal enabling legislation) – a code of conduct for civil servants.[12]

The content of the code[13] was an eclectic amalgam of concerns. It dealt with ethical behavior of civil servants: avoidance of conflict of interest through a variety of transparency and abstention-from-decision mechanisms (though not postemployment, since this was deemed incompatible with constitutional rights), respect for legality, impartiality of treatment, openness in dealing with the public, political neutrality, diligence, responsibility in the use of public resources, etc. However, there are also a range of concerns that appear to stand somewhere between a code of conduct for individual behavior, and a respect for principles which in reality are much more the responsibility of the political tier to deliver – procedural simplicity (a major concern in Italy in recent years), respect for subsidiarity, respect for quality-charter standards in public service, cooperation with processes of performance evaluation exercises, and the process of administrative devolution, in particular. There is also an obligation, linked closely to concerns about Masonic membership in Italy, to make public membership in secret organizations, which might bear on performance in office.

It was this latter group of concerns – together with a general concern on the part of Italian staff unions that the process had been introduced without consultation, in a hurry, and without adequate thought to the precise legal status that the code would have in disciplinary terms – that led to a policy of almost complete noncooperation with the code, and also to intense argument about its legality and purpose. Even more seriously compromising for the code of conduct was that within a few weeks of issuing the code, the government (and hence also the code's chief architect and defender, Sabino Cassese) was out of office, never to return. The following two years saw a general election that brought to office, albeit briefly, the first government headed by Silvio Berlusconi, not a prime minister whose first priority was ethical reform issues, and following Berlusconi a confused and uncertain government under Lamberto Dini. Only in 1996 was a reforming government with anything resembling programmatic purpose and a workable majority returned to office, but Franco Bassanini, the new public service minister, was an individual whose interests in administrative reform took him, at least initially, in a different direction, with a very ambitious program for public-service reform – one focused in its early stages on securing a series of changes to the departmental structure of the civil service (reduction in ministries, decentralization of a range of functions to the regions) and to its management, particularly at senior levels. This took several years, and during this time the code of conduct was left in abeyance, effectively yielding to the opposition put up against it by the staff associations after 1994. The result was that only in 2000 was the issue of a code of conduct returned to with any seriousness. At that point a new version of the 1994 text was issued, clarifying the key legal uncertainty about status by incorporating the code in new contracts of employment, and requiring each government department to set about establishing appropriate units of control and consultancy.[14]

In short, the use made of the code took a decidedly disciplinarian turn. It became a primary document for the imposition of workplace discipline. Management was encouraged to make use of the code for the purpose of addressing very basic problems of productivity performance among rank-and-file staff: a use very different from the notion of a code of conduct serving as a set of ethical guidelines. Thus, in 2002, the Public Service Ministry conducted an extensive investigation to discover how far the code was used as a formal disciplinary sanction, discovering that it had been used in 2000–2001 in 1,725 disciplinary cases, resulting in just over 1,000 penalties in the full range from formal warning to dismissal.[15]

The Italian case, therefore, presents an unusual development. The code started out with many of the appearances of a classic code of conduct, generating a set of guiding principles. It was accompanied by a series of quasi-constitutional precepts about how public services ought to be improved. These precepts looked very much as if they could not be addressed by individual civil servants at lower levels of the service, and certainly not without fundamental structural reform as a precondition. Not surprisingly, without any preparation, the code received an overwhelmingly hostile reception, and in the volatile conditions of Italian government in the 1990s its premature appearance led to its almost immediate shelving for some years. It reappeared in a different climate, the legal ambiguities having been solved by incorporating it fully into formal conditions of service, as a would-be instrument of work-place discipline in one of Europe's public-service workforces where the problems of discipline and productivity are most acute.

CONCLUSION

This chapter has been concerned with analyzing what codes of conduct are in place and why, rather than with showing effectiveness or usage. There is little evidence, other than in the German case, that authorities who have overall responsibility for central civil services have devoted much attention to the effectiveness either of codes or of harder forms of disciplinary mechanisms in combating corrupt or otherwise unacceptable behavior. Measures to combat corruption are generally a combination of responses to particular cases that reach public attention, and a reassertion of values – in this case, basic public service values attaching to the civil service – combined with a proscription, either in a code or in law, of various forms of unacceptable behavior. What actually works seems to get relatively little attention, both because of the need authorities have to demonstrate action, and also because there is a more general cognitive difficulty in assessing effectiveness in the fight against corruption. From the information presented here, we can clearly conclude that the current deployment of codes of conduct for public officials in Europe is patchy and inconsistent, and still in a phase of relatively early development. France and Spain have – the *codes deontologiques* apart – abjured codes of conduct altogether. The UK and Italy have both adopted them, incorporating them to some degree (in the Italian case very forcibly) into conditions of service to deliver a form of potentially extensive workplace discipline. In the Italian case, this has become a central purpose. In the UK case, although the Civil Service Code is extensively referred to in other public service documents, it does not appear in practice to perform this disciplinary role. This is left to the CSMC, where the focus is essentially on postemployment. Both the UK and the Italian codes have also been vehicles for articulating particular aspirational goals in the administrative/ constitutional arena, with values appearing to be projected out to a much wider audience than the civil servants to whom the code is formally to be applied. As a practical and detailed guide to ethics management for managers, and to self-regulation and risk avoidance for individual civil servants, only the German code – an administrative tool not given wide public visibility – seems to get close to what we might think of as a model code of conduct. It is detailed, practical, and apparently taken quite seriously by departments and individual civil servants alike. But it has no formal sanction behind it – it is purely for guidance and reference – and, interestingly, it appears not to have been internally controversial.

How much these differences matter is difficult to judge. Across the criminal law on corruption, administrative law, and civil law obligations that public servants face in relation to negligence and financial liability, labor contracts, and codes of conduct, it might be thought that the underlying ethical features of broader public-service values across Europe are quite similar. Where the values are found, whether the emphasis is on the positive idealism of public service or the negative imperative to avoid conditions that breed corruption, and whether they are articulated in a code rather than hard law, might be regarded as largely secondary issues. In some respects they are. In terms of institutional clarity, however, it is important to understand what different political systems mean when they use the term codes of conduct, just as it is to understand what they mean by ideas contained in, for example, discussions about devolution and subnational government. This article shows that it is not always easy to devise codes of conduct in terms that enable them to mesh with the existing legal and ethical order, and to prevent them being redrafted by those with particular agendas. In turn, this sheds light on the difficulty of making a reality of the introduction of a common code of conduct (and indeed other common ethical vehicles, like regulations on the funding of political parties) along the lines currently being advocated by the Council of Europe/Parliamentary Assembly (2000).[16] Whether there is a case for introducing common codes of this type across widely differing administrative cultures might be thought of as questionable. The doctrine of functional equivalence (convergence as to outcome rather than as to vehicle), which underlies both the OECD Anti-Bribery Convention and the GRECO process, might be thought of as more effective than as an attempt to impose a common model.

NOTES

1. See Transparency International, 2003. Standard deviations do not greatly differ between countries for the 11–13 surveys that make up the composite CPI 2003 Index

for each country. Only France has shifted significantly (down) in the ranking in recent years.

2. It was described by the Lord Chancellor in 2003 as "difficult for our law enforcement agencies to use and the inconsistency, lack of definition and various lacunae might lead to corrupt individuals being acquitted. It shies away from the most important question – it does not have a definition of what acting corruptly means" (Foreword to HMSO, Corruption, Draft Legislation, CM 5777).

3. As the committee reported, "Our task has been made much easier by two recent reports on the Civil Service. The Treasury and Civil Service Select Committee produced a perceptive and thorough analysis of many of the most pressing issues facing the civil service. The Government responded with a positive White Paper 'Taking Forward Continuity and Change,' reflecting the welcome degree of common ground that exists between the political parties about the future of the civil service" (United Kingdom Committee on Standards in Public Life, 1995, p. 58).

4. These cover general principles and rules (with the code as an annex); confidentiality and official information; standards of propriety (with two annexes: one on rules on the acceptance of outside [postservice] employment by civil servants, and another giving guidance to departments and agencies on the rules governing acceptance of such appointments); political activities (with an annex of guidelines and principles on participation in political activities); and disciplinary rules and procedures (with an annex on recovery of losses to public funds including forfeiture of superannuation rights).

5. There is, for example, a long discussion in Sec. 4.3, Annex B, paragraph 8, of whether staff reduction policies might be thought to increase or to reduce suspicion that individuals whose jobs were ending would be more or less under suspicion of offering favors in return for subsequent employment, concluding with the observation that if the run-up to redundancy is less than a year, suspicion is not likely to be significant.

6. For the sake of brevity, the Spanish case is not described here because developments in relation to codes of conduct have paralleled very closely those in France. That is, while Spanish authorities have considered their introduction, especially under pressure from the Council of Europe GRECO initiative (see Council of Europe/ Group of States Against Corruption, 2003), they have to date been unwilling to do so on grounds very similar to those outlined in relation to France.

7. The central civil service, regional and local authorities, and the hospital service.

8. The literature on the phenomenon of political corruption is extensive (see, inter alia, Lascoumes, 1999; Pujas, 2000).

9. Although Italy is often said to lead the field when it comes to prosecution of senior politicians for corruption, the galaxy of well-known French names who have either faced trial or been condemned looks hard to beat, and includes Gérard Longuet, François Léotard, Alain Juppé, Robert Pandraud, Roland Dumas, Dominique Strauss-Kahn, Michel Mouillot, Michel Noir, Bernard Tapie, Robert Hue, Jean Tiberi, and Alain Carignon.

10. Rapport préparatoire Assemblée nationale n° 2941; Sénat n° 61 de 1992/1993; loi publiée au *Journal Officiel de la république française*, 1993, p. 1589.

11. Information for this paragraph was kindly supplied directly to the author by Mme Emanuelle Prada-Bordenave, Maitre des Requetes au Conseil d'Etat, Commissaire du Gouvernement.

12. *Codice di Condotta dei Dipendenti Pubblici: Proposta e Materiali di Studio*, July 1993, issued by the *Dipartimento per la Funzione Pubbli*ca. Although introduced merely as a decree, and therefore having no force of law, the decree was linked to a special enabling clause introduced simultaneously in Art. 26 Dec. Legislativo no. 546/1993.

13. Decreto ministeriale, no.149/1994, Codice di comportamento dei dipendenti delle pubbliche amministrazioni, later superceded by Decreto ministeriale, no. 84/2000, Codice di comportamento dei dipendenti delle pubbliche amministrazioni.

14. Dec. leg. 80/1998 rewrote Art. 58 of dec. leg 29/1993 and made the need for such coordination more explicit. It confirmed Art. 59 of dec. leg. 29/1993, stating that "the typology of the violations and their relevant sanctions is defined by the collective contracts."

15. Presidenza del Consiglio dei Ministri, Ispettorato della Funzione Pubblica, Verifica sull'osservanza delle norme e dei codici di comportamento da parte del personale dei ministeri: Relazione, Dicembre 2002 (Document supplied to the author by Dr F. Giardina, Dip. per la Funzione Pubblica.).

16. Council of Europe, Committee of Ministers, Recommendation no. R (2000) 10 of the Committee of Ministers to member States on codes of conduct for public officials (adopted by the Committee of Ministers at its 106th session on May 11, 2000). The party funding proposal is from a similar source: Council of Europe, Committee of Ministers: Recommendation Rec (2003) 4 of the Committee of Ministers to member states on common rules against corruption in the funding of political parties and electoral campaigns (adopted by the Committee of Ministers on April 8, 2003 at the 835th meeting of the Ministers' Deputies).

Many of the conclusions arrived at in this paper are based upon conversations with:

In Italy: Dr. F. Giardina, Vice-Prefetto (Funzione Pubblica) Minister of Public Service; Prof. Vincenzo Caianello (Presidente del Comitato Etico dell'Autorita' Garante), Communications Authority; Prof. Vittorio Guccione (Magistrato applicazione codice etico dell' Autorita'Garante della Concorrenza e del Mercato), Competition Authority; Dr. Angelo Canale (Corte dei Conti), Court of Accounts.

In Germany: Dr. Birgit Leitenberger (Interior Ministry); Dr. M. Kaup, Bundesministerium des Innern (Interior Ministry); Dr. Markus Lange, Bundeskartellamt (Cartel Office).

In the UK: Anna Hodgson, Home Office; Paul Stephenson, Home Office; Fred Jaeger, Civil Service Commission; Simon Jones, Competition Commission; Sue Gray, Cabinet Office.

In France: M.M.H.-P Lebord (Ser. Centrale Prev. Corr.); Mme Emanuelle Prada-Bordenave (Conseil d'Etat).

REFERENCES

Aubin, E. (2001). *Droit de la Fonction Publique*. Paris: Gualino Editeur.
Council of Europe/Group of States Against Corruption. (2002). *Evaluation report on Germany*, March 8. Retrieved from www.greco.coe.int/evaluations/Default.htm

Council of Europe/Group of States Against Corruption. (2003). *Compliance report on Spain*, October 13–17. Retrieved from www.greco.coe.int/evaluations/Default.htm

Council of Europe/Parliamentary Assembly (2000). Role of parliament in fighting corruption. Doc. 8652. Retrieved from http://assembly.coe.int/Mainf.asp?link= http%3A%2F%2Fassembly.coe.int%2Fdocments%2Fworkingdocs%2Fdoc00%2Fedoc8652.htm

Ferstenberg, J. (1998). *La deontologie de l'accèss du fonctionnaire aux enterprises publiques*. Paris: La Documentation Francaise.

France Commission Bourchery. (1992). *La Prevention de la Corruption et Transparence de la Vie Economique*. Paris: La Documentation Francaise.

Lascoumes, P. (1999). *Corruptions*. Paris: Presses de Sciences Po.

OECD. (2003). Prevention through up-dated regulations and sanctions: The French experience. In: OECD (Ed.), *Managing conflict of interest in the public service* (pp. 147–170). Paris: OECD.

Piastra, R. (2000). Du pantouflage. *Revue du droit public et de la science politique en France et a l'etranger, 116*(1), 121–152.

Pujas, V. (2000). Lacunes et nouvelles dimensions de la responsabilité politique. eléments de politiques comparées. *Pouvoirs, 92*(Janvier), 165–180.

Transparency International. (2003). *Transparency international corruption perceptions index*. Retrieved from www.transparency.org/cpi/2003/cpi2003.en.html

United Kingdom Civil Service Management Code. (1996). Retrieved from www.civilservice.gov.uk/management_information/management/management_code/index.asp

United Kingdom Committee on Standards in Public Life. (1995, May). *First report* (CMC 2850-I). London: Her Majesty's Stationery Office (HMSO).

United Kingdom Committee on Standards in Public Life. (2003, April). *Ninth report. Defining the boundaries within the executive: Ministers, special advisers and the permanent civil service* (CMC 5775). London: HMSO.

United Kingdom House of Commons Public Administration Select Committee. (2003–04). *A draft civil service bill: Completing the reform*. First Report of Session 2003–04, Vol. 1. Report, together with formal minutes, HC 128-1.

POLITICAL ETHICS AND RESPONSIBLE GOVERNMENT

Andrew Potter

ABSTRACT

In 2004, the Canadian government appointed an ethics commissioner reporting directly to Parliament. I show how an appeal of the ethics commissioner finds its traction in three problem areas. First, there is an increasing distaste in Canada for patronage and other similar forms of partisanship in politics, but there is general uncertainty about the constitutional or ethical standards that ought to apply. Second, the language of democratic criticism and reform of Parliament is rooted less in actual constitutional practice than in an idealized sense of how Parliament ought to work, a problem that is exacerbated by the ongoing presence of the American example. Finally, these both feed into a growing disengagement from traditional party politics and a desire for more "independent" or non-partisan checks on government, of which the Office of the Auditor General is becoming a popular exemplar. As an independent, Parliamentary, and non-partisan check on government, the ethics commissioner appears to serve as at least a partial solution to much of what is wrong with the Canadian political system.

Since the mid-1970s, many political jurisdictions at the provincial, state, and national levels have adopted some sort of codified ethics regime for public officials. There are a number of reasons for this, foremost of which, perhaps, is the Watergate effect: concern about scandal, corruption, and abuse in the public sector leading to unprecedented levels of cynicism about politics (Saint-Martin, 2003). But the desire for formalized ethics codes also reflects a more general decline in public deference to governing elites, and a shift to a more managerial or professionalized approach to government.

In its 1993 Red Book election platform, the Liberal Party of Canada promised to restore integrity to public office (after nine scandal-ridden years under the Conservatives, led by Brian Mulroney) by appointing an independent ethics counselor who would be appointed after consultation with the leaders of all parties in the House of Commons, and would report directly to Parliament (Liberal Party of Canada, 1993). Once in power, the Liberals reneged somewhat on this promise: Prime Minister Jean Chrétien appointed an ethics counselor who reported not to Parliament, but to the prime minister himself. There was, in fact, an excellent rationale for this decision, even though neither the government nor the media did a very good job of communicating it to the public. One of the ethics counselor's jobs was to administer the code of ethics for senior public officials, including cabinet ministers. The problem is that since the prime minister has sole constitutional responsibility for the composition of cabinet, for hiring and firing ministers, he also has ultimate responsibility for overseeing their ethical conduct and disciplining them accordingly. Responsibility for the conduct of ministers is a matter for the Crown, and it was believed that having an officer of Parliament – a legislative watchdog – oversee the ethics code would involve improper legislative interference with the executive (Saint-Martin, 2003). Accordingly, it was decided that the ethics counselor would have to be an advisor reporting directly to the prime minister.

This situation was exposed as less than satisfactory when Chrétien was later accused of violating his own ethics guidelines, in the so-called Shawinigate affair. Chrétien was cleared of a conflict of interest by Howard Wilson, the ethics counselor, but for many critics this only served to prove the point: since the ethics counselor was in the end the servant of the man he was supposed to be investigating, he was himself in a conflict, and it was inevitable that the watchdog would become a lapdog (Democracy Watch, 1994).

When he took over as leader of the Liberals and became prime minister in December 2003, Paul Martin introduced a Democratic Reform Action Plan based on the three pillars of democracy: ethics and integrity, the representative and deliberative role of MPs, and executive accountability (Privy Council Office, 2004). In March 2004, the Canadian Senate passed Bill C-4, an act establishing the position of ethics commissioner as an officer of Parliament who will oversee both an improved code of conduct for ministers as well as a new code of conduct for MPs. In late April 2004, former McGill University Principal Bernard Shapiro was named as the first ethics commissioner.

Although the ultimate effectiveness of the office remains to be seen, there is widespread enthusiasm among the opposition parties and the general public for the position of ethics commissioner, and my goal in this chapter is to try to understand that appeal. I begin with the following assumption: there is no serious problem with the ethical behavior of public officials, in particular of cabinet ministers, in Canadian federal politics. That is, there is no evidence that ministerial ethics in Canada are particularly lax, either by historical or international standards, and public officials in Canada are generally held to a higher ethical standard than executives in the private sector (Heath, 2004).

This will strike many people as naive. Yet despite opposition rhetoric and the journalistic enthusiasm for scandal and things ending in "-gate," it is my contention that the real issue, and what actually motivates the underlying appeal of the ethics commissioner, is not worries over government ethics, but concerns about excessive partisanship and majoritarianism. That is, it is not so much that the individual and collective actions of cabinet ministers has earned our disgust, it is that they are increasingly failing to mobilize our consent. Thus, the appeal of the ethics commissioner is part of Canada's so-called democratic deficit, the term used to describe the sense many Canadians have that the federal government has become unresponsive and unrepresentative, and that Parliament is increasingly unable to hold either the government or the bureaucracy accountable. There is a feeling that there is no longer an effective check on executive power, and consequently, Canadians live in either a friendly (Simpson, 2001) or unfriendly (Pue, 2002) dictatorship.

Here, I try to show how appeal of the ethics commissioner finds its traction in three problem areas. First, there is an increasing distaste in Canada for patronage and other similar forms of partisanship in politics, but there is general uncertainty about the constitutional or ethical standards that ought to apply. Second, the language of democratic criticism and reform of Parliament is rooted less in actual constitutional practice than in an idealized sense of how Parliament ought to work, a problem that is exacerbated by the ongoing presence of the American example. Finally, both these feed into a growing disengagement from traditional party politics and a desire for more independent or nonpartisan checks on government, of which the Office of the Auditor General is becoming a popular exemplar. As an independent, Parliamentary, and nonpartisan check on government, the ethics commissioner appears to serve as at least a partial solution to much of what is wrong with the Canadian political system.

POLITICS AND PROFESSIONAL ETHICS

Is politics a profession? Russell Hardin suggests that it is.

> I propose to treat the class of elected officials as a profession, so that their morality is a role morality and is functionally determined. If we conceive the role morality of legislators to be analogous to the ethics of other professions, then this morality must be functionally determined by the purpose that legislators are to fulfill once in office. (Hardin, 2004, p. 76)

Yet some features of politics complicate matters somewhat. First, unlike most professions, there is no esoteric body of knowledge that politicians need to master. Aristotle and academics might consider politics a science, but there is perhaps no other field of human endeavor, apart from sex, in which ignorance and lack of experience is so frequently portrayed as a virtue. Additionally, while professions are typically marked by collegiality, the central feature of democratic politics is partisanship.

Still, politics has a number of characteristics that make it something like a profession. Politics certainly serves a number of vital social functions. Also, while politicians perhaps need not master a given body of knowledge, they do control or have access to a great deal of power and influence. They control the raising and spending of public money; they make, administer, and enforce the law; they possess the ability to raise an army and make war, and so on. In short, politicians have the entire coercive power of the state at their (collective) disposal, and are therefore the sorts of people in which the public has placed a tremendous amount of trust.

If we accept, then, that politicians are at least professionals in the sense of being in a fiduciary relationship with the citizenry, we can ask, with Hardin, what is the role morality of elected officials? Again, a number of problems quickly arise. To begin with, politician, or even elected official, is not a well-defined role. If we restrict ourselves to Canada's Parliament, there are MPs and senators. Among MPs, there are those on the government side and those in opposition. There are also party leaders, members of cabinet, backbenchers, the shadow cabinet, and so on. Even if we treat MPs simply as representatives of a constituency, there are a great many competing theories of representation. Some of these roles are constitutionally defined, but many are not, and it is not clear that there is a single sufficiently clear and robust role description that could underwrite a suitable professional ethic for elected officials.

Let us focus then on the government, i.e., the prime minister and members of cabinet. In a recent paper, Glor and Greene (2002–03) argue that a pillar of ethical democratic government is integrity. In addition to the requirement that elections be free and fair, integrity means that there should be a mechanism for assuring transparent and accountable government, as well as rules for ethical decision making. According to Glor and Greene, ethical decision making includes impartiality, accountability, and the exercise of a fiduciary responsibility. Ministers are caretakers of the public trust, and their prime ethical directive is to refrain from abusing or violating that trust.

The trick lies in determining just what constitutes an abuse or violation of the public trust. The prohibition of conflicts of interest is central to every code of professional ethics, and codes of behavior for politicians are no exception. There are obvious reasons for this: if agents are in a position to achieve private gain from the exercise of their fiduciary duties, there may be a clear conflict between what is in the agent's interest and what is in the principal's interest. When it comes to ministers exercising their executive responsibilities, they have a duty to act so that they do not – or cannot – profit privately from public office. According to the federal conflict of interest code for cabinet, ministers have an obligation to arrange their private affairs in a manner that will bear the closest public scrutiny, which entails preventing real, potential, or apparent conflicts of interest from arising.

Yet the prohibition of conflicts of interest goes beyond simply refraining from taking bribes or accepting gifts or favors in return for the granting of public benefits. As Ian Greene argues, conflicts of interest are prohibited by two unwritten constitutional principles, the rule of law and social equality. Thus, the rule against conflict of interest is part of a general rule against bias: ministers should make decisions fairly and impartially. Not only should they not profit personally from their office, but also they

> may not show favouritism to friends and associates. It may also mean that ministers should not show favouritism to party members and that they must disqualify themselves whenever they might appear to be partial. (Greene, 1990, p. 241)

This ideal of the fair, impartial, and unbiased administration of the law by the executive runs into a number of immediate difficulties. First, there is the question of patronage. If we accept a fairly broad definition of patronage as the giving of appointments, contracts, and other measureable forms of preferment to supporters of the government of the day, then a great deal of what passes for patronage in Canada is neither criminal nor necessarily ethically wrong (Simpson, 1988). Despite its status as a universal term of political opprobrium, patronage has many legitimate and even useful functions. As Jeffrey Simpson points out in his book, *Spoils of Power*, whether certain forms of patronage are ethical or not will not be decidable by explicit rules or principles, but will instead have "much to do with the eye of the beholder, conditioned by the political culture of the country or the province" (Simpson, 1988, p. 9), or even by the relative popularity of the government at a given moment.

A related question is the extent to which the rule against conflict of interest should apply to decisions that have partisan consequences. Again, it is hard to see how a general rule against bias or conflict could help us to distinguish those cases where it might be legitimate for a minister to favor the party's interests from those where it is not (Greene, 1990). The problem is not just that the line is blurry. There is a deeper sense in which politics is about choosing sides, defending one set of interests against another. Democratic party politics is not just a fight over who gets to administer the laws, it is a fight for power. In politics, there are stakes.

The problem of deciding just what counts as a conflict of interest in politics is compounded by three features that distinguish politics from other professions. In the typical professional–client relationship, the professional is responsible for applying (1) a fairly limited and esoteric body of knowledge (medicine, law) toward (2) a single dominant end (health, legal interests), on behalf of (3) a single individual or small group of people. In contrast, the cabinet minister is responsible for (1) the general exercise of power of (2) almost unlimited potential social impact, on behalf of (3) the general population. The minister is simultaneously the agent for a number of overlapping or conflicting principals, pursing multiple, potentially conflicting goals. Consider the various responsibility roles of a minister in the federal government in Canada:

- legally responsible to the Crown for the administration of her portfolio;
- constitutionally responsible to Parliament;
- responsible to constituents for local issues;
- responsible for representing regional or provincial interests (as a political minister);
- responsible to the prime minister;

- responsible to the cabinet as a whole for supporting government policy; and
- responsible to the party.

The problem of multiple goals and multiple principals often serves as a get-out-of-jail-free card, since, when charged with failing to pursue one set of interests, agents can always claim that they were trying to meet another conflicting set of responsibilities (Heath & Norman, 2004). This is exactly what happened with the so-called Shawinigate scandal, when Jean Chrétien was accused of improperly interfering, as prime minister, with the head of a bank. His reply – accurate as far as it went – was that, as an MP, he was merely exercising his duty on behalf of a constituent. To paraphrase Jeffrey Simpson, it is hard to see how the problem of conflict of interest could be amenable to impartial and independent oversight, since what counts as a conflict in politics will often depend on which side of the House of Commons one figuratively, or literally, sits. That is one reason why our traditional mechanism for holding governments accountable for their ethical behavior is not independent and legalistic, but adversarial and political. Through responsible opposition, we ensure responsible government.

THE MEANINGS OF RESPONSIBLE GOVERNMENT

The *Constitution Act, 1867* says that Canada shall have a constitution similar in principle to that of the United Kingdom, which was understood to mean that what underlies the Canadian constitutional order, is a Westminster-style system of parliamentary responsible government. There is considerable debate over the various meanings of *responsible*, but in defining the link between the government and the legislature in Parliament, the term has two essential meanings. In its primary sense, it means that ministers are legally responsible for exercising the executive powers of the Crown. Second, it means that

> ministers are not only responsible *for* the use of these powers, but are responsible and accountable *to* parliament. Parliament, and particularly the House of Commons, is consequently the central forum for discussion about the use and abuse of political power, and is the source of the legitimacy and authority of a government. (Franks, 1987, p. 11)

The essence of parliamentary democracy is the accountability of the government to an elected legislature. The people are represented by the members of the House of Commons, and in order to remain in power the government must retain the support of the majority of MPs.

Under the cabinet system of government, responsible government describes two ways in which ministers are accountable to Parliament. First, each minister bears individual responsibility for the work of his or her department. Second, ministers bear a collective responsibility for government policy. The government must defend its policies and actions before the House of Commons, and it must resign if it is defeated on a bill of substance or on a vote of confidence. The doctrine of cabinet solidarity is central to this system. It began as a device for protecting the ministers, preventing the king from interfering with the government by picking ministers off one at a time. As the English constitution evolved and power shifted from the king to the Commons, cabinet solidarity became just another way of expressing the principle of responsible government: there is a government consisting of the prime minister and cabinet, which has the support of and is responsible to the House of Commons. The cabinet, as a government, stands or falls as a unit.

While this doctrine makes it clear that the government is subordinate to Parliament, it also entrenches the crucial distinction between Parliament and the government. Unless they are members of cabinet, MPs do not – and should not – attempt to govern. Responsible government relies on two distinct domains, "one for ministers to govern and the other for the House to hold the government to account and, if it so desires, to remove the government from power" (Savoie, 2003, p. 33).

There is a third meaning of responsible government that goes beyond the twin doctrines of legal and parliamentary responsibility. This is a broader, or higher, form of responsibility, understood as a set of moral obligations associated with the responsibility of leadership in a constitutional democracy. This higher sense of responsibility is what Amery calls "a state of mind, which weighs the consequences of action and then acts, irrespective, it may be, of the concurrence or approval of others" (Amery, 1964, pp. 30–31). This is the responsibility of leadership, of conviction, conscience, judgment, and integrity. It eschews mere partisanship or majoritarianism, in favor of the pursuit of the public good and the national interest.

We could call it the professional ethic of responsible government, and while it is never strictly codified or even written down anywhere, it includes the unwritten rules and norms that make up a large part of our constitutional heritage. Because the cabinet is able to exercise a great deal of unchecked Crown prerogatives, it is imperative that these standards of obligation are internalized by those in power and accepted as binding regardless of the possibility of being caught or punished. This is not to say that there is no enforcement of the ethical behavior of the government: the check is the system of responsible government, the ongoing oversight of the executive by Parliament.

Yet just what this oversight consists of is not entirely clear, largely because it is not clear just what the relationship between the government and Parliament ought to be. The problem is that we have two conceptions of responsible government, each of which gives a different account of the role of MPs, the relationship between the cabinet and the House of Commons, and the appropriate balance of power between these two central elements of Parliament.

TWO CONCEPTS OF THE CONSTITUTION

The basic parliamentary model affords considerable flexibility in configurations of power, and over the course of the development of the Westminster system the relative powers of the Crown (or government) and the Commons have waxed and waned (Franks, 1987). What we have now are two general understandings of the constitution, two languages that we use to talk about our system of responsible government. There is what Birch (1964) calls the liberal–individualist model, that sees a strong House of Commons and independent-minded MPs as the most effective check on the government. Then there is the executive-centered model that focuses on the central role of the cabinet in setting the parliamentary agenda and on the dominance of party discipline in the Commons. On this model, the most effective check on the government is public opinion, motivated by effective partisan opposition in Parliament.

Perhaps the most well-known proponent of the liberal–individualist concept of the constitution is Walter Bagehot. Bagehot's is an essentially republican view of the English constitution, with power flowing up from voters to their representatives in Parliament, and then from MPs to the cabinet. Responsibility, in turn, flows the other way: from the cabinet to the House of Commons, and from the Commons to the voters. For Bagehot, the Crown now embodies the dignified part of the constitution, liable to move the spirits of the ruder sorts of men, but not exercising any actual effective power (Bagehot, 1867/1974). Bagehot actually describes Great Britain as a disguised republic, with the Commons as an electoral college through which the people choose their president and executive. He says that the cabinet is a committee of the House, a "board of control chosen by the legislature, out of persons whom it trusts and knows, to rule the nation" (Bagehot, 1867/1974, p. 11). Bagehot sees this as superior to the

American system, providing a more effective check on executive power. Under responsible government, the Commons is a continuous election; it "watches, legislates, seats and unseats ministries from day to day" (Bagehot, 1867/1974, p. 22) And unlike the sham American electoral college, the Commons is

> a real choosing body, [it] elects the people it likes. And it dismisses who it likes too. (Bagehot, 1867/1974, p. 116)

To a large extent, this was the view of the constitution during the mid-to-late 19th century. Dicey, John Stuart Mill, Gladstone, and many others held similar views, and by the end of the 1880s the supremacy of Parliament – understood as the dominance of the Commons over the executive – had come to be seen as the cardinal axiom of the constitution (Birch, 1964). As a description of Victorian parliaments, this was a somewhat accurate view. The period between the Reform Acts of 1832 and 1867 was characterized by weak, unstable governments confronting a strong, independent-minded Commons. Many ministries did not last very long, and government defeats on bills were common. But this balance of power did not survive the turn of the century, undermined by the extension of the franchise, the growth of party discipline, and the subsequent domination of Parliament by the executive.

Yet a significant difficulty with the liberal–individualist concept of the constitution is that it confuses the relationship between Parliament and the government. Birch quotes an 1893 speech in the House of Lords by Lord Hartington:

> Parliament makes or unmakes our ministries, it revises their actions. Ministries may make peace and war, but they do so at pain of instant dismissal by Parliament from office ... it [Parliament] does actually and practically in every way directly govern England, Scotland, and Ireland. (Birch, 1964, p. 73)

Hartington's view may be constitutionally inaccurate – Parliament is not the government – yet, as we shall see, it in many ways represents an idealized view of how many people, especially the general public, think the constitution ought to operate.

In contrast, the executive-centered view sees the British constitution as the product of a long process of balance and adjustment between two elements of independent and original authority, the Crown (cabinet) and the nation (Parliament). The long struggle between the two resulted in their fusion, i.e., in the system of responsible government, but they remain distinct entities, fulfilling distinct constitutional functions. The Crown, as represented by the cabinet, remains the wellspring of power and initiative. It is the Crown that sets the agenda in Parliament: it initiates most legislation (and all money bills), it sets government policy, and it directs the administrative bureaucracy. Through the cabinet, the Crown governs in and with – but not by – Parliament. Parliamentary democracy is certainly a democracy, but it is a system of "democracy by consent and not by delegation, of government of the people, for the people, with, but not by, the people" (Amery, 1964, p. 21).

This is very distinct from the liberal–individualist view of the place of the cabinet. In the executive-centered position, it is simply not the case that the cabinet is a committee of the legislature, or even a committee of the majority in the legislature. After an election, the queen (the governor general in Canada) selects as prime minister whoever has the support of the majority of the House of Commons. It is then up to the prime minister alone to choose the cabinet, in what is often described as the loneliest of political jobs. However the decisions are made, the process certainly does not involve election by, or even widespread consultation with, the party MPs. Thus, the prime minister is not primus inter pares in the cabinet, but more like the keystone of the cabinet arch (Amery, 1964). It is the prime minister's cabinet: only he or she chooses it, changes its composition, or brings it to an end through resignation or dissolution. The important point is that ultimately Parliament does not appoint or elect, but rather accepts, a prime minister and the cabinet.

In this respect, there is no fusion of powers. The Parliament and the Crown may be joined through the cabinet, but each exercises distinct functions. The role of the government is to lead, legislate, and direct the affairs of the nation. The role of Parliament is to make a government and hold it accountable. It follows, therefore, that Lord Hartington, Parliament, and its committees should not attempt to govern, set policy, or arrogate executive power; rather, its primary function should be to exercise oversight and control of the public purse and hold the government to account for its actions.

In this view, the most important role of Parliament within the Westminster system of government is to minimize the coercion involved in government by helping to engineer the consent of the governed – in particular, of minorities. Through critical examination, opposition, and discussion, Parliament serves as the great forum of national deliberation through which the government obtains consent for its policies. Its success will be measured by the extent to which it is able to ensure that we have responsible government in the higher sense discussed above. It has long been thought that one of the strengths of the Westminster system is that it encourages this higher sense of responsible government, with the opposition playing a vital role (Amery, 1964). The existence of an opposition that criticizes the government of the day, while remaining loyal to the constitution, helps generate the creative tension through which consent is mobilized. The government proposes, and by

> withstanding the attacks of the opposition and by putting forward its proposals with conviction and vigour, proves the sincerity and the justness of its cause. The process is neither rational nor scientific, but it achieves consent, though through conflict rather than cooperation. (Franks, 1987, p. 15)

Thus, effective parliamentary government requires both responsible government and responsible opposition. The essentially adversarial nature of the system helps simplify the impossibly messy world of politics by offering only two sides to every issue: for or against. This is reinforced by the physical setting of the House of Commons. It is a rectangular chamber, with the supporters of the government on the speaker's right, and the opposition members on his left. Winston Churchill famously endorsed this setup over the semicircular assembly, "which enables every individual or every group to move round the centre, adopting various shades of pink as the weather changes" (quoted in Franks, 1987, p. 144).

The upshot is that the parliamentary model is one that tends to favor the party system. Political parties are certainly not required for responsible government, but in their absence governments tend to be weak, unstable, and – paradoxically perhaps – unaccountable (Smith, 1999). What parties do is support the executive-centered model of the constitution by ensuring the primacy of the government within Parliament. This amplifies and clarifies the underlying adversarial structure by sorting the members of Parliament into a government party (whose job it is to support the cabinet) and opposition members, whose job it is to oppose. Under party government, the cabinet becomes the apex of the governing party caucus, and party discipline is just an extension of cabinet solidarity (Aucoin, 1994).

So, to a large extent, party discipline is crucial to the executive-centered system of responsible government and responsible opposition, by making it clear just who is responsible for supporting the government and who is responsible for opposing. As Sutherland argues,

> party does not empty collective responsibility of its meaning, but gives it meaning. They are the same thing by different names: both are constituted of shared preferences and shared views about how preferences can be acceptably realized. Party makes these visible, arguable, and accountable. (Sutherland, 1991, p. 96)

THE IMPORTANCE OF RESPONSIBLE OPPOSITION

Even Bagehot (1867/1974) agreed that the party system was necessary for effective parliamentary government, although he thought it vital that the parties should not be composed of what he called *warm partisans*.

> The body is eager, but the atoms are cool. If it were otherwise, parliamentary government would become the worst of governments – a sectarian government. (Bagehot, 1867/1974, p. 126)

That is, when cool party feeling turns into hot partisanship, the ability of the Commons to engineer consent will degenerate into raw majoritarianism, as "the party in power would go to all the lengths their orators proposed" (Bagehot, 1867/1974, p. 126).

Aside from the naturally moderate English temperament, Bagehot believed that the parliamentary system was an excellent mechanism for enforcing moderation in party feeling, by keeping party leaders in contact with the world. An opposition party coming into power is like a merchant whose bills are coming due. Having spent a great deal of time saying what they would do once in power, new ministers find that they now have to make good on those promises. Yet reality is always more complicated than it seems from the opposition side of the Commons, "and the end always is, that a middle course is devised which *looks* as much as possible like what was suggested in opposition, but which *is* as much as possible what patent facts ... prove ought to be done" (Bagehot, 1867/1974, p. 128). As they take turns rotating through government and opposition, this reality principle enforces on the competing parties a certain amount of moderation. It gives a system of responsible government and responsible opposition that "makes party government permanent and possible in the sole way in which it can be so, by making it mild" (Bagehot, 1867/1974, p. 128).

Advocates of party-based government argue that it is an effective way of managing two competing demands on government: that it exercises strong leadership, while remaining responsive to public opinion. Party discipline gives a government the strength and stability it needs to implement its agenda, while ensuring that its accountability to citizens for its record is completely transparent (Aucoin, 1999). Unfortunately, it is rather difficult nowadays to find many advocates of the current party system.

For its many critics, party discipline is no longer a means for enabling responsible government; it is an obstacle to it. Firm discipline means that backbench MPs on the government side become mere ciphers, irrelevant nobodies, trained seals standing up or sitting down as the prime minister orders. Meanwhile, the growth in the size and complexity of the permanent bureaucracy has led to the concentration of executive power in a handful of central agencies – the Prime Minister's Office, the Privy Council, Finance, and the Treasury Board (Savoie, 1999). Ministers themselves get shunted aside by the twin forces of the central agencies and the permanent officials, and the cabinet becomes a mere focus group for the prime minister. When all of this is combined with the absence of formal checks on the prime minister, what we end up with is an "imperial prime minister" or an "elected monarchy."

All these contribute to what has come to be known in Canada as the democratic deficit. What is interesting is that the language of criticism, and hence the language of reform, is the language of the liberal–individualist conception of the constitution. Lord Hartington's hope for a Parliament that truly governs looms large in the popular mind, so when it comes to proposals for remedying the democratic deficit, high on the list are things like relaxed party discipline, more free votes in the House of Commons, and the strengthening of bipartisan parliamentary committees to give MPs greater input into policymaking and the drafting and scrutiny of legislation. Of course, what motivates this is not so much nostalgia for Victorian-era Parliaments, but rather an obsessive awareness with the American congressional system of government. The U.S. Congress is seen as the near-embodiment of the liberal–individualist model, with its strong checks and balances and the regime of shared legislative and executive power. For the public, and even for many MPs, the obvious conclusion is that since MPs do not govern, or even really legislate, the House of Commons is simply a weaker and less democratic version of the American Congress (Aucoin, 1999).

Under the spell of the liberal–individualist conception, many critics see the real test of the health of responsible government and the strength of Parliament as lying in the extent to which it is able to force a minister to resign or be dropped from the cabinet. If a minister is forced to resign, it is quite a coup for the opposition. Yet, an embattled minister can be protected by the cloak of cabinet solidarity. By extending that solidarity to the government party as a whole through party discipline, a majority government can effectively check any attempts at picking off an individual minister. Although (as we have seen) the function of cabinet solidarity is precisely to prevent Parliament from picking and choosing among ministers it likes by allowing the majority to govern as a single administration, when it is used to protect weak ministers it is often seen as a "rather low political strategy to protect the inadequate" (Sutherland, 1991, p. 91).

It is actually exceedingly rare that a minister is forced out of the cabinet over violations of public ethics standards. This is borne out by the figures compiled by Sutherland (1991) in her comparative look at the history of ministerial resignations in Canada and Britain. According to Sutherland, by 1991 in Canada there had been 151 ministerial resignations since Confederation. Of these, 28 were for reasons of cabinet solidarity, 62 left to take up patronage posts, and 21 left for health reasons. Meanwhile, 11 ministers resigned for public ethics violations (seven for conflict of interest, three for interfering with a judge), and only two ministers in 124 years resigned over questions of departmental maladministration.

In comparison, of the 98 resignations in Britain between 1903 and 1986, 80% were for solidarity reasons. Five ministers resigned over private moral scandal, and a half-dozen or so were pushed out for political errors. One obvious conclusion is that in Canada, ill health is often easy for the prime minister to arrange (Dawson's joke – see Ward, 1987) while in Britain, the ailing minister picks a fight with the prime minister before he goes (Sutherland's joke). Sutherland draws a more important conclusion: the opposition can force a resignation "only when it can make a case as to lack of personal ethics or probity of a kind for which the minister's own colleagues *refuse* to extend the protection of collective responsibility, or when the cabinet cannot extend solidarity because the government is in a minority" (Sutherland, 1991, p. 105).

Two further points. First, Parliament cannot actually force a minister to resign, in the sense that it does not have the constitutional authority to directly remove a minister from the cabinet. All it can ever do is use strong and effective opposition to make it politically inexpedient or risky for the prime minister to protect an embattled minister. Second, to the extent to which ministerial resignations indicate the efficacy of the accountability mechanisms within responsible government, it would appear that either parliamentary opposition has never been very good at exposing and capitalizing upon breaches of ministerial ethics, or that a widespread lack of ministerial ethics has rarely been a serious problem in Canada.

If you believe the latter, the obvious conclusion to draw is that the best way to continue to ensure an ethical responsible government is to have a strong, responsible opposition. Nothing keeps the government honest like a united and reasonably popular government-in-waiting. But you would be hard pressed to find anyone who believes this. There is a widespread consensus, in Canada and, increasingly, in other jurisdictions such as Britain and Australia, that the Westminster parliamentary system is deeply flawed, if not utterly obsolete. As Michael Atkinson puts it, "so thoroughgoing is this depressing assessment that to argue the opposite – that everything is fundamentally fine – is to court ridicule" (Atkinson, 1994, p. 717).

In Canada, this general rejection of traditional party-based politics is exacerbated by two additional problems. The first is the long-standing feature of Canadian federal politics: there is a single dominant government party that holds power for long periods of time, with a chronic opposition party that occasionally rides a wave of populist discontent into power. The second, more recent problem is that since 1993 the opposition to the ruling Liberals has been far weaker than usual. The feeling that federal politics has reached "Gritlock" (White & Daifallah, 2001) has at least partially contributed to increased public disenchantment, and voter turnout in the last two federal elections has reached all-time lows. What this means is that Parliament's ability to engineer a national consensus is severely diminished. Canadians are turning away from the traditional forms of integrative politics, under which political leaders fought to articulate collective aspirations through reasoned debate and deliberation. There has been a shift in preference toward more individualistic, participatory, or citizen-based forms of government that are suspicious of the old party-based elites (Atkinson, 1994).

So, we seem to have reached the rather unpleasant point where the traditional institutional mechanism for ensuring ethical responsible government is in both disrepair and disrepute. This is a dangerous situation to be in, because what we are left with is a system where "the governing party with a majority can govern with little in the way of partisan–political checks and balances, and thus [has] virtually no incentive to build a broader consensus for its initiatives" (Aucoin, 1999, p. 100). In this case, it is inevitable that the opposition in Parliament, as well as the broader public, will begin to demand other mechanisms for constraining the government. Furthermore, owing to the influence of both the American example and the quasi-republican language of the liberal–individualist concept of the constitution, it is inevitable that these mechanisms will involve trying to give the legislature the means of exercising more direct control of the executive and other senior public officials (Fleming & Holland, 2000).

CONCLUSION

This is the political environment in which the ethics commissioner finds a welcoming niche. It offers the hope of a check on the executive that is independent, nonpartisan, and parliamentary, and its proponents ignore or downplay the constitutional improprieties that might arise. After all, if an ethics commissioner overseeing the executive but reporting to Parliament is unconstitutional because it involves legislative interference in the executive loop, then so much the worse for the constitution (this seems to be the general attitude in Fleming and Holland (2000)). Of course, it might be worth fudging on the constitution if the office of the ethics commissioner is able to deliver the goods as advertised; that is, if we could be reasonably certain that it will help ensure the integrity and ethical behavior that is at the core of building public confidence in government and in the political process (Privy Council Office, 2004).

It may do so. But I want to close by highlighting some areas of concern.

The first concerns the incentive structure it gives to cabinet ministers. The adversarial nature of the party system necessarily puts a premium on public perception. In the highly charged partisan atmosphere of parliamentary debate, especially the question period, the opposition frequently tries to paint the government as corrupt, unethical, and thoroughly incompetent stewards of the nation's affairs, while the government tries to defend itself. Each tries to marshal the support of the media and of the public, and the final verdict on the government's ethical behavior is delivered in the court of public opinion and, ultimately, the voting booth.

The existence of a parliamentary (as opposed to a legal or constitutional) check or limit on government power gives a rather distinctive form of institutional incentive for ethical behavior. Leaders are ultimately held in check by their own sense of duty, responsibility, and professional obligation; Parliament functions as the institutional site of moral socialization (Atkinson, 1994). The move to a written code of ethics administered by an independent officer of Parliament involves a fundamental shift from an incentive-based ethical regime to a control-based one. That is, instead of giving ministers an incentive to internalize the standards of public ethics, the idea of an ethics commissioner starts with the assumption that ministers will exploit their office for private gain if given the chance. What is therefore required is a strict and codified system of external oversight and control.

This move, from a reliance on internalized incentives to external controls, involves a fundamental shift in our regime of public ethics enforcement, and it could well backfire. To draw a Kantian distinction, it may encourage ministers to act merely in accordance with the rules (out of fear of being caught), when what we really want is for them to act out of respect for the rules (because that is what political virtue demands). This might well lead to rule bending and even ethical risk taking, as ministers seek to be seen as adhering to the strict letter of the rules, regardless of what the public good actually requires. It might even result in less accountability, not more, as ministers look for loopholes or other ways of getting around the rules (Juillet & Paquet, 2002).

What underlies all of this is a basic uncertainty over what the point of the ethics code is supposed to be. Is the point to actually improve ministerial conduct, or is it to simply increase the chance that supposedly inappropriate conduct will be detected and exposed? While ideally we should prefer the former, there is evidence that implementing codified rules of behavior for ministers results in the latter (Fleming & Holland, 2000). In that case, the unhappy effect of the ethics commissioner might be increased public cynicism and disgust, by proving what people have always suspected; namely, that most politicians are only in it for their own benefit.

A second, related worry concerns the institutional nature of the office of the ethics commissioner. As a quasi-judicial office, the commissioner's inquiries will have to put a premium on due process and the gathering and evaluation of evidence. When the commissioner becomes involved in investigating a possible ethical breach by a minister, it could have the effect of taking the issue out of the political realm entirely. As a mechanism for holding the government to account, this could backfire by actually making it harder for the opposition to hold the government's feet to the fire. The government might find it easy to get a possible scandal off the agenda by parking it with the ethics commissioner for investigation; the opposition could hardly continue to harass a minister during a question period while the commissioner is conducting an investigation.

There is precedent for this, of course. Canadian governments have always found royal commissions and judicial inquiries extremely useful instruments for burying politically inconvenient issues. For example, the investigation into the treatment of protesters at the 1997 APEC meeting on the campus of the University of British Columbia took three years and cost $10 million. Inquiry Commissioner Ted Hughes replaced the original commission when all three panelists quit after several months of hearings. When his report finally came out in August 2001 there was very little public interest, despite the fact that Hughes found that the Liberal government twice tried to interfere with police operations during the summit (Pue, 2001). The inquiry effectively buried the scandal.

None of this is intended as a knock-down argument against the office of the ethics commissioner or against ethics codes for ministers in general. Bernard Shapiro may turn out to be a useful aid to an increasingly overworked and embattled Parliament as it seeks to fulfill its vital constitutional function of providing oversight to the actions of the government. What we need to resist, though, is the temptation to regard ethics oversight – along with other positions such as the offices of the auditor-general and access to information – as the principal instruments through which we hold the government to account.

To make use of a helpful distinction that John Uhr makes elsewhere in this volume, we must be careful that an obsession with political ethics does not detract from what really matters, viz., ethical politics, or what I have called here the higher form of responsible government. It may be true that Canada suffers from excessively partisan, majoritarian, and executive-centered government. To the extent that this is true, it is largely the result of the long-standing feature of the Canadian political landscape that sees an entrenched government party governing for long periods, punctuated by occasional and short-lived populist revolts. One consequence of this may be that, instead of leading cool and moderate party government, it breeds arrogance on one side and cynicism and apathy on the other. The government grows arrogant because it knows it will rarely be held fully accountable for its activities, while the opposition ceases to offer responsible opposition and turns to scandal mongering.

To the extent that this is true, the only viable solution is electoral and institutional reform. As Aucoin argues in a similar context, we need to guard against

> the perception that partisanship in governance stands against good governance, that is, responsive and responsible government ... The current imperative, accordingly, is to reform the partisan structures of representative and electoral democracy. If for no other reason, the reform of the Senate and the electoral system, as the institutional means to diminish the unbridled power of the executive, needs to be on our political agenda. (Aucoin, 1999, p. 100)

There is no guarantee that these sorts of reforms will give us more ethical government. No reform is politically neutral, and any institutional change that brings more individualized and republican elements into the parliamentary system might do as much harm as good. One consequence of American-style government will likely be American-style politics. In the meantime, a focus on political ethics narrowly conceived will only drain attention and energy from our real concern, which is responsible government.

REFERENCES

Amery, L. S. (1964). *Thoughts on the constitution.* London: Oxford.
Atkinson, M. M. (1994). What kind of democracy do Canadians want? *Canadian Journal of Political Science, 27,* 717–745.

Aucoin, P. (1994). Prime ministerial leadership. In: M. Mancuso, R. Price & R. Wagenberg (Eds), *Leaders and leadership in Canada* (pp. 99–117). Toronto: Oxford University Press.

Aucoin, P. (1999). Responsible government and citizen engagement at the millennium: Are political parties irrelevant? In: F. L. Seidle & L. Masicotte (Eds), *Taking stock of 150 years of responsible government in Canada* (pp. 71–104). Ottawa: The Canadian Study of Parliament Group.

Bagehot, W. (1867/1974). *The English constitution.* London: Oxford University Press (Original work published in 1867).

Birch, A. H. (1964). *Representative and responsible government.* London: George Allen.

Democracy Watch. (1994). Democracy Watch claims ethics counsellor is in conflict of interest and will be ineffective. Retrieved January 12, 2005 from http://www.dwatch.ca/camp/RelsSep2994.html.

Fleming, J., & Holland, I. (2000). Motivating ethical conduct in government ministers. Paper presented at the International Institute for public ethics conference, Ottawa, September. Retrieved January 12, 2005 from http://strategis.ic.gc.ca/pics/oz/flemming.pdf.

Franks, C. E. S. (1987). *The parliament of Canada.* Toronto: University of Toronto Press.

Glor, E., & Greene, I. (2002–03). The government of Canada's approach to ethics. *Public Integrity*, 5, 39–65.

Greene, I. (1990). Conflict of interest and the Canadian constitution: An analysis of conflict of interest rules for Canadian cabinet ministers. *Canadian Journal of Political Science*, 23, 233–256.

Hardin, R. (2004). Representing ignorance. *Social Philosophy and Policy*, 21(1), 76–90.

Heath, J. (2004). A toast to the independent audit. *Policy Options*, 5(May), 60.

Heath, J., & Norman, J. (2004). Stakeholder theory, corporate governance, and public management: What can the history of state-run enterprises teach us in the post-Enron era. *Journal of Business Ethics*, 53, 247–265.

Juillet, L., & Paquet, G. (2002). The neurotic state: Access to information policy and the culture of the Canadian public service. In: G. B. Doern (Ed.), *How Ottawa spends 2002–03, the Security aftermath and national priorities* (pp. 69–87). Oxford, UK: Oxford University Press.

Liberal Party of Canada. (1993). *Creating opportunity: The liberal plan for Canada.*

Privy Council Office, Her Majesty the Queen in Right of Canada. (2004). *Ethics, responsibility, accountability: An action plan for democratic reform.* Ottawa: Privy Council Office, Government of Canada.

Pue, W. (2001). The prime minister's police? Commissioner Hughes' APEC report. *Osgoode Hall Law Journal*, 39, 165–185.

Pue, W. (2002). Bad government: There are no friendly dictators, even in Canada. *Literary Review of Canada*, (January/February), 14–16.

Saint-Martin, D. (2003). Should the federal ethics counsellor become an independent officer of parliament? *Canadian Public Policy – Analyse de Politiques*, 29, 197–212.

Savoie, D. (1999). *Governing from the centre.* Toronto: University of Toronto Press.

Savoie, D. (2003). *Breaking the bargain.* Toronto: University of Toronto Press.

Simpson, J. (1988). *Spoils of power.* Toronto: Collins.

Simpson, J. (2001). *The friendly dictatorship.* Toronto: McLelland and Stewart.

Smith, J. (1999). Responsible government and democracy. In: F. L. Seidle & L. Masicotte (Eds), *Taking stock of 150 years of responsible government in Canada* (pp. 19–49). Ottawa: The Canadian Study of Parliament Group.

Sutherland, S. L. (1991). Responsible government and ministerial responsibility: Every reform is its own problem. *Canadian Journal of Political Science, 24*, 91–120.

Ward, N. (1987). *Dawson's The Government of Canada (6th ed.)*. Toronto: University of Toronto Press.

White, P., & Daifallah, A. (2001). *Gritlock: Are the liberals in forever*. Toronto: Canadian Political Bookshelf.

COMPARING SYSTEMS OF ETHICS REGULATION

Oonagh Gay

ABSTRACT

Parliamentary ethics regimes have grown rapidly since the 1970s, but public trust has not increased. This chapter concludes that no single element of the architecture of ethics regimes is necessarily crucial for their effective operation. A determination to enforce standards, combined with an external element, appears to be the most important determinant of success. Much depends on the overall ethos and culture of the politicians who both operate and are governed by regulation.

To understand ethics regimes, it is first necessary to set out the legal and constitutional principles underpinning ethics regulation, particularly in the parliamentary sector, where questions of self-regulation remain central to the issue. Much of what follows is based on work I undertook for the Wicks Committee on Standards in Public Life in 2002, to enable the committee to place the regulatory system in the UK House of Commons in comparative perspective (Gay, 2002). The committee was established by the then prime minister, John Major, in 1995 to act as an ethical workshop. Its recommendations do not have statutory force, but have great moral authority. I have since drawn further conclusions in *Conduct Unbecoming: The*

Regulation of Parliamentary Behaviour (2004), which I co-edited with Patricia Leopold of Reading University, United Kingdom.

My report for Wicks began by considering the issue of privilege. This was an aspect of particular interest to the Wicks Committee. Parliamentary privilege has two main components:

- freedom of speech, which is guaranteed by Article 9 of the Bill of Rights 1688; and
- the exercise by Parliament of control over its own affairs, known technically as exclusive cognizance.

The first aspect gives protection to comments made in and reports issued by Parliament in relation to the conduct of its members. The power to regulate the behavior of its members and to discipline them if necessary is based on the second aspect of privilege, which also underpins the right to compel witnesses to attend and give evidence. It forms part of the constitutional doctrine of separation of powers, preventing the internal regulation of Parliament from being subject to judicial scrutiny.

In modern times, the justification for parliamentary privilege is that it enables members and officers of each House to carry out their parliamentary duties without interference, thus upholding the ability of Parliament to discharge its functions of scrutinizing the executive and acting as a forum for the grievances of the nation (UK Joint Committee on Parliamentary Privilege, 1999). The value of privilege is that it enables Parliament to consider any matter it chooses, and to react immediately and flexibly to events without resort to statute.

The concept was carried over into the United States during its foundation in the eighteenth century, and the heritage is recognized in Article 1, Section 5 of the US Constitution of 1789: "Each House may determine the Rules of its proceedings, punish its Members for disorderly behaviour, and, with the concurrence of two thirds, expel a Member" – the speech or debate clause. But the power of self-regulation is overlaid by statutory requirements of the 1970s and 1980s, whose wording became incorporated into the House rules. A landmark case, *United States v. Brewster* (1972) established that prosecution of bribery charges does not necessitate inquiry into legislative acts or motivation, an interpretation of Article 1, Section 6 of the US Constitution where the wording derives directly from the Bill of Rights 1689.

The Parliaments of Australia and Canada inherited parliamentary privilege when colonies of the UK, as did their state or provincial legislatures. Privilege was incorporated into the founding constitutional statutes, as also for the previous devolved Parliament in Northern Ireland in the 1920s.

Ireland incorporated certain aspects in its 1922, then 1937 constitution. In contrast the assemblies/parliaments of Scotland, Wales, and Northern Ireland were not given privilege at the time of their establishment. Instead, the rights of the legislature to call witnesses, punish members, and to possess absolute legal privilege in terms of defamation were embodied in the devolution statutes. This represents a break with Commonwealth tradition. The reluctance to confer privilege was not publicly discussed but appeared to be due to the general disrepute in which parliamentary self-regulation was held in the late 1990s, following the Neil Hamilton affair (see Gay & Leopold, 2004). Hamilton, a junior minister in the Major government, was accused of accepting cash payments from Mohammed Al Fayed, the owner of Harrod's department store, in return for tabling parliamentary questions. The existing parliamentary procedures were found to be inadequate for investigating the allegations. Hamilton was defeated in the 1997 general election by an independent standing on an anti-sleaze platform.

Privilege may be codified in statute, as has occurred in Australia in the *Parliamentary Privileges Act 1987*. Statute law covers corruption and bribery of members of parliament, but there remain some difficulties in Australia and Canada as to criminal prosecutions of members, due to the operation of parliamentary privilege. There are similar problems in the UK, where it remains unclear whether MPs are to be treated as public office-holders.

The French also adopted the British concept of privilege insofar as the need to protect elected members from prosecution for opinions expressed in the performance of their duties, as set out in proclamations in 1789/1790. The French model of immunity is wider than the UK counterpart, and has been widely adopted in continental Europe. This has implications for ethics regulation (European Centre for Parliamentary Research and Documentation 2001, p. 11).

SYSTEMS OF PARLIAMENTARY REGULATION

The main types of parliamentary regulation are as follows:

- registration and declaration of interests through a register system administered by a parliamentary official or committee;
- registration through a register system enforced by a semi-independent (and sometimes statutory) commissioner;
- adoption of an internal code of conduct, designed to cover broader requirements than a registration system; and

- a statutory scheme of regulation enforced by the criminal law, with the possibility of specific commissions of inquiry.

Schemes in force can display characteristics of more than one of these main types. An initial mapping demonstrates the variety to be found within one state.

United Kingdom

The House of Commons established a system of registration and declaration of interests in 1974, with a clerk as registrar and a parliamentary committee to investigate abuses. This proved unworkable in the face of scandals prompted by backbench members taking second jobs as parliamentary consultants to lobbying firms. When the parliamentary committee was no longer perceived as offering effective enforcement, the Committee on Standards in Public Life recommended a new semi-independent parliamentary commissioner for standards in 1995 to investigate and recommend penalties to a parliamentary committee, so preserving self-regulation. Members were also made subject to a new code of conduct, which is not designed to police wrong doing by ministers in their ministerial capacity.

The system has worked relatively smoothly, but committee behavior appeared to change when ministers were investigated in relation to allegations about their behavior as parliamentarians. The committee was reluctant to take action, or to follow through on the full implications of the recommendations from the commissioner. In addition, there were strains over the independent status of the commissioner. There was a series of reforms in June 2003, which has given the commissioner a new five-year, nonrenewable term, and has meant that the committee (uniquely among Commons committees) no longer has a government majority. One outstanding issue is the extent to which the procedures for investigation meet the demands of Article 6 (right to a fair trial) of the European Convention on Human Rights (ECHR). The UK Parliament appears to be subject to the ECHR, although recent cases on freedom of speech have allowed the Commons considerable leeway. The House of Lords established a code of conduct in 2002, and uses the law lords as members of the parliamentary committee that acts as the enforcement agent.

The Scottish Parliament has established its own commissioner, as a statutory scheme, but the parliamentary committee still makes the final decision on investigations. Its remit is confined to parliamentarians. The Welsh

Assembly is a unitary body, and so its scheme encompasses ministerial misbehavior as well. It is currently embroiled in a dispute about the sacking of a civil servant. The Assembly has its own independent adviser, but for this investigation the parliamentary ombudsman from Northern Ireland is being used, as free from any prior knowledge of the individuals concerned. Both the Scots and Welsh have members' codes of conduct which are aspirational in nature, and which allow complaints from constituents about the quality of work undertaken by members. This has caused an overlap with the traditional role of the speaker/presiding officer in preserving order.

The Wicks Committee noted with interest that it was possible to introduce statutory regulation of standards. But statutory does not necessarily equate to independent in considering the machinery for the regulation of parliamentary standards. The Scottish commissioner for standards is established by statute, for example, but is subject to powers of direction by the standards committee. The power of direction possessed by the Queensland office of the parliamentary criminal justice commissioner over the initiation of inquiries by its commission illustrates how independence can in fact be diluted by statute.

Australia

Both federal Houses in Australia have schemes for the registration and declaration of interests of members imposed by parliamentary resolution and monitored by parliamentary committees. These systems are based on privilege. Australian state legislatures have adopted the registration and declaration of interests by legislation or by parliamentary resolution. A minority of legislatures has also adopted codes of conduct. New South Wales and Queensland have established statutory commissions with the power to investigate members for official misconduct. This is a step change in the enforcement of rules on parliamentary and ministerial conduct.

The work of the commissions in Queensland and New South Wales has been described in detail by Fleming and Holland (2001). The commissions cover both ministers and parliament, neither of which takes kindly to investigation by a large independent and well-resourced agency. The idea that as a sovereign body the parliament deserved to be naturally trusted seemed to be widespread among its members, along with a perception that investigations were exacerbating the declining public respect for politicians. Unsurprisingly, there have been particular flashpoints about investigations into parliamentary allowances and battles over resources for the agencies. Both states have set up parliamentary officers or committees whose role is to investigate the work of the commissions. These are the Office of the Parliamentary Criminal Justice Commissioner in Queensland, and the Parliamentary Joint Committee in New South Wales. These bodies are responsible for monitoring and reviewing the work of the Crime and Misconduct Commission in Queensland and the Independent Commission against Corruption in New South Wales, respectively. In Queensland, the body has the power to handle complaints against the commission. It has the power to inspect all operational material used by the commission in investigations and to initiate investigations, since the *Criminal Justice (Amendment) Act 1997*. This has caused some unease, with the Law Society of Queensland commenting that "to give the power of direction to the parliamentary committee would enable politicians to use the Commission to target persons or groups in the community" (Fleming & Holland, 2001, p. 134).

Nevertheless, the commissions enjoy a considerable degree of public support among the electorate and in Queensland the commission has been responsible for removing a number of politicians from frontline posts. Both state legislatures also have separate ethics advisers, with a remit of advice rather than investigation. Queensland has in addition a statutory integrity commissioner to regulate members' conduct.

Canada

The Canadian Parliament is about to implement registration and declaration of interests, following a series of reform proposals, including a new position – an independent parliamentary official with both an advisory and an investigatory role – who would report to a parliamentary committee, but not on the detail of individual investigations. Bill C-4 received royal assent on March 31, 2004, and provides for two commissioners, one for each house. The existing ethics counselor, who advises on misconduct in government, will become the commissioner for the Commons and supervise separate regimes for parliamentarians and ministers. His appointment will be preceded by consultation with parliamentary parties. Although the procedures of the new offices were underpinned by parliamentary privilege, a majority of the Senate opposed any statutory scheme for themselves (Young, 2004). The enactment of the Canadian Charter of Rights and Freedoms has posed potential problems for the scope of parliamentary privilege, as there remains doubt as to whether internal processes of Parliament are subject to the charter (see *New Brunswick Broadcasting Co. v.*

Nova Scotia (Speaker of the House of Assembly), 1993). There are clear echoes of the potential ambit of the ECHR here.

Canadian provincial legislatures have generally established statutory ethics parliamentary officers, whose remit extends to both parliamentary and ministerial ethics, apparently under American influence. In fact, most investigations are undertaken into the behavior of ministers. The distinguishing features are:

- The appointment and dismissal is by resolution of the legislature, although government influence can be important in the recruitment process.
- The commissioner has a judicial or legal background.
- The investigation follows an inquisitorial model, with formal statutory inquiry powers, but with the opportunity for the member under investigation to have counsel, make representations, and apply for assistance with legal costs.
- The results of the investigation are presented to the full assembly, rather than to a separate committee.
- The report is published with recommendations as to sanctions.
- The assembly must respond within a set period, usually 30 days.
- The assembly makes the final decision and implements any recommendations for penalties, but must either accept or reject the whole report.

Canadian courts are slow to intervene in areas apparently covered by parliamentary privilege. Two cases at the level of provincial courts of appeal have held that the work of these commissioners in relation to members of assemblies is covered by privilege and that their role was to make recommendations to the legislature, which itself made final decisions and sanctions regarding discipline (*Tafler* and *Morin*) (*Tafler v. British Columbia (Commissioner of Conflict of Interest*, 1985, 1988*)*; *Donald Morin v. Northwest Territories*, 1999). A recent case relating to the dismissal of its commissioner by the North West Assembly has indicated that privilege does not extend to the appointment and removal process where it has been circumscribed by statute (*Roberts*) (*Roberts v. Commissioner of the NWT et al.*, 1999).

Apart from encompassing ethics issues within the executive, the Canadian commissioners appear to be fairly similar to the Westminster commissioner. However, the legislatures they serve are small and often meet on a part-time basis only. The recommendations they make therefore do not have the same national resonance. At central government level, Canada's ethics commissioner will continue to report to the prime minister. The lack of accountability to Parliament is a continuing area of criticism.

United States

The creation of ethical rules in the U.S. legislature began with the adoption by Congress (by resolution) of the Code of Ethics for Government Service in 1958. The House and Senate Ethics Committee have used the guidelines for all government officers and staff, including members of Congress and congressional staff, as a standard for discipline in a number of leading cases.

The Committee on Standards of Official Conduct was first established in the House of Representatives in 1966 and became permanent in 1967, but with major reorganizations in 1989 and 1997. The Senate established its own Select Committee on Standards and Conduct in 1964 after the resignation of a prominent congressman, Senator Bobby Baker, in 1963. Its creation followed recommendations from a Joint Committee on the organization of Congress in 1965 and allegations of misconduct against a former House Committee chairman. It has 10 members and is bipartisan. It must have a majority vote for the issue of a recommendation, whether advisory or following an investigation. Its role is to:

- recommend to the House actions designed to enforce standards of official conduct;
- investigate alleged violations by members, officers, or employees of rules or standards of official conduct;
- interpret the House Code of Official Conduct; and
- administer the gift, outside earned income, and financial disclosure requirements of the *Ethics in Government Act 1978*, and the *Ethics Reform Act 1989.*

INVESTIGATION OF THE EXECUTIVE-POTENTIAL MODELS

The UK systems are unusual in avoiding the regulation of the behavior of ministers, which is left to other nonstatutory mechanisms. The reason for this may lie in the nature of the scandals that gave rise to a perceived need for regulation. In the mid 1990s it was not the behavior of senior ministers which resulted in scandal, but rather government backbenchers or junior ministers. The impetus for the reforms introduced following Lord Nolan's recommendations in 1995 was to deal with the perceived moral laxity displayed by individual Conservative Party MPs. This places the UK rather out of line with continental and U.S. scandals on party funding. The creation of the Electoral Commission in 2000 now provides regulatory mechanisms for campaign expenditure, and already the bureaucracy involved in the administration of the controls has attracted considerable criticism.

Strains between an impartial civil service and the demands of ministers led to a Civil Service Code in 1994, designed to protect civil servants rather than to regulate them. The Ministerial Code was first developed by cabinet secretaries in the mid-twentieth century, but was only published in 1992. Since then, it has attracted the attention of the Committee on Standards in Public Life and parliamentary committees on the public service. At present the Ministerial Code is an uneasy mixture of ethics, accountability, and housekeeping, written mainly for internal consumption. It cries out for a complete redraft and separation into three different sets of guidance. Whoever undertakes primary responsibility, it should be done in a reasonably open, consultative fashion, given its importance in incorporating fundamental constitutional conventions.

A more recent addition is the code for special advisers, developed following scandals involving these temporary civil servants whose role is to add political input to the civil service. The UK is the only country surveyed which has developed a code, but these figures have been familiar in Australia and Canada since the 1970s. The UK penchant for informal codes allows regulation to develop incrementally.

So, developments in the regulation of public servants and ministers in the UK have not yet incorporated an independent investigator. The pace of change has been set by the Committee on Standards in Public Life, which remains a unique British model. It is a nonstatutory and advisory committee of the Great and the Good, whose influence in establishing ethical norms was widespread for the first five years of its existence, producing new rules to regulate appointments to public bodies and new legislation to govern the conduct of local government officials. But its continued existence means that it must keep finding areas to regulate and face the prospect of declining influence.

The extent to which ethics regimes regulate the behavior of public servants as well as ministers is also variable. The Queensland Anti-Corruption Commission takes in the whole sweep of the public sector, and it is common in Commonwealth countries to have some form of statutory regulation of the civil service and anti-corruption legislation. These are often characterized as ineffective in promoting ethical values. Although, the Australian public service commissioner is required to report annually to Parliament on the extent to which civil service values are upheld, in general, oversight tends to be by the executive. In Canada and New Zealand much effort goes into producing guidance on conflicts of interest. Irish legislation is the most all-embracing, reflecting the serious corruption scandals of that state.

In the UK, corruption is not perceived as a major issue, and legislation dating back to 1889 remains unreformed despite a government draft bill in 2003. The Wicks Committee did not suggest any further statutory regulation of public servants. The most developed regime may be found in the United States. The creation of ethical rules began with the adoption by Congress (by resolution) of the Code of Ethics for Government Service in 1958. The House and Senate Ethics Committee have used the guidelines for all government officers and staff, including members of Congress and congressional staff, as a standard for discipline in a number of leading cases.

Ministers tend to report to prime ministers both in terms of discharging their duties and their ethical conduct. Lord Justice Scott recommended an independent parliamentary officer to oversee accountability in evidence to the Public Service Select Committee following his enquiry into the arms for Iraq affair (UK Public Service Select Committee, House of Commons, 1996). But it is difficult to see how the prime minister could not be the prime arbiter in accountability issues, always allowing for parliamentary pressures. Ethics may be a different matter, requiring independent investigation. The latest report from the Committee on Standards in Public Life moves toward this solution, but seems to stop halfway at the Canadian model of an ethics commissioner (Committee on Standards in Public Life, 2003).

There are some interesting boundary issues about the restriction of the UK standards commissioner to the members' code of conduct. Some ministers, notably Geoffrey Robinson, have been investigated for conflict of interest issues. The commissioner does offer a ready-made investigative operation, with independence from government. However the Canadian example is not generally considered a successful model, and the special investigator used in the U.S. has become discredited. The Irish Ethics in Public Government Act 1995 hands over investigations to specialized tribunals. Role creep can be characterized in some of the activities of auditors general in Australia and Canada. In the absence of an independent ethics commissioner, this reputable official has developed a role in uncovering abuses, but the main focus remains the proper and efficient use of public money.

Parliamentary committees may also investigate specific executive wrongdoing, an example being the Australian Senate inquiry into the children overboard affair (Bachelard, 2003). There, an inquisitor was employed to give a more professional and impartial flavor to a traditional parliamentary inquiry. The defects of this model have been amply demonstrated by the

Commons Foreign Affairs Committee enquiry into the David Kelly affair. The nonstatutory Hutton inquiry was far more successful in gaining access to witnesses and documents.

MODELS FOR THE INVESTIGATIVE PROCESS

Whatever the scope of parliamentary ethics regulation, a commissioner is a common feature. There are important exceptions, such as the U.S. or continental Europe which do not favor an investigative official characterized as independent. But the existence of an investigator appears to be linked to the overall efficacy of the regulatory system. This is brought out clearly by Gerard Carney's (2000) study of the Australian systems. The UK Commons had a register of members' interests and a clerkly registrar, but without an effective investigatory official, separate from the staff of the House, there was no effective enforcement of the rules. Whether these are statutory or not becomes irrelevant.

A major issue in the UK has been the status and independence of the investigatory official (Gay & Winetrobe, 2003). The Nolan Committee argued for a nonstatutory scheme, but the decision to leave appointment and tenure in the hands of the Commons administration led to difficulties when the second commissioner, Elizabeth Filkin, was discouraged from seeking a second term. She also felt starved of the necessary resources. At issue was a clash between perceptions – either she was a senior official, employed by Parliament, or she was an independent constitutional watchdog. Reforms in June 2003 have improved security of tenure, but the commissioner is still forced to use the powers of the Committee on Standards and Privileges to compel attendance and disclosure. This makes a close working relationship with the committee essential. Self-regulation is preserved in this model, but public perceptions can be negative, when members are seen to protect their own.

An independent official can be a lonely figure, and so some models prefer a commission, as in Ireland. Whatever the precise characterization and method of appointment, there are fundamental differences of approach to the investigation process. Most of these are related to the extent to which a full judicial approach is followed. One of the major aspects of the UK debate is the extent to which the current Nolan model can be characterized as conforming to Article 6 of the ECHR (the right to an independent and impartial tribunal). This is discussed by Dawn Oliver (Gay & Leopold,

2004). Similar concerns have arisen in Canada with respect to the Charter of Fundamental Rights and Freedoms.

Part of the UK culture is the avoidance of judicial process unless absolutely necessary, and this can be seen in the Scottish model. There, the commissioner does not need a legal background, and the detailed stages of his investigation are subject to statutory regulation. In contrast, the Canadian commissioners are almost always from a judicial background, and the accused are allowed counsel. As might be expected, the U.S. sets out statutory protection for the member under investigation in the *Ethics Reform Act 1989.*

Another issue is the extent to which the advisory and the investigative role should be separated. An investigation might be prejudiced should the investigator previously have offered an opinion on the registration or declaration of an interest. This was of prime concern to the Scots, who retain a parliamentary official to offer advice to members. The U.S. also uses a separate Office of Advice and Education, which represents the hiving off of the advisory function of the Committee on Standards of Official Conduct.

APPEALS, ENFORCEMENT, AND SANCTIONS

Self-regulation allows legislatures the right to suspend and sometimes expel their members. This now conflicts with more modern notions of human rights, and it is becoming important to adopt procedures that do not conflict with external norms of justice. The Commons resolved in June 2003 that the parliamentary commissioner for standards might establish an investigatory panel consisting of himself as chair, plus a legally qualified assessor and an MP who is not a member of the Committee on Standards and Privileges, appointed by the Speaker. This should enable investigations to be carried out more thoroughly and fairly, but ultimately judgments are still made by the Standards Committee and the House, neither of which is an independent and impartial tribunal. However, it is an improvement on the lack of an enforcement regime in the Parliament of Australia and the committee-based system of the U.S.

The Canadian provincial model has attractive features in a UK context. The absence of a committee and the requirement to accept or reject a report in total inhibits the operation of party politics in the consideration of a case. Although these are statutory offices, in general their work has not been subject to judicial intervention, since they are appointed as officers of the assembly. The major drawback to the model is the absence of a right of appeal following the recommendation of a commissioner. This is unfortunate, given the often-serious consequences of an adverse inquiry. For example, the former premier of British Columbia, Glen Clark, was the subject of an investigation by the commissioner there in 1999–2000. The commissioner was successful in preventing his inquiry from being held in public, citing the *Tafler* case. An added difficulty was a criminal case against Clark that ran concurrently (Conflict of Interest Commissioner of British Columbia Assembly, 1999). But appeal to an extra-parliamentary tribunal would inevitably open the question of judicial intervention in the internal disciplinary affairs of a legislature, and so far the Canadians have not been any more successful than the UK Parliament in finding a solution.

WHAT IS BEING REGULATED? CODES OF CONDUCT AND REGISTRATION SYSTEMS

What members must register can vary considerably. In some continental European states, the practice is to disclose all sources of income, but to restrict public disclosure. The UK tradition is different – it requires the interest itself to be determined according to whether it might be seen to influence the behavior of the member. This influence is felt in Australia but not in Canada, where the provincial commissioners collect very detailed information on the assets of each member, which is kept confidential and only a summary made public. Annual interviews are held to keep the declaration up to date.

The U.S. combines the detail of the Canadian process with an interest in transparency. There are bans on honoraria, limits on outside earned income, and restrictions on the acceptance of gifts, which are a feature of the regulation of Congress. These restrictions were initially enforced by the *Ethics Reform Act 1989*, but tightened by a House Resolution on November 16, 1995 (Resolution 250), that banned most gifts to members, officers, and employees. Congressional salaries were increased substantially to compensate for the loss of outside income. An independent electoral commission is also in existence, which administers the bulk of the statute law on campaign expenditure.

The prohibitions on gifts and outside sources of income make explicit the role of members as full-time representatives, in a way not yet considered in the UK or most Commonwealth states. There is an explicit outside earned income limit of 15% of a member's salary and full financial disclosure of income, including that of spouse and dependent children. House rules also require members to treat constituents fairly, with no favorable treatment for supporters. Other differences of approach can be detected in the extent to which partners'/spouses' interests must be declared. This raises privacy issues, as does the interest in registering nonfinancial interests, such as Freemasonry. The Welsh Assembly has struggled to introduce rules that meet ECHR requirements there.

One of the most fundamental distinctions is the extent to which a code of conduct is adopted which is aspirational in form. This was an innovation of the UK Committee on Standards in Public Life, which formulated the seven principles of public life – these have proved to be an influential model, and were incorporated into the members' code of conduct for the House of Commons, as well as the ministerial code. Legislatures in the UK have struggled with the extent to which these aspirations can properly be policed; for example, the standards committee in Scotland has dealt with accusations that members have poached constituents as a breach of their code. Most other parliaments in the Westminster tradition have steered clear of behavioral or job performance issues, preferring to leave policing with the speaker or parliamentary or party bodies.

There has been a lively debate in Australia about the efficacy of adopting codes of conduct, as compared to a basic registration regime. Mancuso's (1995) work in the UK concerning differing perceptions of good conduct in the parliamentary sphere illustrated the value of offering some norms to parliamentarians. But there is skepticism about the mere introduction of a code in place of real changes in behavior.

CONCLUSION

This survey illustrates the variety of regulatory, guidance, and enforcement mechanisms in place in major states. Almost all can be characterized as responses to perceived abuses, and the nature of the abuse tends to affect the regulatory structure adopted. This can be seen clearly in Queensland, where a major commission was developed to investigate the whole public sector, and in the UK, where abuses initially appeared to be concentrated at the level of backbencher, so leaving the standards commissioner without jurisdiction over the executive.

However, the key to a successful system is enforcement. Some degree of independence in the investigatory and decision-making process is vital to sustain public confidence. Where a whole series of investigations take place and the question of ethics is a continuing focus of media attention, it is easy to lose public trust in the ethics of politicians. On the other hand, it must be possible for the public to use the system. The Irish approach is highly litigious – witnesses before parliamentary committees or tribunals face character assassination, and this has an inevitable deterrent effect. No one single aspect of a scheme determines success. Achieving an ethos of honesty and transparency becomes the Holy Grail.

REFERENCES

Bachelard, S. (2003). Executive accountability in the 'Children Overboard' affair. *The table*. London: House of Lords.
Carney, G. (2000). *Members of Parliament: Law and ethics*. Melbourne: Prospect.
Committee on Standards in Public Life. (2003). *Ninth report (Cm 5775)*. London: Her Majesty's Stationery Office (HMSO).
Conflict of Interest Commissioner of British Columbia Assembly. (1999). *Opinion of the conflict of interest commissioner, Hon. H.A.D. Oliver* (August 13). Retrieved from http://www.ag.gov.bc.ca/public/clark/AppendixB.pdf
Donald Morin v. Northwest Territories [1999] NWRJ No 5 (NWTSC).
European Centre for Parliamentary Research and Documentation. (2001). *Rules on parliamentary immunity in the European Parliament and the member states of the European Union*. Brussels: Dick Toornstra ECPRD.
Fleming, J., & Holland, I. (Eds) (2001). *Motivating ministers to morality*. Aldershot, UK: Ashgate Dartmouth.
Gay, O. (2002). *The regulation of parliamentary standards*. London: HMSO.
Gay, O., & Leopold, P. (2004). *Conduct unbecoming: The regulation of parliamentary behaviour*. London: Politico's.
Gay, O., & Winetrobe, B. (2003). *Officers of Parliament: Transforming the role*. London: Constitution Unit.
Mancuso, M. (1995). *The ethical world of MPs*. Montreal: McGill-Queen's University Press.
New Brunswick Broadcasting Co. v. Nova Scotia (Speaker of the House of Assembly) [1993] 1 S.C.R. 319, 1993 CanLII 153 (S.C.C.).
Roberts v. Commissioner of the NWT et al. (1999). NWTSC 68.
Tafler v. British Columbia (Commissioner of Conflict of Interest). (1985). B.C.J. No. 1042 (S.C.).
Tafler v. British Columbia (Commissioner of Conflict of Interest). (1988). B.C.J. No. 1332 (C.A.).
UK Joint Committee on Parliamentary Privilege. (1999). Report HL, Paper 43/HC 214, 1998–99 session.
UK Public Service Select Committee, House of Commons. (1996). HC 313-III, 1995–96.
United States v. Brewster. (1972). 408 US 501.
Young, M. (2004). *Legislative Summary Bill C-4: An act to amend the Parliament of Canada Act (ethics commissioner and senate ethics officer) and other acts in consequence* (February 12). Retrieved from http://www.parl.gc.ca/37/3/parlbus/chambus/house/bills/summaries/c4-e.pdf

CANADA'S UPSIDE-DOWN WORLD OF PUBLIC-SECTOR ETHICS

Andrew Stark

ABSTRACT

Canada's institutions, by comparison with America's, have created a unique normative regime. When it comes to conflict of interest, the main problem in Canada has not been that private interests encumber governmental judgment, but that government itself, and in particular the publicly sourced emoluments controlled by the prime minister, can encumber the judgment of ministers and legislators. When it comes to campaign finance law, the problem is that parties are treated as if they are self-interested entities, while interest groups have often been treated as if they are parties. I explore the institutional causes and regulatory consequences of Canada's unique normative approach.

We Canadians traditionally harbor a robust suspicion that, if we do not keep an eye on them, our governing institutions will generate policies that are more compatible with U.S. norms than with Canada's unique self-conception as North America's peaceable kingdom or just society: think of our debates over free trade, privatized health care, or missile defense. I argue that when it comes to one particular arena of public policy – public-sector ethics – more the reverse has been the case. Our institutions, because of their internal logic, have generated norms idiosyncratic to Canada – norms that precisely invert those that govern in the U.S. – even though we Canadians would do much better if we actually borrowed heavily from our southern neighbor. I make this case by looking at two central domains of public-sector ethics: the conflicts of interest of cabinet ministers and MPs, and campaign finance.

CONFLICT OF INTEREST

I will begin with that I believe is the most profound institutionally generated Canadian–American difference in conflicts posed by personal financial interests. By personal financial interests, I mean to include both the publicly sourced salary and any privately sourced income that an officeholder receives. In the U.S., when a legislator's judgment is impaired by a conflict of interest, what is typically involved is an outside private interest: a stockholding, an honorarium, or a fee from a private party. Conversely, in the U.S., the only widely accepted argument for legislators increasing their public pay is that, in doing so, they will free themselves from having to rely on such potentially compromising private sources of support.

But in parliamentary systems, because of the great power exercised by prime ministers – because they control the public salaries, and more generally the public careers, of legislators through their capacity to promote them to the cabinet, sign nomination papers, and call elections – the idea, certainly historically, has been more the reverse. In Canada, and in Britain too, legislators who rely solely on the public treasury for their income are more likely to evoke worries that their independence of judgment is compromised: compromised by the power of the executive, and in particular the chief executive. Conversely, the only widely accepted argument for members of parliament continuing to possess substantial private interests while in office is that, in doing so, they will free themselves from having to rely on potentially compromising public sources of support.

In a 1978 British debate over pay for MPs, for example, one backbencher declared that "the genuine and individual independent judgment that is so vital to the successful working of the House ... would be jeopardized to some extent if being an honourable member represented a person's only livelihood" (United Kingdom, 1978, pp. 2107–2108). In a similar debate in 1980, another declared that "there is no one so independent of government and the Whips as an unpaid member" (United Kingdom, 1980, p. 175). During one such debate, the *Daily Telegraph* editorialized that "it is not desirable that MPs should become wholly dependent on their parliamentary salaries, [because] parliamentarians wholly beholden to their parties may lose some independence" (MP's pay, 1983). Any similar sentiment has found far less frequent expression in the U.S.

As far as Canada is concerned, up until less than 100 years ago, the law required any MP appointed to the cabinet to resign his seat and seek the approval of his constituents in a by-election. The idea, according to DMacGregor Dawson's (1970) classic text on Canadian government, was to allow constituents to "guard against [their] members being brought under sinister executive control" by virtue of their receipt of increased public emolument as cabinet members (pp. 329–331). And until very recently, any proposed Canadian bills dealing with conflict of interest – as well as the current nonstatutory code governing MPs – have been more exclusively concerned, by comparison with American strictures on members of Congress, on conflicts posed by a member's receipt of public, not private, sources of income: other government appointments apart from the cabinet itself, for example, or federal contracts. The concern was not that a legislator might have any influence over the awarding of such government appointments or contracts, but rather that the executive – which does award them – might thereby be able to exert influence over the parliamentarian (Canada. Special Joint Committee of the Senate and the House of Commons, 1992, p. 10; see also Stark, 1992, 1993).

I stress that this historical tendency – the tendency for Canadians, by comparison with Americans, to be more suspicious of publicly sourced encumbrances on the judgment of legislators, and especially legislators who hope for a cabinet position – takes the form of a comparative propensity, not an absolute dichotomy. Yet it manifests itself even today in the ongoing Canadian debate over the extent to which ordinary MPs, and in particular government backbenchers, should be freed of the whips and allowed to vote against the government. Prime Minister Paul Martin, on assuming office in late 2003, introduced a version of the British three-line whip protocol, which allows his Liberal backbenchers to vote as they wish on most government bills. But it is far from clear that this import from the mother of parliaments will have much effect in Ottawa. Indeed, the early indications are that it will simply allow the prime minister's control over salaries, perks, and careers to come even further to the fore. There is good reason to believe that only government backbenchers who know that they have no hope of entering the cabinet will, even now that the whips are supposedly off, demonstrate independent judgment and deviate from the government line (Some liberals think health deal was too generous, 2004).

A cautionary tale came in the winter of 2004, when Liberal MP Sarkis Assadourian led the backbench against the cabinet in getting the House of Commons to pass a resolution recognizing the Armenian genocide of 1916. Martin's campaign officials put a hold on Assadourian's renomination meeting and sought another candidate (Ibbitson, 2004). Assadourian is no longer an MP, but instead (in stark testimony to the prime minister's capacity to control the public careers of his legislators) now holds a low-level position in Martin's office.

Although Martin's predecessor Jean Chretien did impose the whips on almost all votes, a handful of Liberal MPs who knew they had no chance of making the cabinet – or of getting plum committee assignments, which Chretien also controlled – felt free to thumb their noses at him. Conversely, even though Paul Martin has now eliminated the whips from many votes, still, to the extent that he holds the carrots and sticks of cabinet, parliamentary-secretary and committee offices, as well as Liberal parliamentary nominations, he will meet (and for the most part has met) with little caucus deviation from his line. Indeed, though he may have called off the whips, Martin increased the size of the cabinet to 38, adding a further tier of 28 parliamentary secretaries to whom he has given, for the first time, the extra perk of privy-council membership. As a result, nearly half of the government caucus of 133 now holds executive or quasi-executive positions, with their attendant higher salaries, perks, and career satisfaction. What is more, those left out know that the odds of any one of them joining such already large ranks are good.

The British inner and outer cabinets, by contrast, are much smaller than their Canadian counterparts, while the British government caucus will always be much larger than the Canadian (the British House has 659 members compared to Canada's 308). Hence, there are hundred more government backbenchers in Britain than in Canada who know that they have no hope of entering the cabinet or otherwise rising through the ranks, and so feel free to exert their independence. It is the size of the backbench compared to the cabinet, I conjecture, and not the absence of the whips, that has made the greater contribution to freeing British government backbenchers from prime-ministerial control over their public careers, allowing them to exercise their judgment unencumbered by any publicly sourced interests (with their consequent independence rendering them more vulnerable to their privately sourced interests).

It is unlikely that resolving Canada's publicly sourced conflicts of interest by dramatically increasing the size of the House is politically possible. There would be substantial populist resistance to the notion of, say, doubling the cadre of professional politicians. Another possibility, though – and one that might appeal to populist sentiment – would not be, in British fashion, to double the size of the House but, in American fashion, to shorten the time that individuals can serve there by imposing term limits. I do not mean to suggest that term limits are necessarily a good idea, all things considered, only that one of their virtues would be to increase legislators' independence – to diminish the force of the publicly sourced conflicts of interest that come from prime-ministerial control over their political careers. Knowing that they cannot have lifetime careers as federal politicians, and knowing that the prime minister of the day will not be around indefinitely, they might find themselves less encumbered by whatever control he does retain over their careers.

Term limits might in some ways seem ill-suited to a parliamentary system, given the irregular periodicity of its elections. But there is now in Canada a movement afoot to set fixed election dates – some provinces have already done so – and so term limits might be less out of keeping with Canada's governmental system than they once may have seemed. It is true that term limits have their down sides, one of which is that they make it difficult for the legislature to develop the kind of expertise and institutional wisdom that tenure gives to the executive-branch bureaucracy. The assumption here is that we need to have a repository of embodied wisdom, in the form of the legislature, available to check that other repository of embodied wisdom, the executive bureaucracy. Otherwise, the public service will always be able to manipulate the lawmakers. But maybe instead – and despite the associated immaturity or naivety – the energy, renewal, and impatience that would follow from regular legislative turnover affords a better counterpoint to the stolidity and timidity that necessarily accompany the wisdom embodied in a tenured bureaucracy.

It is true that the U.S. *Federalist Papers* viewed the legislative branch as the repository of wisdom and the executive as the source of energy; but Madison, Hamilton, and Jay were thinking of a relatively small legislature and a single-person executive. A larger legislature, one (such as the Canadian House) with hundreds of members, no longer can claim to represent elite wisdom; and a huge executive branch, one with hundreds of thousands of members, no longer operates energetically. Term limits for MPs – which need not be legislatively imposed but rather undertaken by the parties themselves – would simply recognize this reality: the reality that energy should perhaps become part of the modern legislature's forte, just as institutional wisdom and expertise have become the executive's. In any event, Canada already has its own tenured, wisdom-embodying legislative chamber – the Senate – available, at least in theory, to counter its tenured, wisdom-embodying executive bureaucracy. If publicly sourced conflicts of interest remain a problem for MPs in Canada, then an American-style innovation – term limits – might offer the best prospect for dealing with them.

Privately Sourced Conflicts of Interest

I turn now to Canada's record with the privately sourced conflicts of interest of federal politicians. Certainly, the grosser forms of private impairment on public judgment – bribery of various sorts – have always been of concern in parliamentary systems, and Canada is no exception. But what in the U.S. has come to be called privately sourced conflict of interest (and has been prohibited by statute law since the 19th century) has only in the last 20 years or so become of significant concern in Canada.

Privately sourced conflict of interest is of recent concern in Canada because its principal cause is recent: the election of Brian Mulroney's Conservative government, in power from 1984 to 1993, which featured for the first time in Canada a string of high-profile conflicts of interest involving cabinet ministers and private interests. Until that time, such a conflict-of-interest record – one involving ministers and their private financial holdings – was quite unusual for Canada.

But then again, a Conservative government is something quite unusual for Canada. As a policy advisor in Prime Minister Mulroney's office, I developed the conjecture at the time that Conservative governments are prone to conflicts involving private interests because, being Conservative and not Liberal, they draw a disproportionate number of business people into public life. But – being governments and not businesses – they draw, at the margin, business people who have not been all that successful in business; otherwise they would have stayed in business. Those individuals may see a career in the public sector as a way of helping them succeed in business. And that, perhaps, is why relatively more of them get into conflict-of-interest scrapes.

In the early 1990s, I interviewed Arthur Culvahouse, a former chief White House counsel to President Reagan, whose administration was similarly plagued with conflicts arising from the private business entanglements of its officials. When he was the counsel, Culvahouse told me, he ordered a review of the personnel files of everyone who had fallen into ethical difficulties in the Reagan administration to see whether there were any common factors that might, had they been recognized beforehand, have predicted who would run into trouble. The single most common feature turned out to be personal/business bankruptcy, which provides anecdotal evidence for the idea that many people who go into conservative politics tend to be business people – but not particularly successful ones. Of course, there are exceptions. One thinks of the multi-millionaire Donald Regan, who served as President Reagan's treasury secretary and chief of staff. But then again, Regan did not run into conflict-of-interest difficulties.

In the majority of cases in which the public record is clear, however, the Mulroney-era conflicts of interest did involve ministers with private business debts who were desperately trying to raise some cash. Accordingly in 1988, 1989, 1991, and again in 1992, the Mulroney government introduced bills to regulate conflicts posed by private interests. For various reasons, none became law. But what is noteworthy here is that each of these efforts – although aimed at conflicts posed by private interests – was skewed, by comparison with American law, in ways that reflected both the Canadian executive's power over the legislature, and the parliamentary system's relative nonchalance about privately sourced conflict of interest.

The bills reflected the cabinet's control of the legislature in that, as Ian-Greene (1990) observed, "when legislation came, it was inevitably drafted so as to cover both ministers and other legislators, with little apparent recognition that the appropriate standards of impartiality for these two groups might conflict" (p. 251). This might be an understatement; for when legislation came, it frequently imposed heavier strictures on powerless backbenchers than on powerful ministers. Precisely because the cabinet controls the legislature, one might think that ministers should labor under heavier strictures than ordinary MPs; but precisely because the cabinet controls the legislature – with the cabinet, not ordinary MPs, drafting legislation – more the reverse has been the case. The most extreme example of this phenomenon is 1993's Bill C-116. Under its provisions, a greater degree of public disclosure would actually have been required of ordinary members and their spouses/dependents than of ministers and their spouses/dependents. Ministers would have been able to participate in governmental decisions in which they or their families had interests, while private members would have been prohibited from the same. Ministers would have been allowed to assign or transfer interests to evade the act, while ordinary members would have been banned from doing so. Also, investigative reports into ministerial conflict of interest would not necessarily have been made public, while those for ordinary members would have been.

More recently, Prime Minister Chretien's proposed code of 2002 would have required ministers and members alike to publicly disclose their spouses' assets and earnings. But it, too, would actually have treated MPs more strictly, by subjecting them to the formal rulings of an independent ethics commissioner responsible to Parliament, while continuing to place ministerial cases under the ambit of the informal advisory opinions issued by an ethics counselor reporting to the prime minister. As the *National Post* reported at the time, "some Liberal MPs say the proposed ethics package is designed to divert attention from problem-plagued Cabinet ministers ... to backbenchers, who have little clout and clean record[s]" (Fife & Dawson, 2002, p. A12). The article reported one Liberal backbencher as declaring that "it would be wrong for Mr. Chretien to create an independent watchdog for MPs but not one for Cabinet ministers because backbenchers have the least influence in government" (ibid.).

As for the new code for members, passed in April 2004, it states that a member shall not act in any way to further his or her private interests. The code for ministers and senior bureaucrats, by contrast, says only that such executive-branch officials shall not accord preferential treatment in relation to any official matter in which they have an interest. The new code governing members prohibits the receipt of any gift that is related to the member's position, whereas the code governing ministers and other senior executive-branch officeholders prohibits only gifts that could influence public officeholders in their judgment and performance. The new code allows ethics commissioners to investigate a member not only at the behest of another member, but on their own initiative, and not only must they make their findings public, they may recommend sanctions. The code for ministers/senior bureaucrats does not allow commissioners to launch their own inquiries, nor does it permit them to recommend sanctions. Members, under the new code for MPs, must disclose their families' interests to the commissioner, who then makes available a public summary of such interests (without stating amounts); while, under the code, ministers and senior officeholders make a confidential disclosure and no public summary is issued.

True, a summary of a minister's disclosure will have to be made public by virtue of the fact that he is a member, even if the interests of senior bureaucrats – many of whom are more powerful than ordinary members – will not be. But more generally, as the Library of Parliament's analysis says, the commissioner will apply only one code or the other to any given case involving ministers, not both at the same time. And, the analysis goes on to say, "it may be predicted that most of their actions will be found to be ministerial, and thus the Prime Minister's [less onerous] rules will apply" (Young, 2004, Description and Analysis, Section D500).

Indeed, the very fact that Canadian legislators are less powerful than their U.S. counterparts seems to have suggested, to the ministers drafting various bills or codes over time, that MPs can be subjected to the ultimate remedy of recusal when it comes to voting on an issue in which a member has a direct or particular interest. Recusal of a legislator in the U.S. is thought to disenfranchise her/his constituents, since, whether in voting on laws or in making representations to the executive, one legislator cannot be replaced by another. "Undelegable responsibilities within the executive branch," by contrast, "are comparatively rare" (Association of the Bar of the City of New York, 1960, p. 204); hence, recusal has always been a possibility for U.S. executive-branch officials.

The conflict-of-interest bills introduced in Canada, by contrast, all contemplate the possibility of a legislative member's recusal. And the very reason why ordinary Canadian legislators tend to fall into less egregious privately sourced conflicts than do cabinet ministers – because legislators are so comparatively less powerful – also may explain why the comparatively onerous remedy of recusal has been seen as a possibility for Canadian MPs. Prime Minister Pierre Trudeau once said that Canadian members of Parliament are "nobodies." As if by way of tacit acknowledgment of this view, those in the executive branch who drafted the various Canadian bills showed little concern that an MP's recusal would disenfranchise his constituents. In a real sense, because of the control that leaders exert over their parliamentary caucuses, constituents are disenfranchised anyway. If, because of the prime minister's control over his caucus, each government member is more or less automatically going to support any given bill, then any one government member can substitute for any other, and none is indispensable. And so although Canadian MPs are less likely to fall into privately sourced conflicts than are their American counterparts – because they are less powerful – the conflict-of-interest remedy of recusal will be less disruptive – because they are less powerful.

Apart from the perversities that the cabinet's control over Parliament embedded in Canada's new conflict-of-interest codes, the one governing executive officeholders in particular also shows, by comparison with U.S. strictures, a comparative lack of concern with the privately sourced conflicts of interest they are meant to regulate. U.S. executive officials, by and large, are subject to prophylactic strictures more equivalent to those operating on ordinary Canadian MPs – prohibitions on acting in any way so as to further one's interests or taking gifts in any way related to one's office – and not those operating on Canadian executive officials, which prohibit according preferential treatment to their own interests or receiving gifts that might encumber their judgment. Or, to take another example, the Canadian code also explicitly permits what in the U.S. is commonly called an abuse of office: an official being able to use his official role to affect the interests of a private entity in which he may have no stake, but that is in a position to do business with another private entity whose interests he cannot affect in his official role, but in which he does hold a stake (Stark, 2000, chap. 5). A classic example is Eisenhower's Air Force Secretary Harold Talbot, who was in an official position to award federal contracts to defense firms that had retained the services of Talbot's private consulting company. Even though Talbot argued that he was rendering full private-market services in return for the fees he received from defense companies – and therefore was not beholden to them for any official act – the mere fact that he could have affected their interests while in office was enough to force his resignation. In contrast, in Canada, the code says that "public office holders shall not solicit or accept transfers of economic benefits ... unless the transfer is pursuant to an enforceable contract or property right of the public office holder" (Canada's conflict of interest and post-employment code for public office holders, Part 1, 3(6)) – as, of course, Talbot's were. In other words, Canada explicitly permits what in the U.S. is regarded as unacceptable.

Nowhere is Canada's relative nonchalance toward conflicts posed by private interests more evident than in the two major federal conflict-of-interest cases that emerged after the Liberals assumed office in 1993. As it happens, one involved Prime Minister Chretien, and the other, Prime Minister Martin. There is, I argue, an interesting parallel between the Chretien and Martin affairs. In both instances, the issue was not whether strictures that were being proposed for powerful ministers in a parliamentary system should also apply to powerless legislators, but whether the relatively unfettered regime appropriate to powerless legislators should also apply to powerful cabinet members.

When he was elected prime minister in the fall of 1993, Jean Chretien was the co-owner of a golf course in his Quebec riding of St. Maurice. Chretien has claimed that by the time he was sworn in a couple of weeks later, he had sold his interest. But, it transpired, the person who ostensibly bought it – having had second thoughts – never rendered payment. When it became apparent that, whether or not Chretien still technically owned the shares, he was not going to be paid for them, the prime minister's trustee began to look for a new buyer.

As it happened, the golf course was adjacent to a hotel (the Auberge Grand-Mere) where tourists stayed when they come to golf; the course and the hotel also offered joint packages. As far as the U.S. Office of Government Ethics interpretation of such situations is concerned, Chretien, by virtue of his private interests in the golf course, would have had a private interest in the welfare of the hotel. As long as the hotel was doing well, it would have been easier for Chretien's trustee to unload the prime minister's shares in the golf course, and for Chretien to get paid.

But the hotel was not doing well. And in 1997, Chretien phoned the president of the Federal Business Development Bank – technically an independent agency of government, although the bank's president is a prime-ministerial appointee – and lobbied him to grant the hotel a loan, even though the hotel did not qualify under bank rules. The bank complied, but the president later said that he deemed Chretien's pressing him to have been inappropriate. Chretien did not tell the federal ethics counselor that money was still owing to him for his golf-course shares, although he was obliged to do so. And, his office denied that he had made the call to the head of the bank, although it turned out that he had done so (Clouds of scandal gather in Ottawa, 2001).

What is noteworthy here is the defense that Chretien offered, one that the federal ethics counselor, Howard Wilson, accepted. The prime minister, after all, is also the member of Parliament for St. Maurice, and in phoning the head of the Business Development Bank, Chretien said, he was acting in his legislative, not his executive role. He was doing nothing more nefarious than seeking funds for his constituents, as any legislator does. Even so, though, it is stretching credulity for the most powerful member of the Canadian executive branch to ask to be treated as if he were an ordinary legislator, as if his sway over the agencies that he lobbies is minimal. Ironically, Chretien's own legislation would have made it illegal for an ordinary member, every bit as much as for a minister, to do what he did: lobby the executive branch on a matter in which he held an interest. In the case of his own privately sourced conflict of interest, however, Chretien – instead of holding legislators to strictures more apt for ministers – decided to hold a minister, namely himself, to strictures more apt for ordinary legislators.

Now consider the case of Chretien's successor, Prime Minister Paul Martin. Prior to entering Parliament in 1988, Martin had built a private shipping company, Canada Steamship Lines (CSL), which is currently worth (according to some estimates) U.S. $450 million, and in which he retained voting control. In the run-up to Martin's assuming the prime minister's office in late 2003, the subject of his holdings became a matter of public controversy. Initially refusing to sever his controlling interest in the company, Martin, under pressure, turned it over to his sons in August, a few months before assuming office.

The ethics counselor, Howard Wilson, approved of this arrangement by reasoning as follows: although interests held by close relatives are tantamount to interests held by oneself for conflict-of-interest purposes, Martin could avoid affecting those interests if he simply recused himself, as prime minister, from a narrow set of government decisions having to do with maritime transportation. It is true, the ethics counselor noted, that innumerable prime-ministerial decisions that Martin might make in office would affect the value of CSL, from transport policy more broadly, to agriculture and resource policy governing the commodities that CSL ships to tax, trade, pension, and industrial policy. But to require Martin – or his sons – to divest themselves of their shares in Martin's life's work would, Wilson (2003) said, deter successful business people from going into public life.

Martin's situation, however, is quite unique in two respects. He both occupies high public office and at the same time retains enormous private interests. In cases where even one of these things were not true, there would be no reason for a business person going into government to divest; recusal would work. On one hand, imagine that Martin were running for mayor of Montreal instead of prime minister. Mayors do not control corporate income tax, trade, transport, labor relations, and a host of other policy areas that would affect a company like CSL. On the odd occasion when the mayor's office could affect CSL – something to do with the environs surrounding the Port of Montreal, say – the mayor could recuse himself without impairing his ability to execute 99% of the responsibilities of his office. On the other hand, imagine that in running for prime minister, Martin, instead of being a successful shipping company magnate, was the successful owner of a golf club in rural Quebec. Once again, it would be fairly easy to structure a recusal regime that would allow him to execute his office in the 99.99% of decision-making situations that would have no effect on the golf course. For any official with either less power or less wealth than Martin commands, recusal can work; divestiture is not necessary.

In the U.S., executive officials who hold both powerful public office and substantial private wealth have recognized that recusal cannot work; that only divestment will suffice. In the administration of George W. Bush alone, Defense Secretary Donald Rumsfeld, Treasury Secretary John Snow, former Treasury Secretary Paul O'Neill, and former Budget Director Mitch Daniels each hoped that he could hold his high office while retaining his substantial private interests, recusing himself whenever his decisions affected them. But each soon realized that recusal would not work because most everything he would do in office could substantially affect his interests, and so divested. It is worth noting that, in the American context, the offices that these men have occupied are not as powerful as the prime minister is in Canada, and their wealth (if public estimates are remotely accurate) is not as great as Paul

Martin's. But as a U.S. Treasury (2001) department statement said, in announcing O'Neill's divestment of his approximately $100 million worth of holdings in Alcoa and other companies, the treasury secretary had come to accept "that there is essentially no limit to the range of policy issues that impact the U.S. economy and therefore come before him for review."

So why did Canada's ethics counselor allow Martin to do what O'Neill recognized that wealthy high executive officials should not do: hold onto their interests if they are substantial? The answer seems to be that Wilson chose to view Martin as a legislator, not an executive official. Apart from shipping and maritime-sector issues which could affect CSL specifically or directly, Wilson said, Martin did not need to recuse himself from any other policy decisions affecting the company, since in all other areas – tax policy, trade policy, resource policy – Martin would be affecting CSL only as a member of a broad class of companies with similar interests.

In explaining this arrangement, Wilson (2003) cited provincial rules that allow legislators to vote on matters that affect their own personal interests – interests as taxpayers, consumers, or homeowners – as long as many other citizens share similar interests. But these rules are meant to apply precisely to ordinary members in their legislative roles, not to members who also happen to be cabinet ministers acting in their executive roles. The reason is that when a legislator votes on matters that affect her/his interests, scores or hundreds of other legislators will also be participating equally in the decision. Legislative decisions are collective ones. Whatever bias any given member has will be diluted.

But this reasoning does not apply to officials acting in an executive role. In March 2004, for example, a U.S. inspector general rebuked Interior Secretary Gale Norton for allowing her deputy to participate in a matter affecting his former clients. Norton argued that since the matter "impacted hundreds, if not thousands, of parties similarly," the deputy was not in conflict (Lee 2004, p. A14). Wrong, said the inspector general. That argument does not apply to an executive official even of lower rank, let alone the highest. In effect, Martin – following suit with Chretien – was asking that he be treated as if his executive acts were the acts of an ordinary legislator.

To sum up thus far, in Canada, conflicts posed by publicly sourced interest – and the prime minister's control of the public emolument and careers of legislators – have historically been more consequential than those posed by private interests. Yet, the parliamentary system itself seems unlikely ever to be able, with its own resources, to deal adequately with such publicly sourced conflicts. It must look outside itself, and one option may be some form of American-style term limits.

When it comes to whatever conflicts are posed by private interests, the Canadian parliamentary system at the federal level also seems unable to adequately grapple with them. Because in a parliamentary system, the cabinet is responsible for drafting legislation, it has time and again endeavored to apply the same onerous strictures to powerless members as to powerful ministers. And, turning this on its head – because cabinet members double as legislators – they have, in individual cases, attempted to argue that the same lax strictures appropriate to ordinary members ought to apply to them as ministers. The result is that in recent years, no federal politician has officially been found to be in a conflict resulting from his private financial interests. The separation-of-powers system in the U.S., in contrast, affords a more apt way of crafting appropriate regimes suited to the differences between the legislative and executive branches. Canada should endeavor to emulate that approach, by giving legislators control over the drafting of the conflict-of-interest code for both themselves as legislators and for ministers as executive officials.

Some might counsel against such a move because it would erode the prime minister's constitutional powers of control over the membership of the cabinet. This was the same argument that Howard Wilson and others mounted to persuade Prime Minister Chretien, throughout the 1990s, that making the ethics commissioner report to Parliament would usurp the prime minister's constitutional powers. Hence, the office remained that of a counselor under the prime minister's control (McIntosh, 2002). If that argument has now loosened its grip to the extent that Canada now has an ethics commissioner who reports no longer just to the prime minister but to Parliament even on ministerial conflict of interest, then there is no reason why Parliament should not set the rules that the commissioner is to enforce for ministerial conflict of interest. Nothing would stop the prime minister from setting his own additional criteria. Even if the new ethics commissioner, reporting as he/she will to Parliament, rendered an adverse ruling concerning a minister under rules drafted by Parliament for the executive branch, the commissioner would not have the authority to recommend that the minister be fired or to suggest any other sanction. It would still remain entirely within the prime minister's discretion as to whether he/she demotes the minister, requires an apology or other action, or else expends the political capital necessary to defend the minister – just as it now falls within the prime minister's discretion to defend a minister who has been adversely judged, say, by the auditor general or other officers of Parliament. Allowing legislators to set the rules for ministers would not usurp the prime minister's constitutional powers, though it might have the effect of eroding his/her political capital – but there is no constitutional obligation on anyone to preserve the latter.

CAMPAIGN FINANCE

Just as, in Canada, there is a tradition in which publicly sourced financial interests pose every bit as much a conflict as do privately sourced financial interests, so there is also a tradition – within the campaign-finance laws – in which political parties pose every bit as much a corrupting threat to the electoral process as private-interest groups do.

Once again, the unique Canadian structural context is important. The American cabinet need not be composed of politicians, or indeed even of partisans of the president, and hence it tends to remain isolated from conflict-of-interest scandals involving campaign contributors. Those American cabinet members who do get into such scrapes are invariably former politicians or political operatives such as Mike Espy or Alexis Herman. But nonpolitical cabinet members, such as Janet Reno or Colin Powell, tend to get used sparingly, if at all, as fundraisers for the president's party. They come to office with no personal coterie of political cronies or lobbyists expecting contracts or appointments.

Not so for Canadian cabinet members. Almost all are career politicians, each with his or her own machine. And in Canada there is a long tradition of conflict-of-interest controversies involving ministers and their campaign contributors: not just contributors to the party generally, but contributors to their personal campaigns. When John Manley – who briefly ran against Paul Martin to succeed Jean Chretien – replaced Martin as finance minister in 2002, he jettisoned the Finance Department's ties to a lobbying firm filled with Martin supporters, and substituted one that he found more congenial (Elliott, 2004). Ministers hoping to replace Chretien – notwithstanding their common allegiance to the Liberal Party – openly accused one another of favoring their own particular political organizations in the awarding of contracts.

In the U.S., in contrast, cabinet members are generally not pretenders to succeed the president, and in any case are not career politicians to the same degree as in Canada. Hence, they tend not to get ensnared in controversies involving political contributors. Instead, they are far more likely – because a proportionately greater number of them come from the private sector – to get into scrapes involving their private financial holdings, as evinced by the controversies surrounding James Watt, James Baker, and the late Ron Brown, among others. In fact, post-Mulroney, it has only been prime ministers in

Canada – not the rest of the cabinet – who have gotten into serious difficulties involving their private interests. Conversely, in the U.S., it is principally presidents – think of Bill Clinton's overnighters, or George W. Bush's enormous fundraisers – and not their cabinets who, among high executive officials, raise serious questions involving political contributions.

Of course, when it comes to legislators, conflicts of interest arising from campaign finance are a bigger problem for American congressmen than for Canadian MPs, precisely since the latter are so much less powerful than the former. But when it comes to the cabinet, the conflicts arising from campaign finance in Canada are more serious, since Canadian cabinet members tend to be professional politicians. That, then, is the structural background that shapes the Canadian–American difference in campaign-finance sourced conflicts of interest. Now for some historical background that sets out attempted solutions.

For three decades, up until January 2004 when Canada's new campaign-finance law took effect, the core difference between Canada's and America's campaign-finance regimes was typically said to be the following: In Canada, corporations and unions were allowed to contribute unlimited amounts to parties' and candidates' electoral campaigns, while parties and candidates themselves were limited in their campaign spending. In the U.S., corporations and unions are prohibited from contributing to parties' and candidates' electoral campaigns, but parties and candidates, even during a campaign, are allowed to spend unlimited amounts.[1]

All of the above may be true, but it does not entirely capture two critical differences. First, up until the recent McCain–Feingold soft-money restrictions, although American corporations and unions were prohibited from contributing any amount at all to party electoral campaigns, they could contribute unlimited amounts for broader party-building purposes. Up until January 2004, in contrast, Canadian corporations and unions were allowed to contribute unlimited amounts to political parties for both purposes, electoral and party building; no distinction was drawn between the two. Second, in the U.S., interest groups can be and are restricted in their electoral campaign advertising, while parties can spend unlimited amounts. In Canada, the law limits parties and interest groups alike in their campaign-period, election-related spending, although the specific limits for parties are more generous.

What is key here is that when it comes to contributions from corporations and unions, U.S. law has long recognized a difference between party building and electoral purposes. And when it comes to spending, U.S. law has been more concerned with the difference between interest group and party electoral spending. Neither has been as true in Canada.

Prime Minister Chretien's new campaign finance legislation came into effect on January 1, 2004. As a result, federal law now caps corporate, union, and individual donations – which until then could be made in unlimited amounts to parties – at $1,000 annually for corporations/unions and $5,000 for individuals, requiring that they flow to local party organizations. To compensate the national parties for the lost revenue, Chretien said, each would get an allowance from public funds of $1.75 annually for every vote it received in the previous election. What is of interest here is that although there are now limits on corporate/union contributions where formerly there were none, there still is no distinction between such corporate/union contributions for party building and for electoral purposes.

Conversely, although the law in Canada limits parties and interest groups alike in their campaign-period spending for electoral purposes, lower courts repeatedly struck down the limits on interest-group spending, rendering it unlimited for almost 20 years until 2004, when the Supreme Court upheld them in *Attorney General v. Harper* (1 S.C.R. 827). While in the U.S. party spending on electoral campaigns is unlimited, while group spending is limited, in Canada it has de facto been the other way round up until very recently and, de jure, there are limits on both. While Canada has thus oscillated between periods in which interest-group expenditures have been limited and unlimited, in other words, there is still no distinction, except in degree, between interest-group spending and party spending for electoral purposes (see the useful discussion in Hiebert, 1998).

The question I want to pursue is this: Simply by looking at this jumble of law on either side of the border, would it be possible to find a single principle that underlies the Canadian difference? Let me suggest one. In Canada, parties – and I am referring here to parties outside, not inside of Parliament – are treated as private entities, much closer to private-interest groups than public institutions striving for the public good. The reverse is the case in America. This observation, I think, explains a large part of the difference between the two countries' traditions – not just in laws, which can change, but in the bounds of discourse, the kinds of arguments deemed admissible – in the domain of campaign finance.

Consider allowing corporations and unions to contribute unlimited amounts to political parties, as Canada historically has – and not just for party building but for electoral purposes – identifies parties themselves, by association, as closer to instruments of private interest than bodies propounding their own considered views of the public interest. Or, at least, it shows a comparative lack of concern with protecting the capacity of parties to act as vessels for views of the public interest as opposed to votaries of private interests. True, Chretien's law, which took effect at the beginning of 2004, limits corporate and union contributions, but it does not, as U.S. law does, eliminate them. The president of Chretien's own Liberal party, Stephen LeDrew, objected to the new limitations, lamenting that in their wake, "parties would no longer be seen by some as private institutions" (LeDrew 2002, p. A19). More importantly, as noted, the new law limits corporate and union contributions to parties indiscriminately for both purposes, electoral and party building. In so doing, it fails in its own way to draw a distinction between the party as a self-interested entity intent on periodic electoral victory, and the party as an ongoing institution with a public role in the polity that deserves to be supported.

Up until McCain–Feingold, in contrast, American law has always maintained this distinction. Corporate and union contributions for party-building purposes – so called soft-money donations – were unlimited in the U.S., while corporate/union contributions were utterly prohibited for electoral purposes. What McCain–Feingold embodies is a reluctant realization that this distinction can easily be evaded in practice, and not a renunciation of it in normative terms (see, e.g., Ornstein et al., 2003). As for the critics of McCain–Feingold, many accept that corporate/union donations should not go to parties for electoral purposes: that the danger of a quid pro quo serving the private interests of contributors is just too great. But they attacked McCain–Feingold precisely because – in restricting corporate/union contributions for party-building purposes – it seemed to them to be antiparty, antithetical to the building of parties as institutions (Chinni, 2001).

Turn now from contributions to expenditures. When it comes to spending, the Canadian campaign-finance law on the books limits parties and interest groups alike in their campaign-period, election-related expenditures. True, the limits imposed on parties and interest groups differ in amount, but that means simply that they are seen as distinct only in degree, not in kind. The notion that parties themselves should be limited in their electoral spending, just as interest groups are, implies that parties can be similarly corrupting entities; that, as if they were private interests, they can corrupt the electorate with their expenditures. Viewed through American lenses, Canada's limitations on party campaign spending suggest that such spending amounts to commercial speech – parties hawking their wares – which in America can more easily be constitutionally regulated, rather than political speech, which cannot be.

Chretien's law makes no changes in this area, and the Supreme Court, as noted, recently upheld the law's expenditure caps. But, as it so happens, lower courts over a period of more than two decades had struck down the provisions of the law imposing campaign-period spending limitations on interest groups. The result was that interest groups were able to spend unlimited amounts on electoral advertising, while parties were limited – as if, in the election campaign, it was the party that was the more self-interested entity, since its interests were directly at stake, while the interest group was more public-spirited, having less directly at risk. Indeed, this notion is very much a part of Canadian discourse. In striking down limits on interest group but not party spending, a lower court opined that "[v]oters want the benefit of the independent advice and information on candidates and parties from others [i.e., interest groups] with similar ideologies and without the self-interest involved in candidate and party advertising" (*Somerville v. Canada*, 136 D.L.R. [4th] 205; see also Bakvis & Smith, 1997).

What all of this shows is, that in Canada, there is no tradition comparable to that in the U.S., in which parties are viewed as special, quasi-public institutions, not simply self-interested entities that are, essentially, the moral equivalent of interest groups. Had there been, Canada's laws would have reflected a difference between corporate/union contributions for (legitimate) party building and for (less legitimate) electoral purposes, and they would have reflected a difference between (less legitimate) interest-group spending and (more legitimate) party spending for electoral purposes. Up until recently, the law said that corporations and unions could contribute unlimited (and Chretien's legislation now says that they can contribute limited) funds for both purposes, party building and electoral. The letter of the law says that interest groups and parties alike are limited in their spending for electoral purposes; and in fact, for decades, the courts have said that interest groups alone are unlimited.

Sometimes it seems that wherever one looks in Canadian politics, one can find anecdotes that bear out the idea that Canadian political parties are treated, indeed viewed, as closer to private-interest groups than entities concerned with promoting their view of the public interest. Up till recently – and this has changed with the new legislation – Canadian law placed no spending, contribution, or disclosure requirements on candidates seeking party leadership. Even up until very recently, the government minister who introduced the legislation took the position that parties are private entities whose internal workings should not be regulated (Stock, 2002). That is a far cry from the approach that the U.S. has taken for decades toward party primaries, which are very much seen to be public – and hence regulable – affairs, not private ones.

Or consider some other wrinkles in Chretien's legislation. For a long time, Canadians have been allowed tax credits for their political contributions; the new legislation, in fact, increases that amount to $650. Although there used to be tax credits in the U.S., they were eliminated in the 1986 tax reforms; in any case, those that existed were confined to much smaller contributions ($100–200). What remains in the U.S., of course, is the federal government's provision for publicly matching private contributions to primary campaigns. With matching, the party gets the government's money; while with tax credits, as in Canada, the contributor does. This, it would seem, is yet another way in which Canada treats parties more as private entities, endowing the act of participation with the tinge of a commercial venture: you need a monetary incentive to contribute. In the U.S., it is assumed that you do not need a personal incentive to contribute; rather, it is assumed that voters are more public-spirited. Simply knowing that the cause about which they care will get further support, via public matching, is a sufficient motivation for them to privately contribute.

Of course, in the U.S., taxpayers can also send public money to parties via the check-off on their tax returns. But the check-off – which is the same amount ($3) for each taxpayer – does not reduce a person's tax liability; it simply diverts some of it from general government revenue to the federal government's campaign account. And that account goes to build the party system, to fund both major parties equally, with minor parties eligible for smaller amounts if they have reached a threshold of public support. Canadian taxpayers, in contrast, get a reduction in their tax that varies with the extent of their contributions; more importantly, their contributions go not to build the party system per se, but to the particular party of their choice.

Canadian tax dollars, of course, help assist parties not just via credits for contributions, but also via rebates for election expenses; 50% of whatever a particular party spends is rebated by the Canadian government. In the U.S., in contrast, tax dollars do not rebate but rather replace party expenditures. Campaigns that take public money agree not to spend their own, and the amount provided remains equal for the two major parties – again, an approach that seems far more oriented, in comparison with the Canadian, toward the building and maintenance of a competitive party system. When it comes to Canada's governmental support for parties, public money in the form of tax credits appeals to the private interests of the contributors; public money in the form of rebates encourages parties to rely on private-interest contributors. Neither is true with American public funding for parties. In the U.S., public money matches – instead of rewarding – contributions; and it replaces, instead of rebating, expenditures.

What about the new Canadian law's allowance to each party of $1.75 annually in public funds for every vote it got in the previous election? Would that not introduce a breath of fresh democratic, anti-plutocratic air into Canada's campaign finance? Would it not represent a view of a party more akin to a vehicle for public participation than a private-interest group? Part of the problem here is that unlike in the U.S., where the two major parties get some public support that is dependent neither directly on their electoral success nor on their private financing – public support that is truly meant to build and conserve a party system – in Canada no such public support exists. Not only does Canada not distinguish between corporate/union contributions for party building and for electoral success, but when it comes to contributions from the public treasury, it does not distinguish between a party-building purpose and one designed to reward electoral success.[2]

There is something even more questionable about the new per-vote funding scheme. Its purpose, Chretien has said, is to compensate parties for the loss in funding that they will sustain as a result of the legislation's new limitations on corporate/union contributions (Brown, 2003; Coyne, 2003). In what sense, one might ask, does apportioning money based on votes in the previous election – an ostensibly democratic measure – substitute for apportioning money that would otherwise have come from corporations and unions? It does, and can, only if one assumes that corporate and union contributions are not ideologically motivated. Rather, they follow the winner. The question of whether corporations or unions actually do contribute in this fashion is of course very much an open one, subject to considerable debate on both sides of the border. But that is beside the point here. What is key is that this presumption – the presumption that corporations or unions contribute preponderantly more to whichever party has previously won the most votes – is what underlies the notion that allocating money by votes in the previous election will be a reasonable proxy for lost corporate and union contributions. If giving money to a party based on the votes it received simply shadows the extent to which it would have been funded by corporate interests, then it is less a democratic than a plutocratic principle. Or, less provocatively, in comparison with a principle that would allocate public funds so as to build a competitive party system, Chretien's principle – in which public funding is allocated so as to shadow corporate/union contributions – simply reconfirms the notion that parties are little different from vessels for interest groups.

Finally, there is something revealing in the different ways in which the term *third party* gets used in Canadian and American debates. In Canada, and in the context of campaign finance, the term third-party advertising refers to campaign ads, especially electorally oriented ones, launched by interest groups during campaigns. It is true that in the U.S. the term third party gets used to refer to interest groups as well. But it is also used in another sense. Since the U.S. has a two-party system, debates about whether smaller political parties (i.e., third parties) should be recognized, or whether in fact they are more like interest groups – interferers in party politics – is historically a subject of intense debate. In Canada, then, third parties (i.e., interest groups) have been elevated equal to and, for a long period, even above the status of the major parties. In the U.S., third parties – minor parties – are treated as if they were interest groups external to the two-party system. In Canada, in the term third party the key word is *party*, since as applied to interest groups it rhetorically confers on them party status. In the U.S., the key word is *third*, since it emphasizes the extent to which minor parties occupy a subsidiary role in the two-party system.

All of these various strands – Canada's historical willingness to allow corporate/union contributions to parties, its equation of party spending with interest-group spending (distinguishing between them only in degree, not kind), its encouragement of contributions by an appeal to self-interest, its reticence in using public money to directly support the party system – suggest, when examined through American lenses, a view of parties in which they are not public institutions, but rather akin to private-interest groups. What accounts for this? Certainly, it is not a deliberate wish to erode parties.

Ultimately, I think, the causes are institutional, having to do with Canada's parliamentary system. The core distinguishing feature of Canadian campaign-finance law – from which everything else follows – is the limit on party/candidate expenditures, which, because of the U.S. Supreme Court's interpretation of the First Amendment, do not exist in the United States. In introducing his bill, Chretien identified as its root impetus his horror at the fact that Hillary Clinton had spent more on her 2000 New York Senate race than all Canadian parties combine did in the 2000 federal election.

I am not arguing that this horror is necessarily misplaced. True, in the U.S., the typical riposte is that private interests, such as soup or soap manufacturers, spend even more than that on advertising. Such an argument, however, carries weight only to the extent that political parties are seen as more important civic institutions than mere private interests, and it obviously does not carry weight in Canada. It is this abhorrence of U.S. party electoral spending that lies at the root of Canada's campaign-finance regime, because if parties are to be limited in their electoral spending during a campaign, then, so the reasoning goes, so must be interest-group spending, to keep the playing field even.

The notion that unlimited party spending can sway the opinion of private citizens, and in ways that detach their deliberations from the merits of issues and candidates, certainly figures to some extent in American debate. The difference is that in the U.S., the First Amendment cabins its impact. Canada, being a parliamentary system, did not have a constitutional bill of rights until 1982, eight years after Pierre Trudeau introduced Canada's original campaign-finance law. The result is that we now have a campaign-finance regime in which expenditure restrictions on parties persist – an artifact of Parliament's supremacy, in 1974, in passing laws concerning expression – but in which expenditure restrictions on interest groups were subsequently struck down for two decades as violations of the Charter of Rights and Freedoms.

Canada's distinctive constitutional history thus explains why, when it comes to campaign expenditures, Parliament was able to place parties and interest groups on the same plane, while courts subsequently gave interest groups a leg up. But why, when it comes to campaign contributions, should Canada's regime not have differentiated, as the U.S. has, between corporate and union contributions for party building and for electoral purposes – both until recently being unlimited and now, under Chretien's law, both subject to limitation?

I can offer only a conjecture. In 1974 as today, the largest contributors to the Liberal and Conservative parties were the banks. Canada's banking system differs from America's in that Canada's banks are national institutions, and few in number. Far from betokening a pluralistic riot of economic interests, Canada's banks are (or at least in 1974 could be seen as) national institutions every bit as lofty – perhaps more so – than parties. The source of the contribution thus avoiding the taint of an ordinary interest group, banks' contributions evaded that taint as well. Indeed, banks traditionally contributed to the two major parties, but instead of being seen as a cynical ploy to cover both bases, their doing so was viewed as a way in which major civic institutions could, and should, contribute to sustaining the party system. Because, at that time, Canada did not need to differentiate contributions for party building and more self-interested purposes, the country now inherits a regime that does not when perhaps it should.

CONCLUSION

When it comes to conflicts resulting from personal financial interests, the main problem in Canada, as a comparative historical proposition, has not been that private interests encumber governmental judgment. Rather, because of Canada's parliamentary system, it is that government itself, and in particular the publicly sourced emoluments controlled by the prime minister, can encumber the judgment of ministers and legislators. Indeed, in many instances such publicly sourced interests in Canada can be placed on the same scale of encumbrance as privately sourced interests are in the U.S. This is not in any way to deny that conflicts posed by privately sourced interests ever appear in Canada's parliamentary system, but the parliamentary system has meant that Canada deals with them inadequately. Because it is ministers who draft legislation, ordinary legislators get treated by proposed regimes as if they were executive officials – subject to much the same tough strictures – and because ministers double as legislators, they seek to be treated as if they were ordinary MPs. In America, with its separation of powers, the appropriate distinctions are more readily maintained.

When it comes to Canadian campaign-finance law, the problem has not so much been that private interests corrupt parties as that parties themselves are seen as agents that corrupt the private citizen's judgment. Indeed, Canadian parties are treated in much the same fashion – i.e., their campaign-period electoral spending is limited – as private-interest groups are in the U.S. Canada's parliamentary system – the fact that notions of parliamentary supremacy pre-date the relatively recent Canadian era of constitutional freedoms – allowed this view to animate the law. The result is a legal regime in which parties are treated as if they are self-interested entities, while interest groups have often been treated as if they were parties.

At this stage, my conclusion is that although Canada's institutions have created a unique normative regime, it turns out that this regime is ill-suited to a country with Canada's institutions – and that American norms would be more appropriate. When it comes to publicly sourced conflicts of interest, which continue to plague us, I believe that U.S-style term limits should be given serious consideration as an antidote. As for privately sourced conflict of interest, the law now includes an ethics commissioner reporting to Parliament, charging him/her to enforce whatever code of conduct Parliament sets for itself and whatever code of conduct the prime minister sets for the cabinet. I would argue that both codes – and they should appropriately reflect the differences between the two branches – should be set by the legislature, as they substantially are in the U.S.

Finally, when it comes to campaign finance, it seems to me that the American approach has much more to recommend itself than we in Canada have been willing to acknowledge. Precisely because our Charter of Rights and Freedoms leaves a larger role for Parliament to override it than the U.S. Bill of Rights leaves to Congress, we should be able to accomplish what American campaign-finance law has struggled to do only with great turmoil: to give the campaign-period electoral expression of the parties greater priority than that of interest groups, and the party-building contributions of corporations/unions (and individuals) more scope than those directed toward electoral purposes. It is often thought that Canada's institutions have brought us too close to adopting American norms and ways of life, when something more home-grown would be better suited. Perhaps the reverse is the case when it comes to public-sector ethics.

NOTES

1. More precisely, parties are allowed to spend unlimited amounts as long as such spending remains uncoordinated with candidate campaigns, otherwise such expenditures are then regarded as limitable contributions. They would, in other words, be seen as mere conduits for private interests, who by contributing to the party are in effect contributing to the candidate.

2. It is not surprising that through his new campaign-finance law, Chretien proposed that financing for parties be heavily determined by the will of the electorate, instead of the American-style approach that would fund parties as entities in their own right. He also believed that, in its internal machinations concerning leadership, the party should be subordinated to the will of the electorate, not operated as an entity in its own right with the capacity to change its leader at any time. Specifically, Chretien was aggrieved by the fact that the Liberal Party constitution allows the extra-parliamentary party to review the leader's performance after each election. It was precisely Martin's control of the extra-parliamentary party that ensured that Chretien would lose the post-2000 election review, forcing Chretien's departure. Chretien's retort was that the party should review the leader only after he loses an election (Bryden, 2002), not after he wins one: a provision that existed in the old Progressive Conservative Party constitution. The Liberal Party, Chretien in effect argued, should not be able to thwart the will of the people and deprive a winning prime minister of his party leadership; rather, the will of the people should control the party. Chretien's campaign-finance legislation manifested a similar philosophy. Parties do not deserve funding as institutions in their own right, only to the extent that each reflects public favor in the snapshot of the previous election.

REFERENCES

Association of the Bar of the City of New York. (1960). *Conflict of interest and federal service.* Cambridge, MA: Harvard University Press.

Bakvis, H., & Smith, J. (1997). Third-party advertising and electoral democracy: The political theory of the Alberta Court of appeal in Somerville v. Canada (Attorney General) [1996]. *Canadian Public Policy, 23,* 164–178.

Brown, J. (2003). Chretien ethics package under increasing fire as time for action slips away. *Truro Daily News,* April 19, p. B6.

Bryden, J. (2002). Chretien dares rival to force an election. *Ottawa Citizen*, June 5, p. A1.
Canada. *Conflict of interest and post-employment code for public office holders* (Part 1, 3(6)). Retrieved from http://strategis.ic.gc.ca/epic/internet/inoec-bce.nsf/en/oe01125e.html.
Canada. Special Joint Committee of the Senate and the House of Commons. (1992). *Minutes of proceedings and evidence*, Ottawa, March 24.
Chinni, D. (2001). The future path of soft money. *Christian Science Monitor*, April 26, p. 1.
Clouds of scandal gather in Ottawa. (2001). *National Post*, March 24, p. A15.
Coyne, A. (2003). Campaign finance bill's bad points overshadow its many good ones. *Sault Star*, January 31, p. A4.
Dawson, R. M. (1970). *The government of Canada* (5th ed.). Toronto: University of Toronto Press.
Elliott, L. (2004). Earnscliffe federal jobs total $6 million since 1993. *Ottawa Citizen*, February 9, p. A3.
Fife, R., & Dawson, A. (2002). MP's spouses won't have to declare assets, PM bows to backbenchers. *National Post*, October 9, p. A12.
Greene, I. (1990). Conflict of interest and the Canadian constitution. *Canadian Journal of Political Science*, 23, 233–256.
Hiebert, J. L. (1998). Money and elections: Can citizens participate on fair terms amidst unrestricted spending? *Canadian Journal of Political Science*, 31, 91–111.
Ibbitson, J. (2004). Liberals take no prisoners. *Globe and Mail*, May 5, p. A4.
LeDrew, S. (2002). Don't ban corporate political donations. *National Post*, December 4, p. A19.
Lee, J. (2004). Report faults agency more than top aide in lobbying case. *The New York Times*, March 17, p. A14.
McIntosh, A. (2002). An integrity cop or culprit? *National Post*, June 5, p. A10.
MP's pay. (1983). *Daily Telegraph*, August 16, p. 18.
Ornstein, N. et al. (2003). *Interest of Amici Curiae, McConnell v. FEC*, August 5, p. 13.
Some liberals think health deal was too generous. (2004). CBC News. Retrieved September 21, 2004, from http://www.cbc.ca/story/canada/national/2004/09/22.
Stark, A. (1992). Conflict of interest at the federal level in Canada and the United States: Differences in understanding and approach. *Public Administration Review*, 57, 427–437.
Stark, A. (1993). Public-sector conflict-of-interest at the federal level in Canada and the United States. In: H. George Frederickson (Ed.), *Ethics and public administration* (pp. 52–75). Armonk, NY: M.E. Sharpe.
Stark, A. (2000). *Conflict of interest in American public life*. Cambridge, MA: Harvard University Press.
Stock, P. (2002). Mandate to meddle. *Report Newsmagazine*, January 7, p. 12.
United Kingdom. (1978). *Parliamentary Debates*. Fifth Series. Vol. 954, July 28.
United Kingdom. (1980). *Parliamentary Debates*. Fifth Series. Vol. 989, July 21.
U.S. Treasury. (2001). *O'Neill to divest Alcoa holdings*. Washington, DC: Office of Public Affairs, U.S. Treasury (March 25). Retrieved from http://www.ustreas.gov/press.
Wilson, H. (2003). *Letter to Paul Martin (July 28)*. Ottawa: Office of the Ethics Commissioner.
Young, M. (2004). *Legislative History of Bill C-4 (February 12)*. Ottawa: Library of Parliament.

THE COSTS AND BENEFITS OF ETHICS LAWS

B. A. Rosenson

ABSTRACT

This chapter assesses the impact of ethics laws at the state level in the U.S., focusing on laws that apply specifically to one category of public officials: legislators. I first discuss the positive contribution of ethics laws to the functioning of democratic government. I then turn to the costs of the laws, which are often subtle and counterintuitive. The discussion of the costs of ethics laws draws on a growing body of empirical evidence, and highlights the ways that legislation can have unintended and undesirable consequences.

Over the last half century, the American states have enacted numerous statutes known as ethics laws that limit the activities of a wide range of public officials, both elected and appointed. These laws address potential conflicts between officials' private interests and their public duties, specifically in regard to behavior that lies outside the clear boundary of bribery. For example, ethics laws restrict the receipt of gifts and honoraria, limit post-government employment, ban state employees from providing compensated legal representation before state agencies, and require disclosure of various financial interests. These laws are generally part of the civil rather than the criminal statutes (or in the case of lawmakers, they are often part of ethics rules that govern each legislative chamber).[1] While many of these ethics laws were enacted in the aftermath of Watergate, others predate that landmark event. New York enacted the first generalized state conflict of interest law for public officials in 1954, setting the standard that other states have followed over the last 50 years.

Ethics laws have been the subject of considerable controversy. In recent years, an increasing amount of scholarship has emerged that questions the wisdom and efficacy of these laws. While some works note important benefits of the laws, others have suggested that the laws have unintended and detrimental consequences that need to be taken more seriously (Anechiarico & Jacobs, 1996; Garment, 1991; Mackenzie, 2002; Maletz & Herbel, 2000; Neely, 1989; Rosenthal, 1996; Tolchin & Tolchin, 2001; Rosenson, 2004, in press).

Some states, such as Kentucky, California, South Carolina, and New Jersey, have extensive laws regulating legislators' behavior. These ethics laws include provisions for significant limits on gifts, limits on legislators becoming lobbyists after leaving office, and extensive financial disclosure requirements. Other states, such as Wyoming, Vermont, and North Carolina, have relatively weak legislative ethics laws that lack substantive restrictions on behavior (Rosenson, 2005). Approximately half the states, including Massachusetts, Florida, and Connecticut, have set up independent commissions in addition to legislative ethics committees to enforce their legislative ethics laws, while New York, Ohio, and other states rely solely on committees composed of legislators themselves (Rosenson, 2003a). A number of scholars, and public-interest advocates from groups such as Common Cause, argue in favor of more ethics regulation and stronger enforcement: weak laws should be strengthened (Fain, 2002; Herrick, 2003; Thompson, 1995; Weber, 1999). However, as will be detailed below, an increasing number of analysts of ethics laws argue that caution should be exercised when considering expanding the scope of ethics laws, since the enterprise of ethics regulation contains important challenges, inherent limitations, and often poorly understood costs.

THE VALUE OF LEGISLATIVE ETHICS LAWS: WHY THEY ARE NEEDED AND THE FUNCTIONS THEY SERVE

In *Ethics in Congress: From individual to institutional corruption*, Dennis Thompson (1995) outlines three basic principles of legislative ethics, aimed at guiding legislative behavior in ways that "promote the integrity of legislators and the legislative process" (p. 19). The principles are (1) independence (making decisions based on the merits of the case); (2) fairness (playing by the rules of the legislative institution); and (3) accountability (acting so as to create and maintain public confidence in the actions of individual legislators and in the legislative process). Ethics laws can make a particular contribution to promoting the first and third principles: independence and accountability. By placing limits on legislative behavior in order to discourage lawmakers from acting primarily out of concern for private financial gain, gift restrictions, financial disclosure requirements, and other ethics regulations should promote decision-making on the merits. Rebekah Herrick (2003) concludes that the congressional ethics laws and rules passed since the 1970s have had this effect. She argues that by limiting members' ability to supplement their incomes from interest groups, businesses, and private individuals, the laws "limited the potential for members to base decisions on these interests instead of the merits of policy" (Herrick, 2003, p. 110).

By exposing and reducing the potential influence of private economic concerns on legislators' decisions, conflict of interest laws should also promote accountability and public trust in government. At least this is a critical rationale behind the enactment of these laws. I will later address the counterargument: that ethics laws actually decrease public trust by generating a sense that all lawmakers are fundamentally untrustworthy and strongly motivated by the pursuit of private gain from public office.

In practice, ethics laws cannot eliminate legislators' private financial interests (nor should they) or remove the influence of lobbyists on decision-making. However, ethics and financial disclosure laws do help make such interests public and do circumscribe the influence of lobbyists. The fundamental value of ethics laws is that they set clear standards of conduct, defining boundaries, which separate the acceptable from the unacceptable. As of 2002, for example, 23 of the 50 states prohibited legislators from receiving honoraria (fees for speechmaking). Twenty-seven states had revolving door laws that restricted legislators from becoming lobbyists after leaving office for up to two years. With regard to gifts, nine states had zero tolerance policies, or 'no cup of coffee' laws, which barred legislators from receiving any gifts from lobbyists; an additional 23 states placed limits on the value of gifts (National Conference of State Legislatures, 2002, pp. 35–37, 48–51, 56–58). Such laws place straightforward limits on acceptable activities and interactions between legislators and other parties, specifically interest groups.

Ethics laws make clear that legislators must abide by certain guidelines, beyond the criminal statutes' prohibition on quid pro quo bribery. One scholar has argued that in state capitals where lobbyists once paid the tab for all sorts of entertainment – generating a sense of indebtedness that clouded lawmakers' judgment – public life has benefited from the passage of conflict of interest laws (Rosenthal, 1996). Florida, South Carolina, and Kentucky are states that Alan Rosenthal (1996) argues have gained by the reshaping of capital cultures via the enactment of ethics laws, generally in response to major scandals (p. 213). A similar rationale for the positive impact of good-government reform is often advanced with regard to campaign finance regulations. In April 2004, the New Jersey State Assembly began to look at a 25-point plan to reform state campaign finance laws, in order to change what one assemblyman called a "culture of corruption that had enveloped both of our parties" (NJ Lawmakers to change corruption culture, 2004).[2]

The existence of ethics statutes in general forces legislators to be sensitive to ethically challenging situations and to think about what kind of conduct is acceptable in ways that they might not otherwise do, i.e., if they simply followed their own moral compass. A perennial criticism of ethics laws is that you cannot legislate morality – ethics must come from the heart. This criticism is overly naïve, since the foundation of all law is not to legislate behavior but to proscribe certain activities and attach penalties to their commission. Benefits accrue from defining what is ethically acceptable for practitioners of a given profession, whether it is medicine, law, engineering, or legislating. Because of the complex roles involved in legislating and the myriad pressures that are placed upon lawmakers, they – and the public – do benefit from the outlining of clear standards of conduct, from the enunciation of straightforward 'should nots.' As Frank Anechiarico and James Jacobs (1996, p. 57) suggest, the behavior of two categories of public officials in particular are likely to be influenced by laws that restrict outside activities: (1) those who previously lived by the credo that everything is permissible except that which is clearly prohibited and (2) those who did not previously realize that there was anything wrong with benefiting personally from economic opportunities that arise in the course of public employment.

Ethics laws set clear boundaries on what is acceptable in terms of reaping private benefits from public office. A law that limits gifts to $250 in the aggregate per year from a lobbyist, as exists in California (or Louisiana's $0 gift threshold) does not leave much room for an individual lawmaker to use his or her own discretion. Such laws universalize what is acceptable. To the extent that value is derived from the laying down of universal standards, the laws are beneficial. The counterargument, which I address later, is that removing all discretion is undesirable in the area of ethics because it is demeaning to lawmakers and ultimately harmful to their public image.

Ethics in public life is something no state legislator (or member of the U.S. Congress) today can avoid thinking about, since they generally face a myriad of laws with which they must comply. Over 40 states include ethics training in their new member orientation programs, while 9 offer continuing education programs. The majority of these programs simply include instruction on ethics statutes and rules, but some states go further and provide a forum for discussion of general ethical principles. At least 11 states in 2002 had programs that incorporated principle-based discussions on topics such as honesty, integrity, and value conflicts. In most states such ethics programs are voluntary. However, in 13 states in 2002 it was a statutory mandate that legislators attend such programs. In some states these trainings are conducted by ethics commissions; in others, the legislature itself conducts the sessions. An increasing number of states are also providing ethics training for legislative staff, lobbyists, and other public officials (National Conference of State Legislatures, 2002, pp. 23–33).

Legislators are not always enthusiastic about the time they must devote to understanding the laws of their particular state. Despite this displeasure, having such laws on the books and requiring legislators to invest some time in understanding what the laws demand – and in some states giving them the opportunity to explore what a broader conception of ethics might require – is a good thing when compared to not having such laws or training. However, ethics laws or no ethics laws are not the only alternatives. The argument of an increasing number of analysts is that the legislative ethics laws that do exist have numerous flaws. The key criticisms, which I address in more detail below, are (1) the laws are poorly designed, largely because they often represent hasty responses to scandals; (2) they violate legislators' privacy; (3) related to the violation of privacy and also to the limits they place on outside income opportunities, the laws deter some would-be legislators from running from office; (4) the laws not only hinder recruitment but also drive some lawmakers out early by creating a politicized and unpleasant environment; (5) they contribute to a negative public conception of legislators because laws inevitably lead to publicized allegations of violations, and even if these allegations are later proven unfounded, the stigma lingers; and, (6) they trivialize the concept of political ethics. It is to these criticisms that I now turn.

HOW THE PROCESS OF ETHICS REFORM MAKES A DIFFERENCE

Numerous scholars have noted that political reform generally follows scandals (Hoogenboom, 1978; Katz, 1981; Link & McCormick, 1983; Mackenzie, 2002; Rosenson, 2003a; Rosenthal, 1996; Saint-Martin, 2003; Stewart, 1994).

Watergate is the most well-known example. It helped catalyze the passage of campaign finance reform, the 1977 congressional ethics codes, and the 1978 *Ethics in Government Act*. But there are many less well-known examples, particularly at the state level. For example, beginning in the late 1980s and through the mid-1990s, the Federal Bureau of Investigation and the U.S. Department of Justice conducted a series of controversial sting operations, aimed at catching state lawmakers in the act of taking bribes, in California, Kentucky, South Carolina, and Louisiana. Similar operations were conducted by local law-enforcement authorities and federal prosecutors in New Mexico and Arizona in the early 1990s.[3] Each of these stings, which led to the indictments and convictions of numerous legislators on corruption charges, sparked the enactment of new ethics laws. In Kentucky and South Carolina, where the stings yielded the largest number of convictions, so many new restrictions were placed on legislators' behavior in areas such as gifts and honoraria that the states vaulted to numbers one and two in terms of the stringency of their ethics laws (Rosenson, 2005). Smaller-scale scandals led to ethics reform in states such as Massachusetts in 1978, New York in 1987, and Ohio in 1994. In Illinois in 2003, following the indictment of Democratic Governor George Ryan on corruption charges, the state's gift laws and its ethics enforcement mechanisms were strengthened (see McDermott, 2003).

These laws were not only and not always (indeed, not often) direct responses to the unethical behavior highlighted by the particular scandals that they followed. In many states, the new laws addressed a wide range of behavior, going beyond the activities involved in a given scandal. For example, federal prosecution of state legislators on bribery, mail fraud, and other charges led to the passage of laws banning honoraria and gifts, to post-government and representation employment limits, and to mandatory financial disclosure. The sting operations that exposed state legislators taking bribes could have led simply to stronger bribery laws. Instead, they catalyzed a broad range of conflict of interest laws. There are parallels in this regard to Watergate. As Calvin Mackenzie suggests:

> Watergate was about burglary, cover-ups, lying, and campaign irregularities. [Yet] (n)othing in the Ethics in Government Act (passed in its wake) would have added new deterrents to, or punishments for, those behaviors. (Mackenzie, 2002, p. 44)

As with Watergate, reformers seized the opportunity presented by scandal to push for a variety of new restrictions, many unrelated to the behavior exposed by the scandal. Since 1954 and the passage of the first general ethics law by New York State, good-government advocates outside and inside state legislatures have used the window of opportunity created by scandals to press for the passage of reform proposals that had often languished for years in committee, failing to generate the impetus for a vote. Eager to stem the flow of negative media attention, legislators generally pass many – though by no means all – of these proposals by wide margins (Rosenson, 2005).

The scandal-driven nature of ethics reform has important implications. Scandal-motivated legislation has several negative features. As suggested above, laws enacted in response to scandal are often not well thought out and they are not narrowly tailored to existing problems. In addition, they generally lack deep support from legislators. In Dobel's (1999) terminology, the laws do not constitute excellent political achievement because they are not based on genuine consensus and commitment among elites regarding their value. They are therefore unlikely to endure in the long term, a point I return to in the next section. Scrambling to respond to media criticism, legislators enact laws about which they themselves are highly skeptical. As Rosenthal (1996) points out, ethics laws that lack the support of those who must abide by them are unlikely to succeed. In only about half the states do independent ethics commissions enforce legislative ethics laws, and even then, they do so in conjunction with ethics committees composed of legislators. In the remaining states, legislative ethics committees have sole jurisdiction over the enforcement of ethics laws pertaining to legislators. This means that the support of lawmakers is a critical intervening variable in explaining how, and whether, the laws are firmly enforced. If lawmakers do not believe in the laws, it is unlikely that legislative ethics committees will come down hard on those found guilty of violating them. And it is likely that lawmakers will use a range of mechanisms at their disposal to hobble the independent ethics agencies that they create, from the power of the purse to amendatory legislation designed to remove various powers from the commissions (Rosenson, 2005). Legislators' dislike of ethics laws leads them to implement weak enforcement mechanisms.

REMOVING DISCRETION AND LEGISLATIVE BACKLASH

Another important criticism of ethics laws is that their universality is a vice, not a virtue. This is because they remove discretion from the individual legislator regarding what types of gifts or other things of value may corrupt judgment. In effect, the laws say legislators should not determine for themselves how small a gift is small enough or what types of gifts represent an unacceptable threat to legislative judgment. Many lawmakers find this demeaning and offensive. The result is that the laws often lead to a backlash from the legislators who enacted them under pressure, once the scandals that catalyzed them fade into the background.

For example, in Iowa there is a $3 limit on gifts from lobbyists, enacted in 1994 in the wake of a scandal involving the senate president and his ties to a state investment fund. As of January 2003, the Iowa House Ethics Committee was working on rewriting this law. One representative told reporters that it was absurd and insulting to suggest that a legislator can be influenced by a meal or drink, and that the law had stifled social life at the State House. "It's got to be changed," said Rep. John Connors (D-Des Moines) (Glover, 2003).

The ongoing hostility of legislators to existing ethics laws and to proposals to expand existing laws can also be seen in Maryland. In January 2004, the General Assembly was resisting pressure by the state Common Cause chapter to enact a bill placing their financial disclosure forms online. The aim of this proposal, according to Common Cause, is to make it easier for those who want to obtain that information but now have to visit the legislative ethics committee offices and sign in. Legislators can also request to be notified whenever their records are pulled, which advocates say has a chilling effect on the public's access to public records. One lawmaker, John Arnick (D-Baltimore County) explained his opposition to the proposal, "I don't want (my information) out there for every kook to read" (Levine, 2004, p. B1; Jansen, 1999). Even in the wake of recent scandals involving revelations of lobbyist influence over legislators in Maryland, lawmakers were holding the line with regard to this particular ethics reform proposal, citing their interest in maintaining some degree of privacy.

RECRUITMENT, RETENTION, AND THE POLITICIZATION OF ETHICS CHARGES

Concerns about the invasion of privacy connect to another important claim of the critics of modern ethics laws, namely that the laws hinder recruitment and retention of legislators and other public officials (Anechiarico & Jacobs, 1996; Neely, 1989; Mackenzie, 2002; Rosenthal, 1996; Rosenson, in press). The drafters of ethics laws are highly sensitive to the potential for the laws to deter some individuals from entering public service. The preambles of many state laws explicitly note the balancing act inherent in creating clear standards of conduct, on the one hand, and avoiding a situation in which public service is undesirable due to excessive limits on outside income opportunities or requirements for disclosure of financial interests, on the other. One such example is the preamble to the 1971 Maine ethics code, which stated, "The public interest will suffer if unduly stringent requirements deprive government of the 'services of all but princes and paupers'" (Maine Code, §146: 19-371, Public Laws 1971). Louisiana's 1964 ethics code similarly reflected, "Legal safeguards against conflicts of interest must be so designed as not unnecessarily or unreasonably to impede the recruitment and retention by the government of those men and women who are best qualified to serve it" (Louisiana Code, Title 42, Chap. 15, Sec. 1101).

Although the drafters of ethics laws have generally been careful to avoid making ethics laws overly onerous, there is still evidence that these laws deter some individuals from running for office. For example, I found in my research using multiple regression analysis that financial disclosure laws reduced the number of candidates who ran for open seats in state legislative primaries (Rosenson, in press). The study examined 1,510 primary races across 25 states in the years 1994 and 1996. The stronger a state's financial disclosure requirements, the fewer the number of candidates who ran for any seat that came open. I also found that the passage of representation limits for lawyer-legislators (laws limiting representation before state agencies for pay) contributed to a decline in the number of lawyer-legislators serving in 46 states between 1976 and 1986. Finally, I found that stronger financial disclosure requirements contributed to a decline in the number of business owners serving in the 46 state legislatures during the same time period.

Some may feel it is a good thing to have fewer attorneys and fewer business owners serving in state legislatures. These are still among the most popular occupations for state legislators, so a decline in these categories actually enhances occupational diversity. What is problematic is that ethics laws may be deterring highly qualified individuals from these occupations from serving. The official financial rewards of state legislative service are limited. For example, as of 1998, only eight state legislatures paid salaries above $100,000 per year (Council of State Governments, 1998). Attorneys in states such as Kentucky and South Carolina, which pay relatively low or unprofessional salaries, may decline to run for office because of the limits placed on their capacity to supplement their official salaries by representing clients before state agencies. In states with extensive financial disclosure requirements, such as New York, some business owners are reluctant to publicize their financial interests, choosing to keep them private at the cost of declining to run for office.

While I found evidence of this deterrent effect only for one of the two 10-year periods I examined (no statistically significant effect was found for the years 1986–1995), the fact that I found any deterrent effect must be considered as a downside of ethics laws. One could argue that the individuals who do not run are people who should not serve, due to conflicts of interest. However, it is plausible that at least some could contribute to public life, but do not get to do so because they cannot afford to lose outside income or wish to avoid public exposure of their financial interests. We cannot be sure that only the bad attorneys and business owners are deterred.

In addition to the impact of ethics and financial disclosure laws on attorneys and businessmen, individuals of no particular profession may be hesitant to run for office or serve in appointive positions when they witness the media circus that often attends the accusations of ethics violations. As Suzanne Garment (1991) notes, public servants can face large legal costs, their reputations can be destroyed, their children may suffer fallout, and their spouses may be hounded by reporters. This is an unintended consequence and not an inherent flaw of ethics laws, and the media bears significant responsibility. Again, however, the deterrent effect must be reckoned as a cost.

Similar findings about the deterrent effect of financial disclosure laws on public service have been suggested by Mackenzie (2002) with regard to the national executive branch. Mackenzie (2002) draws his conclusions from the writings of former personnel officers for Presidents Nixon, Carter, Reagan, and George H.W. Bush, who suggested that financial disclosure requirements had been pushed too far and were one of the deterrents to getting people in (to serve as presidential appointees), particularly those from outside Washington from the business community who had the types of financial interests that would have to be made public (p. 127). The former director of personnel for George H.W. Bush added that not only financial disclosure, but also the divestiture requirement and post-government employment restrictions, had harmed recruitment efforts.

In addition to the deterrent effects of ethics laws on recruitment, it is argued that ethics laws may lead to lower retention of legislators by making legislatures into less desirable places to serve (Rosenthal, 1996; Tolchin & Tolchin, 2001). More broadly, the politicization of ethics laws is seen as a serious problem for American democracy (Ginsberg & Shefter, 1990). Susan and Martin Tolchin (2001) discuss the ethics wars in the U.S. Congress. In one chapter they focus on former Republican Speaker of the House Newt Gingrich, whose ethics crusade involved accusing the previous Democratic Speaker, James Wright, of 69 ethics violations. These included improperly taking gifts from a real estate developer and using a book he wrote to enrich himself in violation of the House rules' prohibitions on outside income. Wright was convicted of using sales of his book to evade the House restrictions on honoraria, and he resigned from office.

The ethics process had political overtones well before Gingrich was elected in 1978, but he took it to new heights (Tolchin & Tolchin, 2001, p. 2). Gingrich viewed the process of making ethics charges as a legitimate political weapon. He argued that members of Congress should be held to the highest ethical standards, and that they fell far short. He was especially appalled by the long-time practice of allowing convicted felons to enjoy the full privileges of the House, such as voting, while their cases were being appealed (*ibid.*).

However, Gingrich's use of the ethics process to bring down the Democratic Speaker would come back to haunt him. He unleashed the process only to find it turned against him. Immediately after becoming Speaker himself in 1994, he was charged with unethical behavior for taking a book advance of $4.5 million from publisher Rupert Murdoch. Gingrich gave up the advance and agreed to accept earned royalties in its place. Over 500 additional charges were filed with the House Ethics Committee involving a political action committee (PAC) run by Gingrich to raise money for Republican candidates. He was accused of diverting funds from the PAC to finance two college courses he taught in Georgia. Democrats called it a tax-scam. The charges came primarily from House Democratic Whip John Bonior, Democratic Rep. John Lewis of Georgia, Democratic Rep. George Miller of California, and Democratic Rep. Pat Schroeder of Colorado. Schroeder suggested that Gingrich was no more ethical or law-abiding than the Democrats he had criticized for years: "We might as well rip up all the laws, rip up all the rule books, if the guy at the head can thumb his nose at them" (Tolchin & Tolchin, 2001, p. 6).

Gingrich admitted to failing to get advice from a tax lawyer before teaching the course, and to filing inaccurate information to the House Ethics Committee, although he said it was unintentional. In early 1997, the House voted 395-28 to reprimand him. He was also fined $300,000 by the House Ethics Committee, a fine agreed upon by leaders of both parties. Though Gingrich said the charges against him were 99% partisan, he nevertheless paid the fine (*ibid.*). The congressional charges touched off a three-year IRS investigation that concluded he had acted within the law. Like former Speaker Wright, who said it cost $500,000 in legal fees to defend himself against the ethics charges he faced, Gingrich paid a heavy price in both financial and reputational terms. And both parties arguably suffered from the falls of their leaders.

More recently, House Majority Leader Tom DeLay (R-Texas) has been the target of investigation by the House Ethics Committee. In October 2004, the committee officially admonished DeLay for pressuring another House member to change his vote on a health care bill; for intervening with federal authorities to chase Texas state lawmakers who had fled their state to avoid voting on a redistricting plan aimed at benefiting the Republican party; and for appearing to link political contributions to support for legislation. (DeLay had also been chastised previously by the ethics committee for pressuring trade groups to hire Republican officials.) But in November 2004, the committee also sent a letter to one of DeLay's accusers, Democratic Rep. Chris Bell, saying that the congressman had engaged in exaggeration and innuendo in filing his charges against DeLay. For example, the committee concluded that while Bell had accused DeLay of soliciting a bribe from a Texas energy company, the facts did not come even close to supporting this extremely serious claim. DeLay asserted that he had been vindicated by this letter, despite the committee's admonishment of him, and referred to Bell as a "partisan stalker" (Stout, 2004, p. A1; see also Hulse, 2004).

Acknowledging that members of Congress should abide by the laws and rules of their institution, the bigger concern raised by the DeLay, Gingrich, and Wright cases is the potential for the politicization of ethics charges. Russell Williams (1996), studying the Florida Ethics Commission, found that ethics charges rose in election years and fell in nonelection years, suggesting some degree of political motivation. As parties and candidates trade accusations about ethics violations, this contributes to what Rosenthal (1996) calls a breakdown of trust among members that has dire consequences (p. 12). Put simply, it becomes harder to build consensus needed to make public policy.

Given the increasing ideological polarization between the two major parties at the national and state levels, when ethics is added into the mix it becomes even more difficult to get legislators to work together in a bipartisan fashion. I make the assumption here that bipartisanship is necessary or beneficial in at least some cases, e.g., where neither party has a large majority in the lower or upper house, or there is divided government. Accepting this assumption as legitimate, the potential for ethics laws to be used as a political weapon by partisans becomes a potentially serious issue from the standpoint of the government's ability to govern, since the flinging of ethics accusations can introduce new incentives to policymaking gridlock. Herrick (2003) states, "The use of ethics is likely to increase acrimony and partisanship in the chamber, decreasing the ability of Congress to pass new legislation" (p. 10). Assuming that new legislation is needed under some circumstances, this is a serious problem.

The broader claim about politicization of ethics processes has also been made about the special prosecutor statute, later called the independent counsel statute. This law was enacted in 1978 in response to Watergate, when the attorney general fired Special Prosecutor Archibald Cox on the order of President Nixon. The aim was to prevent the president from encroaching on the independence of special prosecutors appointed to investigate executive branch officials (Saint-Martin, 2003). Mackenzie (2002) and Garment (1991) criticize the independent counsel statute for unduly destroying political careers. Even if someone is later proven innocent, the damage has been done and the financial and emotional costs are tremendous, while the benefits to the public are debatable. A prime example of this is Ray Donovan, secretary of labor under President Reagan, who was ultimately acquitted but paid a huge cost monetarily and in reputational terms (Garment, 1991).

Mackenzie and Garment also point to the cost of independent counsels. The 20 investigations between 1979 and 2000 spent nearly $200 million in taxpayer money in the pursuit of detecting and sanctioning public corruption. The percolating backlash to the independent counsel statute among both Democrats and Republicans, who felt it was used in partisan ways, came to a full boil after the investigation of President Bill Clinton. While it can be argued that Kenneth Starr's investigation was legitimate and defensible since the president should not be above any laws, the investigation was criticized by many as a costly political witch hunt. Congress evidently bought many of the criticisms, declining to reauthorize the statute in 1999.

Returning to the impact of ethics laws on the decision of legislators to leave office earlier than they otherwise might, I did not find strong ethics laws to be associated with higher voluntary retirements, at least in lower houses of state legislatures (Rosenson, 2003b). The study looked at the retirement decisions of legislators in 47 states between 1998 and 2002. However, anecdotal evidence suggests that the passage of ethics laws – such as financial disclosure requirements and post-government employment limits – does lead to some resignations (Anechiarico & Jacobs, 1996, p. 61).[4]

Anechiarico and Jacobs (1996) make an even more subtle argument that ethics laws negatively affect morale and the way that public servants do their jobs. Because many public employees and elected officials view comprehensive ethics laws as presuming their venality and guilt, it would "hardly be surprising if (those) who feel this way were unenthusiastic and ineffective in carrying out their responsibilities" (*ibid.*). This claim is hard to assess, however, in the absence of more empirical evidence, such as interviews with public officials to determine whether ethics laws have had a demoralizing effect on them and their enthusiasm and commitment to their jobs.

ETHICS LAWS, PUBLIC TRUST, AND THE MEDIA

One of the key rationales for the enactment of substantive ethics restrictions, financial disclosure requirements, and other sunshine laws that aim to promote transparency in government, is that they will increase public trust. This goal is particularly significant in the post-Watergate period, which has witnessed a decline in public trust. However, good-government laws may have the perverse and unintentional effect of decreasing public trust. Jeff Milyo and David Primo (2003), for example, found that stronger campaign finance laws in the states were actually associated with lower trust. This may occur because such laws generate constant suspicion of public officials' motives. Mackenzie (2002), for example, criticizes the ethics culture – with its myriad of rules and regulations designed to fend off potential conflicts of interest – as one "rooted in distrust, in the notion that every public official and every candidate ... is suspect" (p. 177). He points to national survey data that shows fluctuations in public trust in the national government have not corresponded to the passage of new ethics laws at the national level.

Herrick (2003) similarly suggests that "the advent of institutional rules related to ethical behavior provided a cache of information about unethical behavior and has perhaps contributed to Americans' low regard for Congress" (p. 9). The media rarely reports on members who are abiding by the ethics laws, since that would not be considered newsworthy. Instead, reporters naturally seize on violations of the laws, even minor ones such as the failure to file financial disclosure forms on time. This increased media attention to ethical lapses, as defined by the possible failure to comply with existing law, may be an important factor in explaining the widespread belief that public officials are corrupt. I have found that in states with strong ethics laws, there is a greater perception of state corruption than in states with weak ethics laws (Rosenson, 2004).[5] My work examines perceptions (by State House reporters) of political corruption in 47 states in 1999.

The critical factor which links ethics laws and lower public trust is the media. Although some scholars of legislative ethics have concluded that legislators today are probably less corrupt than they used to be (Mackenzie, 2002; Rosenthal, 1996; Thompson, 1995), the media does not view or present issues of legislative ethics through this broad, historical lens. Rather, the imperatives of news gathering and media competition impel reporters to focus on current ethical misdeeds – to be the first to report them, or to report them from new angles. With regard to Congress, the number of stories dealing with scandals as opposed to public policy has grown over the years (Lichter & Amundson, 1994).

The existence of ethics laws provides an important clue as to why laws lead to allegations that there have been violations of the laws. These make for stories that are interesting and newsworthy from the journalist's perspective; this is especially true for anti-corruption laws, given the media's interest in political scandals and corruption. The media often emphasizes scandals and corruption, while stories about policymaking or other legislative achievements receive short shrift (Graber, 2002). This is true even though the public does not necessarily want as much scandal coverage of candidates and public officials as it receives (Just, Crigler, Alger, Cook, & Kern, 1996). Consider the revelations about U.S. Rep. Gary Condit (D-California) and his affair with a woman who became a missing person in 2001. Condit became the most recognizable face in Congress, while congressional news about other members and the conducting of institutional business (committee meetings, floor votes, hearings, etc.) was drowned out. One study of network news reporting on Congress in 1989 concluded that two-thirds of the coverage concerned three episodes of scandal (Ornstein, 1989).

Part of the media's emphasis on scandal is due to the long-term impact of Watergate on journalistic culture, but part is an outgrowth of ethics laws that provide easy fodder for journalists' natural interest. Many individuals in the media also may feel a sense of obligation to cover alleged ethics violations in order to fulfill the role of watchdog and expose governmental wrongdoing. If laws define what is wrong, and they appear to have been violated, journalists can justify writing about it by saying they are serving the classic watchdog function, responding to ethical criteria that government has set for itself but officials may have failed to live up to. The media is arguably too aggressive in its pursuit of stories that appear to involve character lapses, acting more as a junkyard dog than a watchdog (Sabato, 1991). The point here, however, is that ethics laws provide a jumping-off point, an objective standard, for reporters' actions and the stories they file. Covering ethics charges is not the same as covering unsubstantiated rumors about political officials. There is a certain objective basis to the former type of coverage that makes it more justifiable than the latter: public officials appear to be violating standards they have set for themselves, rather than standards that journalists choose to apply. The filing of ethics charges is part of an officially sanctioned process; thus, journalists are not merely imposing their own judgments about right and wrong in political life when they write about cases that come before ethics committees and independent commissions.

ETHICS LAWS AND THE TRIVIALIZATION OF POLITICAL ETHICS

Perhaps the most significant criticism of ethics laws is that they aim too low and diminish the concept of what it means to act ethically in political life.

Donald Maletz and Jerry Herbel (2000, p. 10) present this criticism eloquently when they suggest that the requirements of laws such as the Ethics in Government Act of 1978 – such as its gift limits and mandated financial disclosure – lead to a certain trivialization of ethics. The modern ethics reform movement, they argue, suffers from the absence of an ethics of aspiration or excellence (Maletz & Herbel, 2000, p. 37). A growing literature in the field of public administration, of which these authors are a part, has focused on a much broader view of political ethics, one which goes beyond avoiding financial conflicts of interest and emphasizes characteristics such as courage, integrity, and leadership across a wide range of demanding situations that arise in public service (Cooper & Wright, 1992; Dobel, 1999; Hart, 1992; Pffifner, 2003). The content of modern ethics laws, which consists mainly of delineating situations that public officials should avoid rather than providing positive guidelines for action, does not speak to such broader conceptions of political ethics.

This is because ethics laws are deliberately minimalist in nature (Thompson, 1987). They proscribe a small area of conduct, focusing on the domain of financial conflicts of interest. They purposely circumscribe the scope of ethics. This circumscribing has its virtues in a pluralist political system where legislators are likely to disagree on fundamental political and moral values and in which broader agreement on what constitutes ethical behavior is difficult, if not impossible, to achieve. But, the narrow focus on financial conflicts of interest fails to address many aspects of the questions: What does it mean to act as an ethical legislator, or as an ethical public servant more generally? What does it mean for a legislator to exercise judgment well? As Thompson states, "many kinds of influence can erode legislative judgment" (1987, p. 98). As an example, he suggests that legislators who "always use their office zealously to pursue the ... goals of single-interest groups with which they are associated may be distorting legislative judgment no less than those who accept (things of financial value) from special-interest groups" (*ibid.*). The personal financial motives of lawmakers can be an important factor that influences and harms legislative judgment, but it is not the only factor. By focusing exclusively on one factor, ethics laws indeed aim low and must be viewed as possessing important limitations in terms of their ability to promote exemplary moral behavior by public servants.

Another problem raised by the nature of ethics laws is that they focus attention – of the legislators who must abide by them, of the media who looks for occasions on which they are violated, and of the public who consider possible violations presented by the media – on individual corruption rather than on a broader conception of corruption. Thompson (1995) makes the useful distinction between individual corruption and institutional corruption. Individual corruption involves personal financial enrichment from public office. Receiving a bribe is a classic example. Institutional corruption involves political gain rather than personal financial gain. Campaign finance contributions, which are of use in the political process rather than in private life, can be the basis of institutional corruption. Institutional corruption is problematic because it damages the legislative process in a democracy, not because it corrupts individual legislators who may be dismissed as bad apples in the bunch. The Keating Five case is a good example of institutional as opposed to individual corruption. In this case, five U.S. senators called, met with, and importantly, pressured state and federal regulators on behalf of a savings and loan operator whose activities were under investigation. The banker, Charles Keating, was also a major contributor to their campaigns. The senators were ultimately sanctioned by the Senate Ethics Committee (four were rebuked and one was reprimanded) (Thompson, 1995, p. 40).

This conduct, arguably inappropriate and undesirable, does not fit into the narrow category of personal financial gain from office. But it still raises important issues, from the standpoint of legislative ethics, which are worth considering. The senators interfered with quasi-adjudicatory processes, and did so in a way that went against the principle of transparency in government. Ethics laws do not speak to the harm to democracy and to the functioning of the legislative institution that was caused by their actions. In a sense, the exclusive focus on ethics laws on financial conflicts of interest can be used by those accused of unethical behavior to exonerate themselves from charges of acting improperly if their actions do not fit into the neat template of improper financial gain.

This is not to say that minimalist ethics is of no value. As suggested earlier, the delineation of clear standards of conduct, specifically the prohibition of activities such as receiving fees for speechmaking, provides some clear benefits. It is certainly better than the alternative of no ethics laws and leaving decisions about what kinds of behavior are acceptable to the full discretion of legislators. What this article has suggested is that ethics laws contain hidden costs. These costs can be found in their impact on recruitment, in their potential to be used as political weapons by candidates and officeholders, which can lead legislators to leave office earlier than they otherwise might; in their abuse by the media; and in the paradoxical impact they may have in contributing to diminished public trust. More broadly, ethics laws do not speak to the need for a broader vision of ethics in political life and the importance of virtues such as courage and leadership.

NOTES

1. Most ethics and financial disclosure laws carry noncriminal penalties, such as fines or some sort of sanction by an ethics committee, as punishment for violation. For example, Rhode Island's ethics commission can fine violators of the state's ethics laws up to $25,000, Florida's commission can fine up to $10,000, and Connecticut's can fine up to $2,000 per violation. Ethics committees can generally recommend – and the full chamber of each house of the legislature can vote to endorse – sanctions that include rebukes, reprimands, censures, or even expulsion. However, some ethics laws do carry criminal penalties, i.e., jail time.

2. The proposal called for strengthening the powers of the State Election Law Enforcement Commission, increasing campaign finance reporting requirements, increasing penalties for reporting violations, and requiring political fund-raisers to register annually and file reports on their activities (see NJ Lawmakers to change corruption culture, 2004).

3. See Rosenson (2005, Chap. 5) for a discussion of the broader trend involving the shift in the priorities of federal prosecutors toward fighting corruption at the state and local levels after 1976.

4. One anecdotal example is the 1978 Massachusetts ethics law, which among other things created an independent ethics commission, placed a numerical limit on gifts from lobbyists to legislators, and increased significantly the financial disclosure requirements for lawmakers. Bradbury (1996) argues that the passage of this law led to resignations, e.g., of one wealthy legislator who did not want to make his financial profile public.

5. This study, based on a multiple regression analysis that controls for other factors that may influence perceptions of corruption, takes into account what is known as the endogeneity problem. In other words, the model used accounts for the possibility that an independent or explanatory variable – in this case ethics laws – may be influenced by the dependent variable or the outcome to be explained, in this case perceptions of corruption. This modeling issue is addressed through an instrumental variables technique.

REFERENCES

Anechiarico, F., & Jacobs, J. B. (1996). *The pursuit of absolute integrity: How corruption control makes government ineffective.* Chicago: University of Chicago Press.

Bradbury, V. (1996). *Government ethics reform: The Massachusetts financial disclosure law.* Unpublished doctoral dissertation, Boston College, Chestnut Hill, MA.

Cooper, T. L., & Wright, N. D. (Eds) (1992). *Exemplary public administrators: Character and leadership in government.* San Francisco, CA: Jossey-Bass.

Council of State Governments. (1998). *Book of the States,* Vol. 32. Lexington, KY: Council of State Governments.

Dobel, J. P. (1999). *Public integrity.* Baltimore: The Johns Hopkins Press.

Fain, H. (2002). The case for a zero gift policy. *Public Integrity, 4,* 61–74.

Garment, S. (1991). *Scandal: The crisis of mistrust in American politics.* New York: Times Books.

Ginsberg, B., & Shefter, M. (1990). *Politics by other means: The declining importance of elections in America.* New York: Basic Books.

Glover, M. (2003). Key lawmakers agree to revisit gift law. *Associated Press State & Local Wire* (January 30). Retrieved on July 31, 2005 from http://web.lexis-nexis.com.

Graber, D. A. (2002). *Mass media and American politics* (6th ed.). Washington, DC: Congressional Quarterly Press.

Hart, D. K. (1992). The moral exemplar in an organizational society. In: T. L. Cooper & N. D. Wright (Eds), *Exemplary public administrators: Character and leadership in government* (pp. 9–29). San Francisco, CA: Jossey-Bass.

Herrick, R. (2003). *Fashioning the more ethical representative: The impact of ethics reforms in the U.S. House of Representatives.* Westport, CT: Praeger.

Hoogenboom, A. (1978). Did gilded age scandals bring reform? In: A. S. Eisenstadt, A. Hoogenboom & H. L. Trefousse (Eds), *Before Watergate* (pp. 125–142). New York: Brooklyn College Press.

Hulse, C. (2004). House ethics panel says DeLay tried to trade favor for a vote. *The New York Times*, October 1, p. A1.

Jansen, B. (1999). Complaints about ethics bill threaten its toughest provisions. *Associated Press State & Local Wire* (February 17). Retrieved on July 31, 2005 from http://web.lexis-nexis.com.

Just, M. R., Crigler, A. N., Alger, D. E., Cook, T. E., & Kern, M. (1996). *Crosstalk: Citizens, candidates and the media in a presidential campaign.* Chicago: University of Chicago Press.

Katz, A. (1981). The politics of congressional ethics. In: J. Cooper & G. C. Mackenzie (Eds), *The house at work* (pp. 97–118). Austin: University of Texas Press.

Levine, S. (2004). Legislative ethics data find outlet on Internet. *Washington Post*, January 13, p. B1.

Lichter, S. R., & Amundson, D. R. (1994). Less news is worse news: Television news coverage of Congress, 1972–1992. In: T. Mann & N. Ornstein (Eds), *Congress, the press, and the public* (pp. 131–140). Washington, DC: Brookings/American Enterprise Institute.

Link, A. S., & McCormick, R. L. (1983). *Progressivism.* Wheeling, IL: Harlan Davidson, Inc.

Mackenzie, G. C. (2002). *Scandal proof: Do ethics laws make government ethical?* Washington, DC: Brookings.

Maletz, D. J., & Herbel, J. (2000). Beyond idealism: Democracy and ethics reform. *American Review of Public Administration, 30*, 19–45.

McDermott, K. (2003). Illinois House oks overhaul of ethics standards. *St. Louis Post-Dispatch* (November 21). Retrieved on April 27, 2004 from http://1010wins.com/topstories/winstopstories_story_118071802.html.

Milyo, J., & Primo, D. M. (2003). Campaign finance regulation and citizen trust: Evidence from the states (April). Paper presented at the annual meeting of the Midwest Political Science Association, Chicago, IL.

National Conference of State Legislatures. (2002). *The state of State Legislative Ethics.* Denver: National Conference of State Legislatures.

Neely, A. S., IV (1989). Ethics-in-government laws: Are they too ethical? In: A. M. Donahue (Ed.), *Ethics and politics in government* (pp. 74–83). New York: H.W. Wilson.

NJ lawmakers to change corruption culture. (2004). Retrieved on April 27 from http://1010wins.com/topstoriese/winstopstories_story_118071802.html.

Ornstein, N. (1989). What TV news doesn't report about Congress – and should. *TV Guide, 37*(October 21), 11.

Pffifner, J. P. (2003). Judging presidential character. *Public Integrity, 5*, 7–24.
Rosenson, B. A. (2003a). Against their apparent self-interest: The authorization of independent State Legislative Ethics Commissions, 1973–1996. *State Politics and Policy Quarterly, 3*, 42–65.
Rosenson, B. A. (2003b). The effects of ethics laws on legislative retirements. Working paper. University of Florida.
Rosenson, B. A. (2004). Ethics and campaign finance laws and the perception of state corruption. Working paper. University of Florida.
Rosenson, B. A. (2005). *The shadowlands of conduct: Ethics and state politics*. Washington, DC: Georgetown University Press.
Rosenson, B. A. (in press). Political research quarterly. *The impact of ethics laws on legislative recruitment and the occupational composition of state legislatures*, (forthcoming).
Rosenthal, A. (1996). *Drawing the line: Legislative ethics in the States*. New York: Twentieth Century Fund.
Sabato, L. J. (1991). *Feeding frenzy: How attack journalism has transformed American politics*. New York: The Free Press.
Saint-Martin, D. (2003). Should the federal ethics counsellor become an independent officer of parliament? *Canadian Public Policy, 39*, 197–212.
Stewart, C. H., III (1994). *Ain't misbehaving, or, reflections on two centuries of congressional corruption (Occasional Working Paper 94-4)*. Cambridge, MA: Center for American Political Studies, Harvard University.
Stout, D. (2004). DeLay hails ethics panel's rebuke of his accuser. *The New York Times*, November 19, p. A1.
Thompson, D. F. (1987). *Political ethics and public office*. Cambridge, UK: Harvard University Press.
Thompson, D. F. (1995). *Ethics in Congress: From individual to institutional corruption*. Washington, DC: Brookings.
Tolchin, S. J., & Tolchin, M. (2001). *Glass houses: Congressional ethics and the politics of venom*. Boulder, CO: Westview Press.
Weber, R. E. (1999). The quality of state legislative representation: A critical assessment. *Journal of Politics, 61*, 609–627.
Williams, R. L. (1996). Controlling ethical practices through laws and rules: Evaluating the Florida Commission on Ethics. In: J. S. Bowman (Ed.), *Public integrity annual* (pp. 65–72). Lexington, KY: Council of State Governments.

THE EFFECTS OF LEGISLATIVE ETHICS LAW: AN INSTITUTIONAL PERSPECTIVE

Alan Rosenthal

ABSTRACT

This chapter examines the range of possible effects of ethics laws enacted by state legislatures. One objective of ethics law, to reduce corruption, cannot be demonstrated. Other objectives, to placate the media, defend against partisan attack, and permit the legislature to move on, have mixed results, while a final objective, to restore public confidence, is not achieved. Nevertheless, ethics law does affect the process, by somewhat discouraging legislator recruitment and retention, by raising the consciousness of legislators, and by changing the cultures of state capitals.

For the past half-century, American state legislatures have been enacting ethics laws and rules to govern the behavior of their members. Beginning with the adoption of ethics codes in the period before Watergate and continuing with a variety of ethics reforms in the period since, most legislatures have been intent on making legislators act better and look better.

The unethical, if not illegal, behavior of at least a few legislators brought scathing criticism nationwide, and colleagues felt they had to disassociate themselves from the questionable conduct of the few rotten apples in the legislative barrel. According to Beth Rosenson's analysis in her book *Shadowlands of Conduct* (2005a), the factor that best explains the enactment of these ethics reforms is that of scandal. Indeed, it would seem that each new scandal constituted an argument for a new rule. Scandals precipitating legislative action ranged from those in which legislators were indicted and convicted as a result of law enforcement stings in California, Kentucky, Arizona, and South Carolina in the 1980s to those who were punished subsequently for failing to disclose benefits received or accused in the media for using their office in some way for private gain.[1] Not all of the scandals precipitating new ethics laws have been of similar dimension. The major ones, which tended to involve stings, indictments, and convictions, are rare today. Instead, charges and innuendo produced and purveyed by the media constitute much of what currently is considered to be scandalous. In this volume, Robert Williams notes the prominent role that journalists and editors have played in investigating, reporting, alleging, and possibly inventing claims of unethical conduct by politicians. Of course, the negative nature of partisan conflict also has played a part, with accusations of unethical conduct used as a political weapon (Williams, 2005; Ginsberg & Shefter, 1990).

It is worthwhile to examine briefly the various types of law that the states have enacted. The National Conference of State Legislatures (NCSL, 2002) list is a place to start.

(1) *Training and related activities.* Whether by statute, rule, or practice, ethics training is offered in most states, and is mandated in 13 states. The training focuses mainly on compliance with law and regulation, and is designed less to raise the ethical consciousness of members about broad issues than to keep them from getting into trouble on very narrow ones. Advice and counseling are also made available to legislators today, with the same objective in mind – keeping them out of trouble. For the most part, it is up to legislators to seek out formal – either a formal opinion rendered by an independent ethics commission or a legislative ethics committee (usually made public) – or informal advice (sometimes made public by the member in defense of his or her action).

(2) *Revolving door.* To guard against an unethical use of influence, legislatures in 27 states have enacted laws that prevent legislators from employment as lobbyists immediately after leaving the legislature. Six states require legislators to sit it out for two years, 19 for one year, and 2 require a briefer time until legislators can work as lobbyists in their states.

(3) *Nepotism.* Twenty states now prohibit nepotism, the latest being New Jersey, where several legislators were attacked by the Gannett newspaper chain for having relatives on their district office staffs.

(4) *Honorariums.* Twenty-three states now ban legislators from receiving honorariums for addresses they deliver in connection with their public duties. Thus, they are not permitted to use their office for personal gain by way of speaking engagements.

(5) *Gifts.* In 1957, Wisconsin passed the first no-cup-of-coffee law, which prohibited legislators from taking anything of value from lobbyists and their principals. Then, in 1974, as part of Proposition 9, California adopted a limitation of $10 that lobbyists could spend on a legislator's meal. Today, gifts are banned in about a dozen states, although exceptions allow lawmakers to attend receptions to which all members of a legislature, the senate or house, a delegation, or a committee, are invited. In Minnesota, the gift ban has no major exceptions, and members can eat a meal only if they give a speech – which is referred to as the sing-for-your-supper provision. In many states, there are limitations on the dollar amount of gifts legislators can take on a single occasion or annually per source or total. Trips have also been curtailed, either because they are regarded as gifts or because of restrictions on permissible travel. Legislators nearly everywhere, however, are exempt from these provisions when they are attending meetings of legislative organizations such as NCSL, Council of State Governments, State Legislative Leaders Foundation, and American Legislator Exchange Council. In states where gifts are permitted, members (or lobbyists) have to disclose the nature and the amount of the benefit.

(6) *Financial disclosure.* Practically every state requires legislators to make a public disclosure of their assets and sources of income. The rationale for such a requirement is that citizens ought to be able to judge for themselves whether lawmakers' private interests are affecting their public activities. Information subject to disclosure may include assets, income, transactions, and liabilities. Requirements usually pertain to those in one's immediate family, as well as the legislators themselves. Some states have more intrusive requirements and some less ones.

(7) *Conflicts of interest.* States have worked to diminish the possibility that legislators will act on behalf of their own personal, financial interest rather than the interest of the public and/or their constituents. The task is difficult because state legislatures, unlike Congress, are part-time and permit members to earn income from employment outside the legislature. Even in the eight or so virtually full-time legislatures, many

members earn income in addition to what they receive in public salary. Legislatures have tried to deal with the issue in a number of ways: by financial disclosure, counseling, declarations and recusal by individual members, and limitations on outside employment, such as lobbying or lawyer–legislators appearing before state agencies.

(8) *Lobbyists*. For a half-century, lobbyists have been regulated by the states. All 50 states require lobbyists to register. Two-thirds of the states prohibit contingency fees, and a few others require disclosure of such fees. In all 50 states, lobbyists must file disclosure reports, which usually include the expenditures made by lobbyists on legislators. The stringency of lobbying laws, according to one study (Allen, 2002), range among the states, with California, Washington, and South Carolina having the toughest laws and North Dakota, North Carolina, and Wyoming the weakest.

(9) *Independent ethics commissions*. The final important change is the establishment by statute of ethics commissions independent of the legislature with investigative and enforcement powers. Nearly every state has a joint ethics committee or separate senate and house ethics committees, while in two states the presiding officers appoint a special committee when a complaint is filed. In the case of a few such committees, such as New Jersey's, public members as well as legislators serve on the ethics committee. These committees not only render advisory opinions, but also undertake investigations in response to complaints. They also make recommendations to the senate and house regarding the imposition of sanctions on members who have acted unethically. In addition to legislative committees, about 20 states now have independent commissions with jurisdiction over legislative ethics, a few of which not only investigate but can also punish ethics violations by legislators. Usually, however, after an investigation a commission's findings and recommendations are transmitted to the legislature for action.

DETERMINING THE EFFECTS OF LAW

The question is frequently asked, "What difference have ethics laws made in the states?" The question is occasionally addressed, but rarely answered. I shall address it here, but with no attempt to try to measure effects. There are a number of reasons to avoid precision, and these reasons are worth brief discussion at this point.

The first challenge of any analysis is the decision as to just what ought to be included as legislative ethics law. We have reviewed the types of measures enacted by legislatures in the past 50 years. Should we anticipate, on the one hand, that particular laws, or types of law, will have distinct effects – financial disclosure will impact one way and gift restrictions will impact in a very different manner? If that is the case, each measure has to be considered on its own, independent of all the rest. Yet, controlling for other measures will be virtually impossible to do. Or should we expect, on the other, that the totality of legislative ethics law is what matters, and not any single measure? If that is the case, the expectation is that the more law and/or the more stringent the law, the greater the effect will be. Each approach requires specification of provisions state by state, either to be used category by category or as a totality. Whatever the approach, the measure or measures will have had to have been in effect for some time before any consequence can be expected. How long would that be? It is difficult to even estimate. But the longer the time period, the more likely that the effects will have been subject to a combination of other factors coming into play.

Another issue pertains to enforcement of legislative ethics law and compliance with it. The possibility that there is slippage in the law cannot be dismissed. For example, it is estimated that in California there is some underreporting of meals lobbyists buy legislators, but not very much. Ways exist to evade restrictions on travel, as when the California association of prison guards meets in Hawaii and invites legislators. The legislators pay in their own way, but the association reciprocates by contributing to their campaign accounts. In New Jersey, legislators no longer take gifts of seats in skyboxes at Giants Stadium to watch professional football. Instead, they buy their own tickets in the stands, but still visit skyboxes at the invitation of lobbyists and their principals. Despite slippage, laws do receive overall compliance. Take financial disclosure, which is required practically everywhere. In New Jersey, for instance, 100% of legislators file. Yet, there is really no way to check on the accuracy of each item of information disclosed without enormous effort and expense. Enforcement depends on the aggressiveness of ethics commissions and committees, and also on adequate budgets.

Rosenson (2005b) suggests that legislators' dislike of the ethics laws they adopt leads to weak enforcement mechanisms. That may be the case when an internal body, such as a legislative ethics committee, has jurisdiction. It is less likely when an external body, independent of the legislature, is overseeing the conduct of members (Saint-Martin, 2005). Generally speaking, independent ethics commissions such as those in Connecticut,

Massachusetts, and Rhode Island have been more proactive than legislative committees in their policing of legislative conduct. According to Earl Mackey (2003, pp. 149–158), the former director of the commission Kentucky established in 1993 as part of a comprehensive ethics law, "the effectiveness of legislative ethics laws can be measured in large part by a single standard: the authority of an independent commission to initiate investigations on its own motion." In its first year, the Kentucky commission conducted four investigations in response to complaints and initiated 14 on its own. A few years later, the legislature took away the commission's power to investigate possible ethics violations on its own initiative, thus marginalizing what Mackey had characterized as the strongest law in the nation. The change in the Kentucky commission's authority and membership led to a change in approach. While the commission no longer has the authority to initiate investigations, its members can file complaints and thereby prompt investigations. But members do not do so, because the commission is no longer prosecutorially oriented, playing to the media and public. Instead, it now plays to the legislature, trying to keep members out of trouble. "It is much easier to keep Humpty Dumpty on the wall," explained the commission director, "than to try to put him together again."

If enforcement counts as much as is suggested here, then the existence of more or less law or stricter or looser law alone may not make a difference. In that event, it would be necessary to factor in enforcement, so that the effects would stem from not simply the law itself but also how the law is carried out.

In any case, tracing effects is a complicated business. Working backwards, one approach is to identify major changes that have taken place and then consider whether and how they might be attributable to ethics law. One such change, for instance, is the greater dispersion of power within the legislative institution. Legislative leaders have somewhat less power than formerly, while rank-and-file members have somewhat more. Can this be attributed to ethics restrictions? Not according to any plausible reasoning about how legislatures function. Clearly, there has to be a presumption that the change could result from the imposition of ethics restrictions. We would have to ask, how have legislatures changed in the past 10 years or so, and how have ethics laws contributed to this change? Another major change in legislatures has been the adoption of term limits in almost half the states, and its maintenance to date in 15. Did the states that adopted term limits have more ethics restrictions, or fewer? Did ethics law, or the lack thereof, lead to term limits? There is no reason to believe so. With the sole exception of Louisiana, the states that adopted term limits were those in which initiatives could be put on the ballot by petition and then voted on by the statewide electorate. Constitutional and statutory initiative provisions offered an opportunity, organized term-limits proponents provided the push, and the unpopularity of politicians and legislatures ensured that there were more than enough votes for provisions to remove politicians from office. The Florida legislature has been transformed in the past 15 years – but not so much by ethics law as by the increasing strength of Republicans in the senate and house, and by term limits.

It makes more sense to approach effects not by working backward, but by working forward, starting with ethics law, and trying to figure out the consequences. The problem in reasoning along these lines, of course, is that so many other factors may also be contributing to any observed effects. Take the change in the capital cultures of the states, which we shall return to later on. The social atmosphere is not what it used to be. The entertaining of legislators by lobbyists is much less a part of the scene today than 30 or 40 years ago. Ethics restrictions and disclosure requirements have had something to do with the change in capital cultures, but they are among other changes that have worked in the same direction.

One reason for less entertaining is that contemporary legislators are different from their predecessors. They drink less, are more serious, work harder, and want to get home to their families if possible. Moreover, legislators nowadays have more to do. Entertainment is both distracting and tiring. Living arrangements in capital cities have changed. No longer do legislators stay at the same hotel or hotels during the session, except in a few small states such as Wyoming. Legislative leaders behave differently than their predecessors did. Vern Riffe and Stan Aronoff, Ohio's speaker of the house and president of the senate during the 1980s, illustrate an older style. They held forth at the Galleria restaurant, and members flocked there to be near their leaders. Their successors – JoAnn Davidson and Larry Householder in the house, and Richard Finan and Douglas White in the senate – did not hold forth; therefore, hanging out was no longer the thing to do.

Another contaminating change is the attitude of legislative leaders nowadays as compared to the past. Contemporary leaders take greater responsibility for the conduct of their members. During the 1970s, after three California senators were indicted and convicted in the Shrimpgate sting, David Roberti, president pro tem, maintained that his role did not include that of being a nursemaid to members. Today, no legislative leader would offer such an excuse. Few, any longer, would – or could afford to – wink at behavior of members that had been challenged on ethics grounds. Indeed, there is some evidence that leaders come down hard on members who cross the line (Rosenthal, 1999).

Despite measurement difficulties, we still ought to think about how ethics law has been working, what it accomplishes, and what it does not. My purpose here is to specify the objectives of legislative ethics regulations, mainly (but not entirely) from the perspective of the legislature and legislators. What do legislators want to accomplish, and what do they accomplish? In thinking about this subject, I rely on my own observation and study of legislatures over the years, on a survey done by NCSL, and on interviews I conducted for this paper with 20 individuals from 13 states, including legislators, legislative staff, and members and staff of ethics commissions.

REDUCING OR PREVENTING CORRUPTION

One objective of legislative ethics law is the reduction or prevention of legislative corruption. Neither legislatures nor most legislators, however, explicitly or implicitly hold this as an objective. They do not acknowledge any need for further law to achieve this. In short, they do not admit to corruption or even tendencies in that direction. Whatever anticorruption law is necessary is already on the books. Nevertheless, the reduction or prevention of corrupt behavior by legislators ought to be considered as a possible effect of law. If such an end were achieved, the result would be noteworthy indeed. Greater regulation would be a powerful deterrent, keeping legislators on the straight and narrow. The outcome would be fewer indictments and fewer convictions for illegal acts.

A distinction must be made at the outset between scandal, on the one hand, and corruption, on the other. The two are not the same thing. A scandal need not be related to illegal behavior, but rather it may involve behavior that looks bad or has been made to look bad. To a large extent, scandal is a product not only of behavior, but also of its communication by the media and how it then appears to people. Even if the conduct is actually legal, the public may perceive it to be illegal. Whatever the public perception, legal and illegal conducts differ, however. According to Suzanne Garment (1991, pp. 61–69), anticorruption efforts may actually contribute to an increase in scandals. For her, scandals resemble rituals through which we try to expel the impurity of politics from political life. Corruption, by contrast, involves the misuse of public power for private gain.

The definition of corruption has changed over the years to include more types of official and private conduct. What was legal a generation ago is considered corrupt today, whether it is legal or not. And the definition keeps changing, as evidenced by Dennis Thompson's (1995, pp. 67, 103) distinction between personal and institutional corruption. In the case of the former, a legislator may be offered something of value and then provide a service in return. The connection is the legislator's motive. In the case of the latter, no motive need exist. Instead, the offer and service are connected through the practices and norms of the legislature itself. The notion of institutional corruption, which Thompson believes is the problem today, expands the definition of corruption broadly.

Because the definition of corruption has been expanded conceptually, and also for reporting purposes, the incidence of corruption ought to have increased. G. Calvin Mackenzie (2002, pp. 102–107) found that the number of indictments and convictions of federal officials prosecuted for public corruption increased from nine in 1970 to 480 in 1999. Yet, because of definitional change, this comparison over time is faulty. There are many more laws to be broken nowadays, prosecutors have become more zealous, and resources at their disposal have become more plentiful. Mackenzie also examined 40 years of newspaper articles about corruption and ethics in the federal government, and concluded that there was more smoke than fire: "Press stories about corruption or ethics violations ... are often about innuendoes, unverified and never-proven charges, pregovernment implications, political pot shots, and the kind of minor oversights that are neither very surprising nor very criminal in the lives of busy leaders" (Mackenzie, 2002, p. 101). Whether the indicator is indictments and convictions, on the one hand, or press coverage, on the other, we cannot be confident that the incidence of corruption at the federal level has either increased or decreased as a result of additional law. The amount of substantial corruption at the federal level, years ago as today, is extremely low in any case.

If one looks at anticorruption activity at the state legislative level, it would appear that there are fewer violations today than there were 20–25 years ago. During the 1980s FBI sting operations uncovered legislative corruption in California, Tennessee, Kentucky, South Carolina, Illinois, and Louisiana, while local law enforcement stings did the same in Arizona and New Mexico. Over 50 legislators were indicted or convicted as a consequence of all this investigative and prosecutorial activity. Other legislators were the subject of criminal or ethics charges in Michigan, Minnesota, Texas, Florida, Massachusetts, and Wisconsin. For most state legislatures the worst violations appear to be in the past. Wisconsin, however, may be an exception. There, from 1997 to the present, a number of breaches occurred (most related to campaign finance and the use of state facilities in campaigns), involving legislative leaders in both chambers and from both parties (Dresang, 2003).

Legislative ethics committees have had fewer serious cases in recent years. Take Maryland, for instance. In the late 1990s the joint legislative ethics committee dealt with several ethics violations, including that of a legislator who was forced to retire and another whom the senate expelled. Since then, the committee has written a letter reprimanding one legislator, but went no further. It also found no cause to launch an investigation of the senate president, who had allegedly brought pressure on state judges. His communication, in the committee's view, may not have been proper, but no ethics law was violated. Currently, on average, Maryland's legislative ethics committee conducts one investigation a year, usually prompted by a story that appears in the press. Otherwise, the major committee activity is rendering advisory opinions. The Ohio legislature also had to deal with a number of serious issues in the 1990s, but has less ethics business today. The only major recent case involved a legislator who accepted travel and lodging from a lobbyist, but should not have done so. On the recommendation of the ethics committee, the legislator was reprimanded and stripped of his committee chairmanship (which meant losing an $8,000 leadership stipend).

If the activity of legislative ethics committees and commissions is a reliable indicator, then corruption is not a major problem. A survey of state legislatures conducted by NCSL (2002, pp. 4–5), covering the period from June 2001 through June 2002, established that only 2% of legislators had complaints or charges brought against them. Only 3 out of 3,166 legislators in the states who responded to the survey were found guilty of any ethical violation during the period. In fact, according to the survey, only 0.013% of the legislators reported on had been found guilty of any infraction during the previous five years.

Is the low incidence of ethics violations, as reported by state ethics committees and commissions, a product of ethics law? It is extremely doubtful. At any rate, with so few cases it would not be possible to examine variation among states with stronger and weaker laws. Another survey, by two political scientists (Boylan & Long, 2003), relied on state house reporters for an evaluation of corruption, and asked them what percentage of legislators were corrupt. Such a ranking, however, is much too dependent on the perceptions of journalists within each state, who have varying but probably exaggerated definitions and perceptions of corruption by legislators.[2]

In 2002, the Better Government Association (BGA) ranked the 50 states on the relative strength of laws that protected against corruption and promoted integrity in the operation of state government. These laws pertained to freedom of information, whistle-blower protection, campaign finance, gifts, trips, honoraria, and conflicts of interest. They applied generally, but not specifically to state legislatures. At the top of the ranking were Wisconsin, Rhode Island, Kentucky, Hawaii, and California. At the bottom were Louisiana, Alabama, New Mexico, Vermont, and South Dakota. The Corporate Crime Reporter (2004) took the BGA ranking, compared it to the annual report documenting the number of federal prosecutions and convictions of individuals, as compiled by the Public Integrity Section of U.S. Department of Justice, and ranked the states on corruption. The period covered was 1993–2002, with the corruption rate standardized for state population. According to this measure, the most corrupt states were Mississippi, North Dakota, Louisiana, Alaska, and Illinois, in that order. The least corrupt were Nebraska, Oregon, New Hampshire, Iowa, and Colorado, in that order. The Corporate Crime Reporter concluded: "Our review of public corruption convictions in the states indicates that there is apparently little correlation between strong laws and integrity – if a public official wants to violate his or her trust, the laws don't stand in the way" (Corporate Crime Reporter, 2004, p. 7). Rosenson (2005a) has also ranked states, according to the strength of their legislative ethics laws. The strongest laws are in Kentucky, South Carolina, California (each of which had been shocked by FBI stings), and Texas (where legislators also were involved in scandals). The weakest laws are in Wyoming, Vermont, South Dakota, and Idaho (all of which are small states with citizen legislatures). There is, however, no adequate measure of corruption to which to relate Rosenson's index. The NCSL survey provides too few cases to even begin to attribute a lack of ethics violations to the strength of ethics law.

WHAT THE LEGISLATURE HAD IN MIND

Normally, legislative action is intended to address a particular problem. Ethics reform is different. It generally results from the exposure of corruption or scandal, but it seldom is designed to prevent such corruption or scandal from occurring. That law is already on the books. Seldom does the legislature, of its own accord, put ethics reform on its agenda, although some members may be inclined to do so. Instead, the agenda is almost wholly determined by outsiders – by prosecutorial indictments, or by ethics charges and discipline, and by what the media chooses to report on, with what intensity, and for how long.

Legislative objectives in enacting ethics law tend to be twofold: first, and most immediate, to placate the media, defend against partisan attack in the next election campaign, and be able to move on to other lawmaking business; second, and longer range, to restore public confidence in the legislature and legislative process.

In the short term, legislatures succeed in their pacification efforts. The legislature passes legislation and takes credit for ethics reform, and the media relent for a time. Maryland serves as an example. The legislature enacted a package of reforms after an investigative report in the *Baltimore Sun* led to the expulsion of a member of the senate. Perhaps as a result, the concerned media – that is, the *Baltimore Sun* and *Washington Post* – relaxed for a while, paying less attention to ethics issues than they had previously.[3] But by no means did the media drop ethics entirely. It continued to be on the prowl for evidence of ethical lapses by legislators. New ethics law, however, may make the job of the press somewhat tougher. The gray areas are reduced. A Kentucky legislator put it this way: "The media is less able to embarrass us." Where the law is spelled out, legislators go along, and journalists have to be more resourceful in their search for stories. For instance, a capitol reporter for the *Louisville Courier* inquired into receptions hosted by lobbyists at three national meetings, and even into a retreat held for senate Republicans in Kentucky. There was little entertaining to target in Frankfort.

No matter what the extent of the law, the media does continue to dig.[4] When a legislature enacts disclosure requirements or gift restrictions, the media sifts through the information for stories explaining how legislators vote and how they make their money. Such reporting, according to journalists, furnishes the public with what it needs to know. Legislators point out that only the media is interested in and benefits from the information filed; the public does not care.

New Jersey offers a case of a state that in the past had enacted significant legislative ethics reforms, ranking in the top fifth of the states on an index of legislative ethics law. Nonetheless, the legislature was fair game for an extensive investigative report in 2003 by Gannett's New Jersey newspapers, led by the *Asbury Park Press*. In what has been referred to as advocacy journalism, the Gannett series: criticized the ethics of almost half of the state's 120 legislators and impugned the ethics of the legislature as an institution; sent one of its own disclosure forms (adapted from that used in Washington State) to all members of the New Jersey Legislature; created its own six-point plan for ethics reform, and demanded that legislators support its plan as a condition for newspaper endorsement; succeeded in defeating the Republican senate co-president in his bid for reelection; contributed to the defeat of a few other incumbents; and helped the Democrats maintain control of the assembly and gain control of the senate.

In response to the series and the election, the New Jersey legislature in its lame duck session quickly brought up bills banning nepotism, double-dipping in health insurance coverage, and the acceptance of trips and gifts above a certain dollar amount. In the 2004 session, the Democratic majority in the Assembly put together a package of 25 bills covering a wide swath, while the Republican minority criticized the package for not going far enough. The result, of course, was more ethics law.

The legislature manages to move on, but the media does not always let up. After the first series on the New Jersey legislature had run, the *Asbury Park Press* did not relent. It continued with other stories critical of legislative operations. Other statewide newspapers joined in, pursuing somewhat different avenues to uncover unethical behavior in Trenton. Indeed, sometimes an ethics coup by one newspaper leads to another newspaper seeking to compete, at the legislature's expense. In 1996, for example, the *Baltimore Sun* published an investigative report on a member of the Maryland senate, who was subsequently expelled, and ran a story on a member of the house, who resigned before the ethics committee had completed its investigation. As a result of the *Sun*'s impact, editors at the *Washington Post*, which also covers Annapolis, instructed their staff to investigate the legislature as well. In an effort to catch up with its rival, the *Post* targeted Maryland's speaker of the house. The *Post*'s coverage, however, had little impact, and the legislature's ethics committee, after a preliminary inquiry, decided that there were insufficient grounds for investigation.

Whether the media pursues legislative ethics investigations or not depend on their own incentives, agenda, and circumstances. It does not depend on the amount of ethics law already on the books or the overall ethical conduct of members of the legislature. In New Jersey the media has kept digging, but at some point the focus is likely to shift. In Maryland the focus shifted, although ethics stories crop up now and again. There is little reason to believe, however, that the way in which the media cover the subject has anything to do with the nature or amount of legislative ethics law in the states. The coverage can be just as intense (and unfair) when there is more law as when there is less.

According to Saint-Martin (2005), legislators are likely to continue adopting more ethics laws. They are difficult to resist, especially since the expansion of ethics regulations has produced more public controversy over the ethics behavior of public officials. The regulation of political ethics is what Saint-Martin refers to as a case of policy lock-in, with self-reinforcing processes that make it extraordinarily difficult for legislators to change direction.

If the first objective in enacting law has had mixed results at best, the second produces even less of what the legislature would like to see happen. The legislature's longer-term objective, as the legislative histories of ethics reform demonstrate, is to restore public trust or confidence. This has been the theme at the national as well as the state level. Reformers and legislators both agree that such an objective is not only worthwhile, but is also possible to achieve. The National Conference of State Legislatures (2002) sums it up by saying that legislatures pass stricter laws to increase the public's confidence in government. Its survey of legislative ethics committees and state commissions finds the widespread belief that public trust can be enhanced by more and stricter law.

However laudable the intent, there is little reason to believe that the public's confidence changes as a result of changes in ethics law. The post-Watergate explosion of restrictions has not produced higher levels of trust in the federal government, at least not as measured by the American National Election Studies (ANES) of the Survey Research Center of the University of Michigan. NCSL's ethics survey also suggests that, although legislative ethics are improving, the public still does not believe that legislators can be trusted. But, from a political point of view, legislators do not need to restore public confidence – but they have to appear to be making the effort.

Indeed, ethics law may have the effect of producing more rather than less distrust. There is an assumption in the law itself that politicians generally cannot be trusted with the regulation of their own ethical conduct (Uhr, 2005). And the very tone of the discussion over ethics law conveys "a clear lack of trust and respect for public officials" (Dobel, 1993, p. 151). Even ethicist Michael Josephson (NCSL, 2002, p. 25) has speculated that ethics codes passed in reaction to scandals may hurt rather than help, because they are considered by the public as an admission of legislative guilt. Laws, thus, may feed distrust and make legislatures even more suspect than otherwise. Legislators are reluctant to adopt new laws, because they send a negative message about those who serve in the legislatures and encourages more, not less, public cynicism and a culture of mistrust.

No one has made a persuasive case that law helps as far as the public is concerned. But, some participants and some observers still believe that, on balance, law has proven useful. A Maryland staffer admits that public confidence has remained unchanged, but law, in his opinion, enables legislators to defend themselves better against public distrust. "They can reply," he suggests, "that Maryland has one of the toughest ethics laws in the country." That may help a little, but the most intriguing defense of law is offered by Thompson (1995, p. 177). He acknowledges the loss of confidence in Congress, but denies it means that the reforms of recent years have had no positive effect; without them, he asserts, the decline might have been worse.

Why, in any case, ought we to believe that law would have independent effects on public trust? Distrust stems from many factors, including the inability of people to appreciate the operating practices of representative democracy, the way ethics are used in partisan political combat, the treatment of political institutions and political people in issue advocacy campaigns, and – probably more than anything else – the media's coverage of legislatures and ethics. Mackenzie concludes that ethics regulations have not led to greater trust, but rather have produced more investigations. "The real state of public integrity," he writes, "is thus less important in determining levels of public confidence than the magnitude of news headlines that pierce public attention" (Mackenzie, 2002, p. 112).

HOW LAWS AFFECT LEGISLATORS AND THE PROCESS

Legislative intentions to placate the media in the short run and reassure the public in the longer run are largely unfulfilled. New law also has little to do with reducing or preventing legislative corruption. Still, it may have effects, albeit less intended ones, on legislative behavior and process.

It would be a remarkable achievement if legislative ethics reform had created more moral politicians. If, however, morality and pleasure are inversely related, then legislators today may be more moral than they used to be. Legislators derive less pleasure from their jobs than in the past. According to veteran members, the legislature is not nearly as much fun as it used to be. In part, this can be attributed to ethics laws that curtail socializing and gift taking. Moreover, because of intrusive financial disclosure requirements, legislators have less privacy. And they face a more cynical public, whose negative views of all legislators but their own representatives have not been assuaged by ethics reforms.

If cautious legislators are more moral ones, then the level of legislator morality has risen. Because of financial and gift disclosure requirements, in particular, legislators take greater care than ever before; most display an avoidance mentality. Not only individuals but also the caucus and the body as a whole exercise greater care. So do lobbyists. A close observer of the California legislature concluded that legislators there are more ethical today, mainly because they are under intense scrutiny. With a watchdog like the Fair Political Practices Commission, enforcement is taken very seriously and California legislators are kept on their toes.

Legislators nowadays tend to seek advice on ethical issues. Some of it is informal, obtained from colleagues or ethics committee staff. Some of it is of a more formal nature, such as an ethics committee advisory opinion. On the basis of a survey of the states, NCSL (2002) estimates that anywhere from 10% to 50% of legislators annually seek advice from commissions or committees on ethical matters. In Ohio, for example, the legislature's inspector general gives roughly 40–50 informal legal opinions a year, mainly on conflict-of-interest questions. This advice not only relates to the letter-of-the-law, but it may also deal with the appearance of impropriety. In Maryland, counseling is mandatory. Every year, members have to meet with the ethics advisor to review their private financial interests and receive counseling on a confidential basis. On a few occasions, counseling may have helped to keep legislators from getting into trouble.

Because legislators are much more cautious today than earlier, it may be that legislative ethics law has some deterrent effects. It does not deter legislators from corrupt behavior, but rather from questionable behavior. Such effects cannot be measured, but they probably lead to the conclusion reached by most informed observers that the integrity of legislators is greater now than it used to be. Law may also offer legislators cover. When challenged by the media or a political opponent, members can use informal or formal advisory opinions in defense of their actions.

Still, law has its perils, even for the wariest of legislators. The requirement for detailed financial data, for instance, can lead to inaccuracies and omissions. Josephson recognizes that a growing body of law poses a possible trap for legislators. Some legislators suspect that, in enacting more law, they are setting themselves up. In view of the political ambitions of prosecutors and the "gotcha" mentality of the media, they feel that they are sitting ducks, with each law on the books providing additional ammunition for the firing squad (Rosenthal, 1996, pp. 214–215).

Legislating ethics, in the opinion of some observers, may actually make legislators less ethically conscious than they might be otherwise. What is referred to as principle-based ethics may run against the legislative grain. Legislators live in a concrete world of elections, demands, bills, votes, etc.

For them, morality and ethics are abstractions that do not conveniently fit into the framework in which they operate. In term-limited legislatures, where members have shorter horizons, the focus is even more particularistic and immediate. Ethics law aggravates the problem. It induces compliance-based ethics, what Mackenzie (2002, p. 23) refers to as rule-driven ethics rather than character-focused ethics. In addition to compliance-based ethics, today's legislators concern themselves with appearance-based ethics. It is not so much how they conduct themselves, but how they appear to be conducting themselves. The appearance of impropriety is enough to do them in politically.

The danger is that compliance- and appearance-based ethics will drive principle-based ethics further out of the picture. As Michael Josephson (1992, pp. 34–41) puts it, "laws coerce from the outside, ethics controls from the inside." Legislative ethics training, for example, tends to emphasize regulations and restrictions rather than broader-based matters. Given the limited time and attention available to members, few legislatures have the luxury of exploring values, responsibilities, and gray areas; they have to familiarize members, and especially new ones, with the minefields that they have to traverse every day. The director of the Kentucky Legislative Ethics Commission acknowledged the problem of ethics law: "The down side is that legislators think that by complying with a code of conduct they have fulfilled their ethical responsibilities." In his view they have not, because their responsibilities extend further.

The possible effects on recruitment of individuals to serve in the legislature also deserves mention. A number of legislators, and veterans especially, believe that ethics laws and disclosure in particular discourage some qualified people from running. "With disclosure," a Kentucky legislative leader observed, "people have to be ready for their whole life to flash before them." A wealthy Kentucky businessman, for instance, who was being recruited to run, refused. "Not a prayer," was his response, fearing that his business would be done damage by the media's treatment of it. It is not simply ethics law per se, but a number of related factors that may discourage recruitment. These include the public's attitude, the intrusiveness of the press, the no-holds-barred nature of campaigns, and the time required to do the job nowadays. Ethics law may operate in the same direction. That is the conclusion of Rosenson's (2004) analysis, which shows that financial disclosure laws depressed the number of candidates who ran in state legislative primaries for open seats; limits on lawyer–legislators representing clients before certain state agencies led to a decline in the number of lawyer–legislators serving; and financial disclosure requirements led to a reduction in the number of business owners serving. These effects were not uniform during the period under study, but she concludes that these laws do have some deterrent effect on legislative service.

Undoubtedly, the ethics laws that have had the greatest impact on the legislative process are those that ban or limit gifts (including meals, entertainment, and travel) from lobbyists or their principals, or laws that simply require their disclosure. In most states these laws have reduced gift giving and gift taking, because legislators want to avoid the appearance of deriving private gain from their public office and, even more important, the inference that they are providing something in return. They do not want it reported in the press that they rank first, second, tenth, or anywhere on the list of members who have received lobbyist largesse. Thus, legislators are much more sensitive to their interaction with lobbyists.

Gift bans and gift disclosure requirements have been highly effective nearly everywhere. At the outset, they introduced a fear factor into legislative service. Members did not want to incur the risk. The fear factor has declined somewhat over the years, but most legislators have become used to practicing avoidance; so have lobbyists. Take California, for example. It is simply not worth the trouble for members to take anything. They do not want to endure the hassle of having to disclose and they do not want to incur any bad publicity. Nowadays, they may have an occasional meal with a lobbyist, but each pays his or her own way. As one lobbyist commented, "I just don't take reportable people to lunch." Meals shared by a legislator and lobbyist in California, as elsewhere, are fewer than formerly. In some states – Florida and Ohio are examples – lobbyists used to maintain an open tab at some popular watering hole. It allowed legislators, unaccompanied by their hosts, to charge food and drink to a lobbyist's account. That is no longer the case. Furthermore, members and lobbyists mingle and socialize much less than they once did.

The nature of legislator–lobbyist interaction has changed. Clubs and watering holes are on their way to extinction. The change in California is illustrative. Legislator–lobbyist clubs were the principal gathering place in Sacramento in the 1970s. They were succeeded by Frank Fats, a restaurant where Assembly Speaker Willie Brown held forth. By the 1990s, with Brown gone, another Chinese restaurant, which Senate President Pro Tem Bill Lockyer frequented, was the spot. Today there is no dominant hangout in Sacramento (Michael & Waters, 2002, p. 86).

Socializing still occurs, but it is less chummy than earlier. Receptions for large groups have replaced more intimate dinners; one-on-one dealings have been succeeded by events where legislators and lobbyists bounce from one person to another. In most states, receptions are excluded from personal gift disclosure requirements, so legislators go where there is safety in numbers. Consequently, intimacy between legislators and lobbyists has decreased and distance has increased. The other contemporary gathering, where some mingling occurs, is the fund-raiser. It is now the center of social life in California, as well as in most of the large states with professionalized, two-party legislatures.

Because of ethics laws, among other factors, lobbyists have to operate differently – more on the basis of the information they bring to bear, on their persuasive skills, and sometimes on grass-roots efforts, but less on the basis of purely social relationships. More than in the past, lobbyists today have to make a case if they want to influence legislative action. The current system of interactions among lobbyists and legislators looks much better, at least to close observers of the process. Appearance to the press and public, however, has not changed much at all.

Probably the major effect of all this has been a transformation of the cultures of most (but not all) state capitals. In places like North Dakota and Wyoming, with their citizen legislatures, ethics law has had little impact on capital cultures. That is because there was not much entertainment before the enactment of gift laws, and there is not much now. Wining and dining is minimal, lobbyists continue to buy legislators an occasional meal, and nobody seems to object. In the period before the 1980s, most capital cultures were different from those in North Dakota and Wyoming. They were relatively cozy, perhaps too much so. That is no longer the case. The current generation of legislators is less interested in socializing.

Legislators today rush home if they can, and they spend more time at office- and constituency-related work after a floor or committee session than at socializing. Even Louisiana is not at all like it used to be in the 1970s (with its motto, "Let the good times roll!"), in part because the legislature is far more active than it used to be. In some term-limited legislatures, moreover, new members are fearful of getting too close to lobbyists lest they be contaminated. By the time they figure out that lobbyists are part of the representational system, they would have left office.

New generations of legislators with different tastes, dispersed living, increased work, and term limits are among the factors leading to cultural shifts. But gift restrictions and gift disclosure requirements also have contributed to the transformation. Old timers regret the changes; they prefer the good old days when there were benefits to be had. But fewer old timers are around any longer. Now in states with term limits, like California, Michigan, and Ohio, no one remembers the old days or old ways.

Furthermore, in some southern states there is a relief, among legislators and lobbyists alike, that the good-old-boy culture is out, or on its way out. Just about everywhere, few members regret the passing of the summer camp type of relationships. And when new members hear about the way things used to be, they do not believe that things actually were the way that is described.

The downside of the new culture is that members socialize with one another less. Lobbyists formerly served to bring members – from the two houses and the two parties – together. Without such hosts, and due to other factors as well, legislators are less inclined to get together and talk things over. "Something has been lost," comments a legislative ethics regulator in Ohio. In Columbus, Annapolis, Trenton, and other capitals, camaraderie is diminished, but it still exists. That is because relationships among legislators and between legislators and lobbyists need not depend on socializing. Instead, they can grow out of common concerns and working the process together.

The effect of law in this regard has made the process fairer, and probably more ethical. What is sometimes referred to as benefit passing has declined. Members no longer live, as they once did, on the lobbyist's dime. Office is no longer used for petty types of personal gain; legislators pay their own way. On their part, most lobbyists are relieved; they no longer are shaken down the way they used to be, although they are still expected to buy tickets for fund-raisers and contribute to political campaigns. The old culture disproportionately favored wealthy interests; the new culture levels the playing field, at least somewhat. Lobbyists no longer have privileged access by virtue of entertaining. Now, campaign support is far more important in most places. Also more important than before is the quality of information that lobbyists provide (that is, the substantive and political case they make), and who they represent. A veteran California lobbyist summed up the change that he attributed partly to the adoption of gift laws by saying that the process is fairer today. Arguments are based more on the merits and relationship lobbying is less important than it used to be. It changes the way of doing business, but it does not change the result. But this way of doing business – reaching settlements by assembling majorities at various stages – is what the legislative process is about, no matter what the particular result.

On balance, laws restricting gifts to legislators have resulted in more gains than losses. While the process is not entirely different than it used to be, it is marginally better as a result. In terms of Thompson's (1995, pp. 18–25) formulation, standards of independence and fairness have been advanced. This is because chances of petty personal gain are diminished, and chances of decisions based on the merits are enhanced. The integrity of the process is greater as a result.

CHANGING STANDARDS

The past 35 years have witnessed an increase of ethics law and regulation to which legislatures and legislators have had to adapt. All of this seems to have had little, if any, effect on reducing legislative corruption, building public trust, or satisfying the media. Nor has it produced more moral legislators. But law and regulation have succeeded in transforming legislative cultures in ways that promote integrity in the process. Along with everything else, new standards have been defined, and it is to these standards that legislatures and their members are now being held accountable.

Today's standards are stricter than they used to be. Conduct that was acceptable, if not the norm, earlier would now lead to expulsion. These new standards both help shape the public's expectations and provide guidelines for legislators to follow. As Michael Malbin (1994, p. 1155) points out with regard to Congress, the new standards themselves are catalysts for bringing attention to situations that once might have been accepted without question. Thus, legislators are more at risk now than formerly, but both members and their institutions seem to be adjusting.

What is more disturbing is the ethical standard that, in practice, has become the dominant one for legislatures. That is, appearance. At one time what mattered was behavior; legislators were prohibited from engaging in bribery, extortion, and other forms of improper influence. Their intentions were the issues then. In contrast, today what matters is the appearance of impropriety. From a philosophical point of view, "appearance ethics is problematic because it detracts from the primary ethical referent, motive" (Morgan & Reynolds, 1997, p. 36).

Appearance has being gaining in ethical power since 1965, first at the federal level and then in the states. And it is justified in the strongest terms by Thompson (1995, pp. 124–130), who ranks among the leading scholars of political ethics. The question, however, is to whom does the appearance of impropriety (or the potential for the appearance of impropriety) appear? In theory, the arbiter of appearance is a fair-minded or reasonable person. Practically speaking, only one arbiter exists – the media. Appearance is what the media says it is, since the media's words and pictures are all the public has to go by. As a standard, appearance leaves much room for interpretation. Anything in the gray areas of politics can easily be made to look bad, and much that is not bad at all is made to look bad. The media mainly reports what is bad (or what can appear to be bad), but rarely what is good. So, the press is the big winner from the ethics explosion, which has expanded what is deemed to be bad. And, with the acceptance of appearance as a standard, the press has plenty of grist for its mill.

If appearance remains the standard, neither the media nor the public is likely to be satisfied as a result of ethics law. The public buys the media line because it confirms what is already conventional wisdom – neither political people, institutions, nor processes are trustworthy. The legislature has an almost impossible battle to persuade anyone of the contrary, even as it enacts more ethics law that raises the bar even higher.

NOTES

1. After Watergate, Congress also responded, passing the Ethics in Government Act of 1978 and prompting additional restrictions in the states. The result, according to one analysis, was the largest government ethics reform effort in history (Morgan & Reynolds, 1997, pp. 70–72).
2. Rosenson (2005a) found that in states with strong ethics laws there is a greater perception by state house reporters of political corruption.
3. The electronic media usually follow the lead of the print media in their coverage of state legislatures.
4. This is because, if nothing else, the very nature of the news enterprise impels them to continue. Scandals sell copy, and the more scandalous the better. In addition, editors and journalists are more distrustful of politicians today. So the media continues to dig, often resorting to inference rather than evidence to make their case.

REFERENCES

Allen, D. (2002). Corruption, scandal, and the political economy of adopting lobbying policies. *Public Integrity*, *4*, 13–42.
Boylan, R. T., & Long, C. (2003). Measuring public corruption in the American states: A survey of state house reporters. *State Politics and Policy Quarterly*, *3*, 420–438.
Corporate Crime Reporter. (2004). *Public corruption in the United States*. Washington, DC: Author.
Dobel, J. P. (1993). The realpolitik of ethics codes: An implementation approach to public ethics. In: G. H. Frederickson (Ed.), *Ethics and public administration* (pp. 158–176). New York: M. E. Sharpe.
Dresang, D. L. (2003). Mr. Clean gets dirty. *Public Integrity*, *5*, 319–330.
Garment, S. (1991). *Scandal: The crisis of mistrust in American politics*. New York: Times Books.

Ginsberg, B., & Shefter, M. (1990). *Politics by other means: The declining importance of elections in America.* New York: Basic Books.
Josephson, M. (1992). The best of times, the worst of times. *SPECTRUM: The Journal of State Government, 65*(4), 34–41.
Mackenzie, G. C. (2002). *Scandal proof: Do ethics laws make government ethical?* Washington, DC: Brookings Institution.
Mackey, E. S. (2003). Dismantling the Kentucky legislative ethics law. *Public Integrity, 5*, 149–158.
Malbin, M. (1994). Legislative ethics. In: J. Silbey (Ed.), *Encyclopedia of the American legislative system* (pp. 1155–1170). New York: Charles Scribner's Sons.
Michael, J., & Waters, D. (2002). *The third house: Lobbyists, money, and power in Sacramento.* Berkeley, CA: Berkeley Public Policy Press.
Morgan, P. W., & Reynolds, G. H. (1997). *The appearance of impropriety.* New York: The Free Press.
National Conference of State Legislatures (NCSL). (2002). *The state of state legislative ethics.*
Rosenson, B. A. (2004). The effects of ethics laws on legislative recruitment. Working paper.
Rosenson, B. A. (2005a). *The shadowlands of conduct: Ethics and state politics.* Washington, DC: Georgetown University Press.
Rosenson, B. A. (2005b). The costs and benefits of ethics laws. This volume.
Rosenthal, A. (1996). *Drawing the line: Legislative ethics in the states.* Lincoln: University of Nebraska Press.
Rosenthal, A. (1999). *The ethics process in state legislatures: Disciplining members in a public forum.* Denver, CO: National Conference of State Legislatures.
Saint-Martin, D. (2005). Path dependence and self-reinforcing processes in the regulation of ethics in politics: Toward a framework for comparative analysis. This volume.
Thompson, D. (1995). *Ethics in congress.* Washington, DC: Brookings Institution.
Uhr, J. (2005). Professional ethics for politicians? This volume.
Williams, R. (2005). The ethics eruption: Sources and catalysts. This volume.

MANAGERIAL LEADERSHIP AND THE ETHICAL IMPORTANCE OF LEGACY

J. Patrick Dobel

ABSTRACT

A good theory of leadership unites personal integrity, moral commitments, legal authority, and accountability and effectiveness. This chapter presents leaving a legacy as an approach to organize managers' and leaders' ethical reflection. It unites personal meaning with organizational mission and connects a person's significance with organizational results. It embeds leaders in an historical setting, linking their inheritance and their obligations to the future. Thinking of a legacy guides leaders to a less controlling style, supporting people and institutions capable of adaptation and growth. While legacy does not capture all aspects of managerial leadership, it maps broad and rich understanding of leadership and responsibility linked to trusteeship.

> And on the pedestal these words appear:
> "My name is Ozymandias, king of kings:
> Look on my works, ye Mighty, and despair!"
> Nothing beside remains round the decay
> of that colossal work, boundless and bare

The lone and level sands stretch far away.
Percy Bysshe Shelly, *Ozymandias*

A long moral tradition conceives of public office as a trusteeship where public officials exercise power and responsibility as a trust to work for the good of the public. The United Nations enshrines this view in its *International Code for Public Officials* that states that public office is a position of trust (United Nations, 1996). A trust means officials act as stewards of law and institutions. At a deeper level, officials have obligations to attend to the long-term welfare versus the short-term and attend to the equity and dignity of persons. Trusteeship or stewardship presumes a range of discretion for public officials who serve as leaders and managers (Terry, 2003; Greenleaf, 1991; Cooper, 1991, 1998; Bloch, 1996; Armstrong, 1997). The challenge of the trust conception and its wide range of discretion is always to articulate the nature of judgments permitted and the mechanisms of accountability to counteract pressures toward corruption (Adams & Balfour, 2004; Huber & Shipan, 2002; Dobel, 1976, 1999). Theories of public trusteeship range from insistence upon strict adherence to law and procedure to emphasis on the importance of principles to inform judgments to the contention that only virtue and character address the unpredictability of life and sustain persons through the tribulations and temptations of public life (Burke, 1986; Denhardt, 1988; Cooper & Wright, 1992).[1] Alternative traditions epitomized by Rousseau with modern variations in reinventing government movement and the post-modern critiques emphasize that no individuals should be trusted with the power and discretion to prescribe reality, and that public officials per se pose threats to human freedom. Human dignity and efficiency require that political power reside in democratic participation or discourse, which guide public officials (Osborne, 1993; Osborne & Plastrik, 1998; Farmer, 1995).[2]

If we accept the inevitable and desirable role of discretionary judgment by public officials – elected, appointed, and career – a good theory of public trust should unite personal integrity, moral commitments, legal authority, and accountability, and effectiveness (Burke, 1986; Rohr, 2002; Cooper, 1998; Huber & Shipan, 2002; Dobel, 1999). Ideally, a model of public trust should incorporate these issues but in a united fashion, since each captures a critical aspect of public trust but on its own will not cover the full moral and political complexity of public discretion. Public trust integrates legal and process commitments, the long-term and externality dimensions, and the regime values and character that support deliberation and action. Public trust also should build in accountability and limits upon power. Finally, an approach to public trust should avoid what John Rawls (1971) calls the *strain of commitment*, and be livable and usable by individuals to act with integrity and effectiveness. Because discretion requires judgment, it entails an element of leadership where individuals assess, decide, and act in ways that are not predetermined, but require initiative and responsibility. The leadership element – changing the world and people through self-initiated action and interaction – remains inextricable with discretion. Persons should be able to use this model to judge and live in a way that sustains their emotional and moral commitments, technical expertise, accountability, and effectiveness.

This chapter presents leaving a legacy as an approach to organize managers' and leaders' reflection. The concept itself often arises in a valedictorian setting where people comment upon what a person accomplished and the meaning of his or her life. Funerals, retiring, or moving to another job evoke such reflection. This chapter argues that an individual's legacy actually unfolds daily through cumulative judgments and actions. This method reveals how people make a difference in the world and emphasizes personal responsibility and significance.

Legacy's relation to meaning indicates its advantages to thinking through the frames and obligations of leadership. First, it unites personal search for meaning with an organizational focus on mission. Second, it connects the individual's preoccupation with self-worth and significance with organizational results (Denhardt, 1989, 2000). Third, it embeds leaders in an historical setting linking their inheritance from the past and their obligations to the future. Finally, thinking of a legacy can guide individuals to a less controlling leadership style, supporting people and institutions capable of adaptation and growth. While legacy does not capture all aspects of managerial leadership, it maps a broad and rich understanding of leadership and individuality linked to trusteeship. Legacy unites many of the best aspects of the most common normative explanations of trusteeship. Thinking this way highlights the moral reality that everyone leaves a legacy. The chapter explores the concept of legacy, metaphors that elucidate the range of human legacy, the dimensions of time in action, and the possible problems with using legacy as a way to organize deliberation.

THE CONCEPT OF LEGACY

When people depart, the consequences of their actions upon people and the physical and social world endure as their legacy. Why care about a legacy? It seems a concept more at home with death or retirement than leading for the future. It can seem egotistical. As one head of a state social service agency remarked, "If I thought of this as *my* legacy, I'd start putting myself before the public." Yet legacy matters, because the idea joins responsibility and consequences with a person's search for meaning. Hard but fundamental questions such as: "Why am I here?" or "What difference does it make that I have lived?" remind people that finding meaning in life remains of elemental importance for human moral and social life (Baumeister, 1991; Wolf, 1990). Human mortality adds urgency to these questions. People usually only ask the questions as they approach the end: "Has my life had any meaning?" "Is the world a better place because I have lived?" While most prefer to avoid these questions or segregate them from work, most people entering public life seek a sense of meaning in public work (Goodsell, 1985; Bloch, 1996). More than a few prominent leaders have spent their later years writing memoirs or trying to craft an understanding of their legacy after the fact.

People are not gods who never die and who infuse meaning in reality by acts of will and power. Persons cannot control or determine transcendent purpose for the world. Many persons relate to God or a transcendent purpose to find meaning and structure that guide decisions (Warren, 2002; Daloz, Keen, Keen, & Parks, 1996, pp. 140–151). These relations reflect human mortality and the yearning for transcendent or immanent purpose to secure meaning. Living as mortals with limited time on earth infuses urgency to the question of meaning. Committing to others or organizations seldom happens if life feels futile, purposeless, and devoid of meaning beyond personal satisfaction (Denhardt, 1989, 2000; Csikszentmihalyi, 2003). This type of commitment can be a temptation to transcend death by contributing to something immortal or beyond oneself.

To have meaning in life provides psychological and moral resources to order commitments and make decisions about what fits or does not fit within one's life and integrity (Dobel, 1990, 1999; Carter, 1996; Petrick & Quinn, 1997). The thought of leaving a legacy connects to meaning by insisting that the consequences of what people do matters and should be taken seriously. When individuals cease to exist physically, their actions still affect people, institutions, and the environment – the world differs for good or bad because of a human's presence. Much of the meaning that can be culled from life arises from the outcomes of living that provide tangible proof that a person made a mark. Recognizing that all individuals leave a legacy buttresses responsibility by insisting that each human contributes.

The word legacy derives from the word *legate* – one to whom is delegated responsibility. Both words derive from the Latin root for laws (*leges*) and attending to the public dimensions of life. The concept fits naturally with the tradition of public leadership as a trust where leaders hold office as a temporary legate, steward, or trustee for the good of individuals. The ideal of legacy bridges with the trustee model when individuals who take leadership positions make promises. Their moral legitimacy depends upon their promise to obey the law, frame their judgments by statutory intent and principle, be accountable to authority, consult with the public, and be competent and efficient in performance. The promise has an implicit requirement that the leaders attend to the institution and hand them on in better shape. The vulnerability of citizens and colleagues who depend upon organizations for service heightens leaders' obligations. Each public leader inherits an office with legal obligations and moral webs of reliance supporting those obligations. They hold responsibility as trustees of the legitimacy and public point of view of institutions that go beyond the welter of advocacy surrounding a public organization (Rohr, 2002; Cooper, 1991; Huber & Shipan, 2002).

When an individual realizes that he or she leaves a legacy, it also means that the person realizes that he or she inherits a world and has responsibilities toward the inheritance and the legacy. Any person who claims credit for the good of a life or institution must also take responsibility for the harm or bad of that institution and life. Too often trustees and legatees focus only upon the good they want to be remembered or pursued, but the historical responsibility of a legacy orientation entails acknowledgment and responsibility for the good and the bad.

The idea of a legacy scales to a context. A legacy orientation helps organize public reflection because leaders experience life as a series of entrances and exits, whether they enter a meeting, a new agency, or leave a project group or organization. Attending to legacy as a managerial leader helps individuals to bridge these comings and goings intellectually and morally, for an individual can leave a legacy with each human interaction. These can be as casual as a piece of advice, a comment which impacts a person's worth or performance, a slight or recognition, or an act as powerful as firing. Each interaction can change another human being. The scale extends to groups, meetings, projects, teams, or organizations. An individual's impact could ripple out through other groups, families, or interactions within and outside organizations. Actions can affect a particular person whom an individual serves one-on-one, or affect hundreds when a policy changes because of an individual's contributions. A person can always ask of himself or herself, "What do I wish to leave, or what have I left behind?" in each interaction, precedent, meeting, rule or policy. The cumulative impact or aggregated impact of actions adds an almost strategic scale to legacy. Often the quality of individuals one leads changes not with one inadvertent or swift interaction, but due to the accrual of modeling, educating, and feedback. This can be positive or negative for the person.

The temporal and spatial scales connect the immediate with the long term. Once individuals realize that actions accumulate in their impact, then the dichotomy of sweating for small things and keeping an eye on the big things fades. Legacy scales in time with consequences moving out into hours, days, weeks, and years. Small things and big things meld over time in the individual's responsibility, contributions, and realities of life. A physical or social environment changes through aggregated accumulation of waste or neglect or the opposite. A building does not run down all at once and an office does not deteriorate without slow, persistent neglect. Cultural norms of interaction or styles of disagreement change over time, seldom suddenly. Legacy is amplified when a group or organization reaches a tipping point and individual actions help transform norms or patterns (Kelling, 1999; Gladwell, 2000).

Legacy endures after individuals depart and no longer control a situation. The paradox is that life consists of an infinite number of arrivals and departures, and legacies accumulate continually through every moment and interaction. Those touched by an individual's actions or their consequences carry on in their lives. This carrying on may be as before or may be enabled by a person's actions, or it may differ in some ways because of a leader's actions. Becoming aware of one's legacy focuses upon the questions: "Who carries on and how do they carry on because of my actions? What is different about the world or the people in it because I acted?" It raises to self-consciousness a person's initiation of differences in the world that resonate or endure.

The concept of leaving a legacy exists in the shadow of the counterfactual of what would have happened if "I" had not been there. The job may still get done, the laws may still get passed, but the nuance and style of the doing of the job, the exact wording or implementation of the law, the cumulative impact of outcomes on people, and interactions on those with whom one works can be immense – ask anyone who has had a good or bad boss while working in the same position. This focus upon legacy underlines moral responsibility and emphasizes the consequences of being there.

At an abstract level legacy extends in several dimensions. The first covers the range of our contribution. This includes the magnitude of contributions to actions, but also the temporal proximity to the consequences. Many of the most interesting or compelling consequences occur down the line from the actual contribution, such as a report read later that influences people, or individuals helped by social service who later make good or bad lives for themselves. It is possible, but not predictable, that the farther away from an individual's contribution to results, the less responsible a person becomes. It could also be that what an individual did thoughtlessly might seem trivial at the moment but may grow in importance for a person or system over time, and an individual's responsibility increases. Second, the issue of the temporal durability and traceability of consequences follow from the contribution. Some consequences can evanesce. Some consequences are immediately apparent and endure; others may seem to have no impact but turn out to have significance later. Actions can resemble ripples or seeds, or engender receptivity in people for future change. They can also erect concrete monuments or foundations. When Abraham Lincoln crafted the Gettysburg Address to commemorate those who had died at the Battle of Gettysburg, he gave the words considerable thought, but at first the speech made barely a ripple. Over time the address grew to become one of the foundational documents of the American political creed (Wills, 1992). Third, the meaning of actions and consequences is mutable. Actions and consequences possess no one stable meaning. Individuals may have one intention and they may battle to ensure that their interpretation of their action's meanings dominate memory and deliberation; other people, however, may have very different interpretations of the meaning of actions (Lynn, 1987; Levi, 1989, 2001; Wolf, 2004). Even if everyone agrees on the meaning of an act at one time, this meaning can still mutate over time as individuals or society change. Finally, a legacy is often linked to a person who seeks or receives credit or blame for the results; this can affect individuals both when they are alive and also their reputation after death. This is especially important if persons are motivated by the desire for fame and renown as a solution to meaning and mortality (Braudy, 1986). Individuals may desire recognition for their legacy, but often their actual contribution may be unknown to those affected. Even if recognized and memorialized, over time the memory and meaning may fade. As with monuments, the original intent may be forgotten, ignored, or reappropriated (Goodsell, 1988). More than a few monuments named for forgotten dignitaries exist in shaded parks – a home for pigeons or a meeting place for young lovers or drug dealers.

Legacies can extend to people, the world, and domains of the physical, ecological, social, or psychological. Often all realms interact, such as when a leader creates a physical space that affects the institutional perceptions of authority and equality in a way that changes people's self-perceptions (Goodsell, 1988). This in turn could affect the quality of service they deliver to the citizens who depend upon them.

Legacy and trusteeship situates individuals in these dimensions:

(1) the physical, social, and psychological impact of what is immediately done and the perceivable consequences that flow from actions;
(2) durability of impacts and whether they endure, permute, or dissipate, as well as how far out they might impact;
(3) temporal and physical proximity to actions and whether consequences occur immediately or reverberate down the road, impacting people and organizations;
(4) indirection as a proximate and long-term factor. Influenced individuals or environments may change or assimilate influences in indirect or long-term ways; people affected may be enabled to act later, having forgotten the impact. Many outcomes will be unknown, delayed, or unacknowledged;
(5) responsibility identifies persons with contributions and dignity. It emerges in the search for reputations and claims of credit or blame;
(6) cumulative impacts mount over time, sometimes imperceptibly. Rather than isolate one critical action for an assessment, many of the most important results of leadership and management occur over time and gradually transform an institution; and
(7) meanings of a legacy will be contested. While one's intentions may motivate the contribution, the interpretation of the meaning of actions will be contested by others, and meanings will vary and change.

These dimensions frame reflection and responsibility that flow from leaving a legacy. A legacy orientation acknowledges responsibility, dignity, and contribution. It deliberates in a temporal continuum where individuals attend to what they inherit in their position, what occurs while they live in office, and the consequences of actions after they move on. These contributions and impacts exist in dimensions of temporal and physical proximity. Individual contributions possess short-term direct as well as long-term or indirect effects. Many consequences flow from enabled actions others take because they were helped through service or mentoring. Results evolve over time, usually not as one-time sudden impacts. In theory, one could map the magnitude and proximity of contributions, the areas in which it occurs, the durability over time, and the contested meanings, to refine how a person might think about legacy.

MODES OF LEGACY

Everyone leaves a legacy, whether they want to or not. I believe legacies can helpfully be understood as metaphors that depict the ways people influence the world. The ones I discuss were developed in an iterative process using case studies and a series of interviews with senior public and nonprofit officials.[3] Interestingly, many of the metaphors have long historical antecedents in past stories of leaders. Obviously other metaphors could be used, and these metaphors, while distinct, can overlap and reinforce understanding, such as when a monument serves as a foundation or a seed grows inside a womb. Senior public officials responded powerfully to these metaphors, and used them often in their speech. The metaphors integrate the abstract aspects of legacy and create heightened awareness of how individuals make a difference.

Monuments

All political cultures create monuments. Pyramids, aqueducts, tombstones, or walls come to mind as enduring reminders of the successes and failures of governments. A monument focuses upon the physical presence left after a person leaves, and physical reminders leap to mind when people think of legacies. Yet few managers spoke of monuments per se, but often mentioned building monuments to ideals or good people. Monuments stand out by their autonomous existence, durability, and obviousness. They are usually physical, like buildings, memorials, public spaces, art, writing, or law. Monuments can serve functional purposes or can reflect attempts to memorialize something or someone for history. Many government buildings try to do both by memorializing a person or event but also by creating a public space that permits debates over conceptions of governance and legitimacy (Goodsell, 1988; Wolf, 2004). A monument can reflect a collective attempt by a society to enshrine memories or recover aspects of identity. Leaders who create monuments can bring society to deliberate over social understandings. The existence of monuments can become a gathering point for social and political reflection about its meaning and the meaning of the events memorialized or the people or ideals remembered. Modern archeologists believe that building the pyramids, for instance, served not as megalomania for pharaohs but as a national enterprise uniting the country and reaffirming its identity and gods. The Jefferson Monument, engraved with his magnificent defense of human freedom, reminds people of unfulfilled dreams as well as the fallibility of humans when a great leader and slaveholder preaches liberty. Creating a monument often reflects social deliberation about what a society values and wants to remember. The creation of a memorial to the women veterans who served in Vietnam began with one woman who served in Vietnam and believed that the role of women had been ignored in the history of the country and war. She and her allies worked for 10 years of discussion and political conflict. The process forced the public, government, and military to rethink their own self-definition and standards of heroism (as noted in the dedication's program, *Celebration of Patriotism and Courage: Dedication of the Vietnam Women's Memorial*, November 10–12, 1993).

Foundations

Buildings cannot survive without strong foundations. Buildings can also be torn down and rebuilt on the same foundations. Learning in areas like language or math depends upon individuals acquiring a foundation set of skills upon which more advanced skills can be built. Individual character becomes the foundation of good judgment and supports sustained action in the face of obstacles (Norton, 1976; Sherman, 1989). With skill or character as foundations, people can act with independent deliberation. The most interesting paradox about foundations as a metaphor for legacy is that people can build upon them things that have not been anticipated or controlled by those laying the foundations. Foundations of character and knowledge become a source of freedom and empowerment, but can also be a socialized means of control and limitation. Leaders who mentor people lay future possibilities for growth, but the knowledge they impart can be used in many different ways. Creating healthy environments or public safety provides foundations that enable communities and individuals to flourish and act in ways uncontrolled by fear, which can make legacy unpredictable, potentially liberating, or imprisoning (Kelling, 1999). The foundation of an organization permits those who follow to work from existing capacity to construct new policy and actions.

Wombs and Incubators

Special environments permit new life to gestate, grow, and be born into the world. Individuals, organizations, groups, and projects can all engender interactions among individuals, a place and time to gestate new possibilities and give birth to fresh lives, ideas, creations, or decisions in people and institutions. From earliest civilizations people have identified the womb (both in women and the earth) as a source of creativity and mystery. More than one manager described him or herself as a midwife as they thought about their impacts on others. The famous Lockheed skunk works for aircraft development, or development teams like the computer team described in Kidder's (1997) *The Soul of a New Machine* generate organic cooperation that gives birth to relations that form not only ideas and creations but often individuals who go out as different persons. Institutions like the Social Security Administration, Wells Fargo Bank, Proctor and Gamble, or the US Marine Corps are noted as organizations that give birth to strong leaders who later influence other organizations. Strong leadership provides the social space and institutional protection and resources where people, ideas, and practices can be born and grow to influence others. Incubating leadership and management aims to succor the growth of autonomous individuals, ideas, and policy.

Coral Reefs

Quotidian life accumulates minute by minute, day by day, imperceptible in its impact on people and places, much like a coral reef. In a healthy reef, after an individual dies or moves on, the place they occupied becomes a possible home for others or a new anchorage where others can add to the life of the reef. The reef life generates interdependence and nurtures a system where other individuals and organizations thrive in relation to the reef. In high performing and successful organizations built to last, managers and leaders see themselves as contributing to a project of lasting duration (Collins & Porras, 1977; Collins, 2001). Allies, groups, schools, and clients cluster around, not just as sycophants but as part of a thriving organizational ecosystem (Perrow, 1993). The reef-building metaphor reminds us that even if one's accomplishments seem insignificant, they are not. The reef grows and contributes because of individuals' help, and the shell of what one accomplished, whether building an office, a record, or a space, becomes a potential building block for another. This person can enter the space (which might seem empty) and use it as a place from which to work and continue the mission. It means that leave taking leaves an addition for carrying on or renewal.

Webs

Management and leadership occur through relations (Lynn, 1987; Bloch, 1996; Bryson, 1992). Actions create or impact networks of relationships. In the primordial story of the *Odyssey*, Queen Penelope and the goddess Athena both refer to how they weave plans and patterns to lead (Homer, 1997, pp. 2.90–142, 19.149–180, 23). Webs can be woven in complex ways that create elaborate hierarchies, convoluted spheres, or webs of webs with horizontal threads. Webs can unite people in new and unique ways and from these relations different lives and consequences flow. Like the goddess Ariadne, they can also trap people in webs not of their own choosing. These relationships generate new patterns of action and communication. The web reveals or creates interdependencies and connections that might have been missed or never existed. Webs can create alternative arrangements, where true leaders work with each other rather than work under imposed hierarchy (Wren, 1994). Especially in modern public life, public leaders build relations across sectors and organizations. In a classic metaphor identification test, one range of executives always identify themselves as spiders, not because they capture people in webs to devour them, but because they bring together and create community, communication, and possibility where none existed. These webs make possible not only new ideas, but coordination and accountability as well as feedback. If the webs grow strong, they can become sources of self-initiation and non-hierarchical coordination (Collins, 2001; Bryson, 1992). The web metaphor means every system presents opportunities for bringing together and coordination where relations have not existed – or becomes frayed or strangling.

Sowing Seeds/Cultivating Soil

Max Weber called politics "the slow boring of hard boards." His metaphor emphasized the importance of tenacity and patience for durable accomplishment. Ancient Thebes, on the other hand, believed its people grew from the dragon's teeth planted by the hero Perseus. Ancient agricultural civilizations treat the rite and metaphor of planting and harvest as central and sacred. Planting and cultivation provide another way to think of patient influence that recognizes durable and healthy change grows often from small insights or possibilities. Successful change needs to grow roots in a community, organization, or person. This understanding sees change as occurring over time and identifies responsibility as its initiator. The cultivation aspect recognizes the need to prepare others and achieve consent. Thoughtful interactions with a long-term view involve conversation and interactions that plant seeds of ideas, policy, or different ways of being. Seldom does such planting take immediately: often seeds need to be replanted or cultivated. Every interaction with people and organizations plants seeds of possible change and action. William F. Schulz of Amnesty International likes to speak of seeding as the major activity of human rights activists (Schulz, 2003). Good leaders spend time planting seeds of knowledge and possibility, and nurture them for the right moment when the window of opportunity opens for action. One senior social services manager described her day as "spreading seeds of possibility among stakeholders." She discussed the need to "fertilize and make people and places receptive to ideas." Sometimes with "patience you can harvest ideas, and sometimes others harvest the results, it doesn't really matter."

Sometimes seeds lodge in dry ground; cast to the wind they settle where they might and either shrivel or bring forth fruit quickly. The fruits can be harvested by others or oneself. An Ethiopian health ministry official pointed out that a leader might spend time thinking about the right type of seed to plant in a particular environment. The challenge of constantly fertilizing soil can often exact too high a cost to sustain. He mentioned, "I must know the ground first to pick the right seed for the earth, then it will grow within the people." Most top-initiated change fails because the initiatives never take at the lower levels of the organization and wither as soon as the leaders leave (Collins & Porras, 1997; Kotter, 1996). Engendering receptivity in people, language, and culture and adapting initiatives to them are vital forms of leadership.

Ripples

Actions reverberate like the ripples of stones dropped in a pond. The ripples move out in concentric circles and touch, disturb, or change the direction of things around them. Sometimes they barely rustle the world. At other times the ripples collide, intersect, and overlap, growing arithmetically into waves. The ripples move out far beyond the person who tossed the stone, and often the effects are hidden from the originator. Those affected may not know who moved them, and people find themselves moved as others disturb social norms, generate emulation in others, and move people to action. An executive director of a humanitarian relief organization commented, "I think it's the ones who simply stand up and say 'no' or 'yes.' They disturb the order, and others see it can be done and they move also." Multiple stone throwers create ripples that merge into tidal waves like social movements.

Lenses and Dreams

People's quality of mind and imagination can change under the tutelage of individuals and experience. Plato portrayed leadership as a form of getting new sight by moving from the cave of shadow to the light. Cognitively, individuals focus attention and organize the world with frames of reference that order perception and provide context and meaning (Morgan, 1997; Senge, 1990; Bolman & Deal, 1997). Imagination expands when individuals learn to see the world in new ways or picture other possibilities for themselves. Old frames are replaced or supplemented by new frames of reference. Individuals discover aspects of reality they had missed. Their perception can be sharpened or their imaginations made more supple, and they learn to see situations in different ways rather than being trapped in one comfortable internalized frame (Daloz et al., 1996; Morgan, 1997). In his Nobel Prize lecture, Bellow (1994) could have been describing good leaders when he suggested that artists "should give new eyes to human beings, inducing them to view the world differently, converting them from fixed modes of experience" (pp. 88–97). Movements to restore the dignity of marginalized groups involve not just collective power, but changing how members of the group and members of society see themselves – to understand that actions once acceptable can no longer be accepted because of the injustice hidden beneath them. The aspirations of individuals can be changed by leaders who believe in them and manage them in ways that they see new possibilities in their lives for growth and change. As one local utilities manager said, "The most important leader can be the one who sees possibilities for you that you do not see in yourself." A Pakistani World Health Organization official described how a small, low-tech program provided training for village girls at power looming to provide economic benefits for their local rural community outside of Karachi. This changed their self-understandings and initiated a ripple of change where the girls, in an unprecedented event, united to convince the mayor of their small village to convert part of the government center into a community center. Young girls ensconced in traditional families with no options slowly grew into a new image of themselves. At a local meeting a young woman spoke up and stated simply, "We have dreams too."

Each metaphor highlights a range of influence individuals can have upon people and the world – good and bad. They expand the ways of seeing how people lead. Acknowledging them deepens a leader's array of strategies and sense of responsibility.

The dimensions and metaphors of legacy also illuminate three paradoxes.

1. An individual's goals may not turn out to be his or her legacy. The goal orientation of managerial leaders can blind them to the accumulating impact of their actions on people, processes, and relations. These indirect impacts may influence people more than the putative goals.
2. People do not control the final meaning of their legacy. Because legacies entwine with meaning, they will be contestable. Debates over the meaning of actions will occur among those who view them and those who experience them. The meaning of an action may change over time as individuals reinterpret experiences in light of experience. Because legacies transcend the results, they are entangled with meaning issues. Mutable expectations will be a profound influence on legacies.
3. The actual nature of good and bad legacy can be very complicated. Levi (1989) points out that "the memories which lie within us are not carved in stone; not only do they tend to become erased as the years go by, but often they change, or even grow, by incorporation of extraneous features" (p. 23). Often, actions individuals initially experience as wrong or negative can induce changes in people or policy that end with positive developments. A public organization forced to face private competition can fail, or adapt and become more efficient and creative in how it deploys resources and understands its actual goals (Osborne, 1993; Kettl, 2000). More than a few managers commented upon the paradox of how a bad or painful experience with leaders changed them in complex ways. One senior transportation authority manager commented, "My experience with Bill made me a better leader. When I thought of what Bill would do in this situation, I did the opposite." A senior military officer reflected, "I thought it was the worst experience of my life. But I learned my strength and how to recover. I can't thank him, but if I hadn't experienced how badly he treated me and others I'd never known how to become a good leader." One young deputy executive director resigned after an intensely bad experience and noted, "We all felt trapped with no way out, but within five months, the entire staff had left. My act came from despair but it freed others." Time and again what people experienced as harm does harm them, but becomes a chance to grow if they learn from the experience. The learning is not guaranteed to be positive.

Survivors of traumatic experiences fall into three categories: those who decay under the sense of failure and pity, those who adapt and restore their life to normal levels, and those who become more at peace and stronger people (Csikszentmihalyi, 1990).

The legacy approach to leadership reminds individuals about the connections among people and the world. The connections mean each action can contribute to wombs and incubation, foundations, ripples, reef coral, lenses, or seeds that influence how people act. This viewpoint reinforces the relationship between present and future.

TIME AND HISTORY

Managerial leaders inherit people, institutions, relationships, expectations, and culture. People in organizations and environments possess memories and a sense of purpose and legacy. The inherited personnel are the guardians of what exists and what has been accomplished. The mission, history, and culture remain alive in the personnel (Schein, 1985; Denhardt, 2000). Every leader who attends to his or her legacy should attend to the inherited legacy – for good or bad.

This approach asks for more humility about the fabrication of goals and missions without the sustaining support of people and the political system. It asks for more diffidence about univocal definitions of success. It asks for reticence about ego involvement while demanding energy and commitment. It requires attending carefully to the history and culture of an organization. Creating an institutional legacy begins with understanding inherited meanings, accomplishments, and stories. This understanding enables leaders to anticipate how staff will interpret actions or respond to initiatives. An institutional legacy needs to be adopted by the members of the institution and stakeholders, co-creating the meaning and mission. Whether a leader wishes it or not, personnel and clients will create their own meanings for their actions (Schein, 1985; Morgan, 1997).

Legacy-oriented leadership requires a continuity strategy that addresses mission and organizational practices and norms. This builds upon the foundation that exists with care, moving internally from within the meanings available. If it means significant changes, so be it, but leaders need to be aware of the levels of resistance and changes emerging from the existing matrix of meaning and commitment.

Thinking of a legacy and inheritance reminds leaders that they owe respect to those who have come before and built the inherited legacy. This gives leadership a chance to honor and build upon the foundations and recognize the monuments. But true respect means honesty – no legacy is flawless. Even fine legacies can be contested and entail unanticipated consequences. Humility should inform the quest for a new legacy and evaluations of the past. An inheritance should be honestly evaluated and brought forward with good intact, not undermined by hidden resentment or unrecognized failures. To claim the good of inheritance imposes the obligation to not make things worse, but also to correct the wrong done in the institution's name. At times, it may involve destroying part of the inheritance.

Any realistic interpretation of legacy should incorporate cumulative and time dimensions. This refocuses leadership upon the present, the daily interactions and performance, not just the enticing game of high-level policy change. The Emperor Marcus Aurelius, in his *Meditations*, reflected,

> Even if you're going to live three thousand more years, or ten times that, remember: you cannot lose another life than the one you're living now, or live another one than the one you're losing ... The present is the same for everyone. (Aurelius, 2002, p. I.14)

Later, he reminds himself to stay attuned to the present and stop drifting (p. III.14). He could be speaking to all managerial leaders when he tells himself,

> Life is short. That's all there is to say. Get what you can from the present – thoughtfully, justly. (Aurelius, 2002, p. IV.26)

The small stuff matters for a legacy. Leaders manage the quality of relations with people and organizations, the competence and performance of individuals, the technology, political support, and structure to sustain the organization's effectiveness. These emphases keep leaders and personnel coupled and emphasize that the most durable legacy left will be the quality of people led and served. Impacts upon people, environments, and policy remain largely cumulative. Windows of opportunity can permit sudden changes to occur. These significant changes depend upon the webs, seeds, cultivation, changed lenses, and dreams that laid the foundation for movement.

Attention to the present means working hard to achieve results that accomplish good and impact others in intended ways. It focuses upon the real impact and the reality of what people and institutions face. This focus fights against the temptation of many senior managers and leaders to focus upon big policy change as their legacy. An experienced state and local executive remarked, "Leaders tend to underemphasize management because they want the big score, the notch on their belt, and then after the policy victory, they move on." An honest legacy encourages leaders to ensure that people see the connection between competent daily work and the legacy for citizens and colleagues who benefit or suffer from it. Leaders need to help all their colleagues see their own legacy by seeing the worth and impact of their work. Establishing a connection between competent daily work and its legacy fights the cynicism, boredom, and exhaustion that erode performance and self-worth (Petrick & Quinn, 1997; Csikszentmihalyi, 2003).

Building an institution or policy legacy means the slow, hard work of acquiring the resources to hire, train, and direct people. Even competent, caring performance does not guarantee continuing support. To sustain performance and the impact on lives of individuals even after one leaves requires attending to the politics of building support. Laws, policy, and institutions do not survive on automatic pilot but live through deep roots, strong foundations, and webs of support and power.

Focusing leadership on legacy naturally leads to a performance emphasis, which underlines the reality that people are creating their legacy on a daily basis. Performance focus demands that leaders and workers ask what they are seeking to accomplish and to connect their actual work with the legacy impact they seek. It engages the realities of accomplishments, failure, and improvement and gives more reality to the belief that people are better off because individuals perform their jobs well. Performance over time means building an institution's capacity with strong support structures, but also with training and competence.

Legacy links so profoundly with the meaning of action that it converges on culture building. The question for leadership becomes what type of culture helps individuals to achieve a legacy. People who work in institutions will construct their own meaning of actions. This insight invites leaders to engage meaning as part of managing and leading (Schein, 1985, 1999). A managerial legacy that focuses upon the quality of individuals as well as performance devotes time and effort to build the meanings, practices, stories, myths, and symbols for people (Doig & Hargrove, 1987).

The time dimensions of legacy present the greatest challenges and paradoxes. Once it becomes a focus of judgment, the challenge of legacy building for leaders is to reflect upon what it means to leave behind accomplishments that matter and endure without one's will to nourish them. Time acts as a prism, refracting unpredictable meanings and purposes. Emphasizing what remains after one leaves and the fragility and uncertainty about how actions will be understood underscores the importance of humility in transmitting a legacy.

This future orientation links with the concern to create something that endures. The durability issue meshes with the agendas of both public management and administration (Lynn, 1987; Rainey, 1991). Concentrating upon durability means working on culture where the commitments are imbedded in organizational practices and passed on. It means learning, training, and persuading so personnel continue to commit to goal competencies. If individuals who come later are not committed to the same issues and beliefs, all the institutional stability and resources will not make much difference. The legacy will end differently than intended. A legacy requires building support among authorizers and stakeholders to sustain the organization and policy. But a supple legacy should also leave the freedom and creativity for people to adapt to new changes in the environment. Foundations, webs, roots, corals, soil and seeds, and dreams and lenses provide the means and ends of this approach to legacy.

The future holds little but uncertainty. Environments change, policy changes, people change, evaluations change, and unanticipated consequences, for good or bad, emerge. Organizational or mission survival will not continue in pristine form. Organizations that cannot adapt to changed demands will not flourish. The mission itself will permute as people learn about the full implications of their goals and adjust to mistakes or credible changes of emphasis and direction. A future-oriented legacy always exists in the lives enabled by competent public service. However, it should not exclusively focus on rigid but clear outcomes. Any achievement is tenuous and open to future interpretations. Performance measures simply provide baselines for learning and growing, not permanent answers. The battles over the meaning of accomplishment and failure launch their own momentum to address or rectify actions. True leadership legacies generate wombs, webs, foundations, and soil and seeds that become the source for others to grow, adapt, and achieve autonomy without one's sustaining will.

The writer of the *Bhagavad Gita* wrote, 3000 years ago, that

> You have a right to your actions, but never to your actions' fruits. Act for the action's sake ... The wise man lets go of all results, whether good or bad, and is focused on the action alone. (*Bhagavad Gita*, 2000, pp. 2.45–2.49)

The reality of legacy is that once an individual leaves, he or she should leave and let people and institutions change or even die on their own. Anything humans build will change, die, be destroyed or rebuilt over time. Yet individuals will be lured by the indispensable person temptation where they believe only they can lead the institution. Consequently, leadership demands a strong sense of humility in leaving legacies. This is compounded by the need to welcome accountability and to adapt to the changed will of legislatures, people, and the environment, as well as the capacity to adapt to unanticipated consequences and new information. To build a legacy in a liberal democracy means to be humble, and willing to not only learn, but also accept that learning will change the shape or meaning of one's legacies. In this light, one of the most enduring legacies will be the quality of people helped. They will move on to live or continue a leader's work in new and unpredictable ways, even as the leader moves on. As a teacher, a leader sows seeds of skills, ideas, and commitment, and these grow in new and different ways. Often individuals will not even know the final results of a legacy. Individuals should remember that they enable people to achieve in ways they could not have without help.

LIMITS AND PROBLEMS

Focusing on legacy is not a panacea for organizing the cognitive attention and moral evaluation that go into deliberation (Petrick & Quinn, 1997). Like all concepts used by mortals, it has problems. The trouble arises because the concept intimately links to the self and the search for meaning. Too often the individual seeking to leave a legacy overinvests in both a specific legacy and meaning for that legacy. While I have insisted upon the importance of humility, another strong tradition of politics emphasizes that individuals enter public life seeking glory, reputation, and advancement (Braudy, 1986; Machiavelli, 1992). This desire for glory and fame provides powerful motivation for action and mixes together with more public-spirited motives. Yet the desire to stamp a legacy with one's name can cause several problems. First, the approach can encourage organizational rigidity. Second, it misunderstands the importance of memory and limits of control. Third, it tempts people to grandiosity. Fourth, it tempts people to focus on the physical rather than the human. Finally, it encourages people to confuse fame with legacy.

Building strong political support for policies or organizations and constructing sturdy cultures are hallmarks of legacy-oriented leadership. Ironically, these very attributes can induce organizational rigidity and impermeability. Supporters, commitment, and success raise a form of organizational fundamentalism that shores up institutional inertia. This conflicts with both accountability and adapting to the environment. This organizational rigidity can become a serious problem and lead to unanticipated consequences, harmful adaptations, and goal displacement, where serving past practices becomes a substitute for achieving public purposes. When Ralph Burger took over as the head of A&P after the retirement of the founders, the Hartford brothers, he spent his decades of leadership asking the question, "What would Mr. Hartford do?" This insistence upon the dream and lenses of the founders trapped him and the company into a spiral that limited their adaptability and led to its decline (Collins, 2001).

The notion of legacy can presume that those who come after one leaves actually remember and acknowledge one's contributions. More interestingly, it can presume people will continue to interpret one's contribution in the terms desired by the legatee. Several problems undermine this assumption. Human memory is notoriously unreliable, selective, and changes over time. Others' memory or interpretation of legacy-intended actions may not be congruent with an individual actor's intent. For example, as we age, our evaluation of how our parents behaved changes. What seemed bad or troubling once may be seen as helpful later on. What seemed like a good idea at one time may turn out to cause problems later.

More dangerously, a person's intention and legacy can fuse in their mind. It is extremely difficult, however, to control the meaning of actions in others. While successful leadership requires strategic attention to influencing how stakeholders interpret meaning (Lynn, 1987), leaders cannot always control how they are perceived. Different individuals will read actions in different ways, although they may publicly go along with a manager's interpretation if the manager has great power. The desire to control how others interpret action induces individuals to spend time and resources to control the meaning and to imprint organizational and political rigidity rather than attend to the actual impact upon lives. At its logical extremes it leads to an authoritarian insistence on control or a leadership cult.

Paradoxically, many legacies will be unknown or forgotten by recipients. Changes in people's character or competence may occur gradually under the tutelage of several individuals. The cumulative changes matter, but the actual memory of exact personal impact may fade before a general sense of change. The lenses a person uses later in time may change how they view impacts people had on them earlier. Often the impact of an action will not be known to those who benefit from them. Supervisors and mechanics who fix a problem in a bus or a senior manager who solves a scheduling glitch will not be known to those who benefit, like riders or drivers who benefit from reliable, safe service. Contributions to clients that seem routine may enable significant changes in their lives without clear acknowledgment to those who helped, yet all produce legacies.

An aggrieved sense of inadequate recognition or the slipperiness of human memory tempts many individuals to focus upon the big picture, the big score, and the big policy. A widely experienced senior state appointed official and governor's advisor commented, "Policy folks always look for the big score. It makes their reputation ... They don't have much time. They leave the details to others." This temptation leads a person to see legacy as big change, a major innovation, and something that visibly endures. This tempts people to grandiosity and a sense of their indispensability. The heroic mode of managerial leadership with its emphasis upon what "I" can hold together by force of my talent and will distorts the legacy orientation. This approach can help agencies flourish but forgets that people create meaning and legacies together. It undervalues how others will function on their own without the heroic leader. The heroic model can subvert attention to capacity building for a narrow focus on the leader's direction. Organizational culture and the depth or quality of people falls by the wayside in the search for high-profile outcomes. Organizations flourish but do not develop people or the capacity to adapt to new environments after the leader departs (Collins & Porras, 1997; Collins, 2001).

The dynamic of focusing on the physical rather than the human impels many managers to think concretely, as in bricks and mortar. A long-time city council member took pride in his legacy as "changing the way we think about delivery of social service to at-risk kids. That's my real accomplishment." At the end of the interview, however, his senior staffer interjected, "We are spending lots of time on rebuilding the station. We want something physical that we can point to, to prove we left something behind." Monuments scale from the simple, such as new paint jobs, furniture, or technology, to creating laws or buildings. Government and nonprofits starve for physical or technical infrastructure and successes there are obvious and endure. New equipment remains in place. They upgrade personnel with Hawthorne effects and help citizens in direct ways such as a new park structure that invites children to play and families to congregate. A new public space or art can contribute to a new culture and respect for an organization. With these rewards, leaders often concentrate upon physical achievements and pay less attention to the quality of people or whether staff can use the new technologies or keep up the new buildings or systems.

A legacy focus easily confuses fame with legacy. As with Ozymandias, many think of their legacy as their solution to a mortal world. Memory, like the songs the Greeks sang of their heroes, grants them a surrogate for immortality. This focus upon wanting to be remembered for doing things usually gets in the way of leaving a good legacy. It can paralyze a person with the temptation to grandiosity or incite people to underachieve because they are less willing to give credit or share power in achievement. Aggrandizing one's ego and enshrining correct memories of oneself displace the real goals of making life better or even making a difference as opposed to making 'my' difference and making sure everyone knows it. It can redirect energy into building reputation or monuments at the expense of real achievements. At the same time, it makes legacy out as a possession of the great and powerful and discourages everyone from understanding the real differences individuals make in the world. This denies humans a deepening of their own dignity and worth.

Human memory and human change haunt all the problems with legacy-based leadership. To return to the lure of concrete, a building might be perfect and cutting-edge when built. Ten years later it might be seen as a stagnant artifact of an architectural fad. A space embodying the latest human-relations insights becomes obsolete in five years. In a virtual world where half-lives of computer programs are six months, new technologies will be passed by as they are installed. Even a park or monument can end up a dangerous, unused space or become nest for pigeons. To ask too much durability and too much interpretive stability invites abuse of power and goes beyond what individuals should reasonably seek.

CONCLUSIONS

I have several ideas about how to think about leaving a legacy as leaders and managers. They flow from seeing individuals serve as stewards of a trust given by those who came before and handed on to those who remain.

(1) *Beware of pigeons on your monuments.* Monuments and foundations matter as social memorials, achievements, foci of action, and touchstones for the future. However, focusing mainly on the monumental or physical and insisting on credit invites disappointment and distortion of personal energy and aspirations.

(2) *Begin sooner rather than later.* A person's legacy unfolds every day, from the beginning. An individual's cumulative actions, relations, precedents, and attention contribute to create a slow and almost imperceptible influence that reaches into organizations and people. People can think they are going along and staying low as they wait to get power and position – then they will really make a difference. This misreads the slowly accreting influence of actions and people's ability to control the meaning of

actions. At the end, when individuals feel freer, they often possess less leverage. To think people can make a legacy late and fast ignores that people have already engendered much of it. Much of what a person actually does builds upon the wombs, foundations, seeding, monuments, webs, and corals they helped earlier.

(3) *Accept the inheritance as a prelude to legacy.* Individuals do not manage or lead alone, and leaders build upon or are trapped by what came before. Leaders have obligations to learn the history – the true good and the true harm done by an institution and its people. The true history should be integrated into strategies for action. Respecting, truth seeking, and sometimes destroying are central to legacy creation.

(4) *Scale actions.* Every job carries with it a reasonable scope of action. The temptation to go big and permanent when thinking of a legacy downplays the present work to look beyond to what really matters. This is a fundamental mistake. Communication and relations sustain the quotidian legacy and enable other people to link their commitment and meaning to their service. The scaling of action and aspiration from person, to group, to institution; from purpose to institution; from immediate to long term permits legacy to unfold as an organizationally enduring phenomena, not an imposition of will. It aligns with the need to build foundations, weave webs, change lenses and dreams, build reefs, start ripples, or prepare soil or plant seeds.

(5) *Link the small and large.* Insist upon the connection and meaning from the smallest acts of the present to the deepest aspirations of the future. Enable colleagues and workers to appreciate the meaning and legacy of their actions and communicate this endlessly. Legacies depend upon the linkages and feedback loops between broader goals and daily interactions. Each modeled behavior or interaction trains and directs in this way. When leaders hand on knowledge and inculcate behavioral expectations and norms, they connect real action with purpose. Every person touched in these interactions can become different, for good or bad. Every person served by competent performance benefits in their life for good or bad.

(6) *Not controlling the final meaning.* While influencing meanings is a necessary aspect of strategic and tactical leadership, in the end, the meanings of a legacy will emerge from dialogue, accountability, and impacts. Memory and history will exact their own costs, as memories will change or forget the original intent. Too much time spent controlling after one leaves not only distorts one's own efforts, but also the truth of the legacy.

(7) *Leading and letting go.* The paradox of leading for a legacy resides in learning to let go. The *Tao te Ching*, agreeing with the *Baghavad Gita*, comments that

> He who clings to his work will create nothing that endures ... [J]ust do your job, then let go. (Lao Tzu, 1988, chapter 24)

The old wisdom argues that the capacity for accomplishments to endure and continue to help the public good resides in the ability of the individuals and institutions to adapt and recreate their meaning and performance in changed circumstances. One of the true bequests of leadership is that webs, foundations, corals, lenses, dreams, and wombs enable other persons to grow, move on, and build their lives and successes from an individual's contribution. This means understanding that what endures must do so without the will and ego of the 'I' to sustain it or control it. This humility should not sap the drive to do good or the strategic need to fight for agendas and educate the public. Individuals should take work seriously but hold it lightly.

Everyone leaves a legacy, whether they want to or not. This knowledge remains central to democratic leadership. In ancient Athens, when the young men reached the age of citizenship, they took an oath. One of the central promises in the oath was that they would hand on their city, not less, but greater, better, and more beautiful than they received it. Remembering this and organizing ethical reflection around it offsets the tendency to emphasize ends over means and stresses their inherent connections. Understanding this links ethics, responsibility, position, and action. The self-understanding permitted by legacy-oriented leadership asks individuals to understand the full range of impact they can have on life, institutions, and people. The reality of legacy reminds people that they are stewards with significance and power.

NOTES

1. The debate over whether strict adherence to the law or character-based discretion never really ends. Plato (1974, 1980) discussed both alternatives in *The Republic* and *The Laws*. The Chinese legalists argued with the Confucians about the relative importance of the two (Wren, 1994, pp. 13–35). In America the classic argument between Herman Finer (1941) and Carl Friedrich (1940) covers the need for legal adherence and accountability versus the stress on expertise and character, and reflects a debate that has no definite answer but will always be with us given the limitations of human beings and of the two models.

2. Rousseau's combined critique of human nature made trust of autonomous or trustee power impossible, while his emphasis upon the capacity of human beings to participate together and free themselves from the tyranny of autonomous government power laid the basis for most modern variations of these themes. Recent postmodern thought in public administration tends toward the same direction with its denial of any independent and legitimate position and responsibility to government or public officials given its epistemology. At the same time, modern critics of government that focus upon reinventing often see themselves not only as guardians of efficiency, but also as creating better accountability and moving government close to citizens.

3. This chapter draws upon over 50 semistructured interviews with middle to senior managers from 10 countries. I conducted the interviews from 1998 to 2003 under strict confidentiality. The interviews occurred in Seattle, Washington; Washington, DC; Kansas City, Missouri; Hanoi, Vietnam; Mexico City, Mexico; and Addis Ababa, Ethiopia. The citations are based upon my personal notes.

REFERENCES

Adams, G., & Balfour, D. L. (2004). *Unmasking administrative evil*. Monmark, NY: M.E. Sharpe.
Armstrong, J. (1997). *Stewardship and public service: A discussion paper*. Ottawa: Public Service Commission of Canada.
Aurelius, M. (2002). In: G. Hays (Trans.), *Meditations*. New York: Modern Library. Citations to book and line.
Baumeister, R. F. (1991). *Meanings of life*. New York: Guilford Press.
Bellow, S. (1994). *It all adds up*. London: Seeker and Walburg.
Bhagavad Gita. (2000). In: S. Mitchell (Trans.), *Bhagavad Gita*. New York: Harmony Books. Citation to book and line.
Bloch, P. (1996). *Stewardship: Choosing service over self interest*. San Francisco, CA: Berrett-Koehler Publications.
Bolman, L. G., & Deal, T. E. (1997). *Reframing organizations: Artistry, choice and leadership*. San Francisco, CA: Jossey-Bass Publishers.
Braudy, L. (1986). *The frenzy of renown: Fame and its history*. New York: Oxford University Press.
Bryson, J. M. (1992). *Leadership for the common good: Tackling public problems in a shared-power world*. San Francisco, CA: Jossey-Bass Publishers.
Burke, J. P. (1986). *Bureaucratic responsibility*. Baltimore, MD: Johns Hopkins University Press.
Carter, S. L. (1996). *Integrity*. New York: Basic Books.
Collins, J. C. (2001). *Good to great*. New York: Harper Business.
Collins, J. C., & Porras, J. I. (1997). *Built to last: Successful habits of visionary companies*. New York: Harper Business.
Cooper, T. (1991). *An ethics of citizenship for public administration*. Englewood Cliffs, NJ: Prentice-Hall.

Cooper, T. (1998). *The responsible administrator: An approach to ethics for the administrative role* (4th ed.). San Francisco, CA: Jossey-Bass Publishers.
Cooper, T., & Wright, D. N. (1992). *Exemplary public administrators: Character and leadership in government.* San Francisco, CA: Jossey-Bass Publishers.
Csikszentmihalyi, M. (1990). *Flow: The psychology of optimal experience.* New York: Harper Collins.
Csikszentmihalyi, M. (2003). *Good business: Leadership, flow, and the making of meaning.* New York: Viking.
Daloz, L. A. P., Keen, C. H., Keen, J. P., & Parks, S. D. (1996). *Common fire: Leading lives of commitment in a complex world.* Boston, MA: Beacon Press.
Denhardt, K. G. (1988). *The ethics of public service: Resolving moral dilemmas in public organizations.* New York: Greenwood Press.
Denhardt, R. B. (1989). *In the shadow of organization.* Lawrence: University of Kansas Press.
Denhardt, R. B. (2000). *The pursuit of significance: Strategies for managerial success in public organizations.* Prospect Heights, IL: Waveland Press.
Dobel, J. P. (1976). The corruption of the state. *American Political Science Review, 72,* 958–973.
Dobel, J. P. (1990). Integrity in public service. *Public Administration Review, 50,* 354–366.
Dobel, J. P. (1999). *Public integrity.* Baltimore, MD: Johns Hopkins University Press.
Doig, J. W., & Hargrove, E. (Eds) (1987). *Leadership and innovation: A biographical perspective on entrepreneurs in government.* Baltimore, MD: Johns Hopkins University Press.
Farmer, D. J. (1995). *The language of public administration: Bureaucracy, modernity and post-modernity.* Tuscaloosa: University of Alabama Press.
Finer, H. (1941). Administrative responsibility in democratic life. *Public Administration Review, 14,* 335–350.
Friedrich, C. J. (1940). The nature of administrative responsibility. *Public Policy, 1,* 3–24.
Gladwell, M. (2000). *The tipping point: How little things can make a big difference.* New York: Little Brown and Company.
Goodsell, C. (1985). *The case for bureaucracy: A public administration polemic.* Lawrence: University Press of Kansas.
Goodsell, C. (1988). *The social meaning of civic space: Studying political authority through architecture.* Lawrence: University Press of Kansas.
Greenleaf, R. K. (1991). *Servant leadership: A journey into the nature of legitimate power and greatness.* New York: Paulist Press.
Homer. (1977). In: R. Fagles (Trans.), *The Odyssey.* (Introduction and notes by B. Knox.) New York: Penguin Books. Citation by book and line.
Huber, J. D., & Shipan, C. R. (2002). *Deliberate discretion: The institutional foundations of bureaucratic autonomy.* Cambridge, UK: Cambridge University Press.
Kelling, G. L. (1999). *Broken windows and police discretion.* Washington, DC: US Department of Justice, Office of Justice Programs, National Institute of Justice.
Kettl, D. F. (2000). *The global public management revolution: A report on the transformation of governance.* Washington, DC: Brookings Institution Press.
Kidder, T. (1997). *The soul of a new machine.* New York: Modern Library.
Kotter, J. P. (1996). *Leading change.* Cambridge, MA: Harvard Business School Press.
Lao Tzu. (1988). In: S. Mitchell (Trans.), *Tao te Ching.* New York: Harper Perennial.
Levi, P. (1989). *The drowned and the saved.* New York: Vintage International.
Levi, P. (2001). *The voice of memory.* New York: The New Press.
Lynn, L. E. (1987). *Managing public policy.* Boston: Little Brown.

Machiavelli, N. (1992). In: R. Adams (Trans.), *The Prince*. New York: Norton.
Morgan, G. (1997). *Images of organizations*. Thousand Oaks, CA: Sage.
Norton, D. (1976). *Individual destinies: A philosophy of ethical individualism*. Princeton, NJ: Princeton University Press.
Osborne, D. (1993). *Reinventing government: How the entrepreneurial spirit is transforming the public sector*. New York: Plume.
Osborne, D., & Plastrik, P. (1998). *Banishing bureaucracy: The five strategies for reinventing government*. New York: Plume.
Perrow, C. (1993). *Complex organizations: A critical essay* (3rd ed.). New York: McGraw-Hill.
Petrick, J. A., & Quinn, J. F. (1997). *Management ethics: Integrity at work*. Thousand Oaks, CA: Sage.
Plato. (1974). In: G. M. A. Grube (Trans.), *The Republic*. Indianapolis: Hackett Publishing Company.
Plato. (1980). In: T. L. Prangle (Trans.), *The Laws*. New York: Basic Books.
Rainey, H. G. (1991). *Understanding and managing public organizations*. San Francisco, CA: Jossey-Bass Publishers.
Rawls, J. (1971). *A theory of justice*. Cambridge, MA: Belknap Press.
Rohr, J. A. (2002). *Civil servants and their constitutions*. Lawrence: University Press of Kansas.
Schein, E. H. (1985). *Organizational culture and leadership*. San Francisco, CA: Jossey Bass Publishers.
Schein, E. H. (1999). *The corporate culture survival guide*. San Francisco, CA: Jossey-Bass Publishers.
Schulz, W. (2003). *Tainted legacy: 9/11 and the ruin of human rights*. New York: Nation Books.
Senge, P. (1990). *The fifth discipline: The art and practice of the learning organization*. Garden City, NJ: Prentice-Hall.
Sherman, N. (1989). *The fabric of character: Aristotle's theory of virtue*. Oxford, UK: Clarendon Press.
Terry, L. D. (2003). *Leadership of public bureaucracies: The administrator as conservator*. Armonk, NY: M. E. Sharpe.
United Nations. (1996). Action against corruption & annex international code of conduct for public officials (Resolution 51/59, 82nd Plenary Meeting, December 12). Retrieved May 5, 2003, from http://www.un.org/documents/ga/51/a51r059.htm
Warren, R. (2002). *The purpose driven life*. Grand Rapids, MI: Zondervan.
Wills, G. (1992). *Lincoln at Gettysburg: The words that remade America*. New York: Simon and Schuster.
Wolf, J. B. (2004). *Harnessing the holocaust: The politics of memory in France*. Stanford, CA: Stanford University Press.
Wolf, S. R. (1990). *Freedom within reason*. New York: Oxford University Press.
Wren, D. A. (1994) (4th ed.). *The evolution of management thought*. New York: Wiley.

PROFESSIONAL ETHICS FOR POLITICIANS?

John Uhr

ABSTRACT

Democracies typically impose onerous regulation on the conduct of bureaucratic officials and remarkably light regulation of the conduct of elected officials. The traditional presumption was that politicians should be allowed to self-regulate. In many democratic regimes, politicians have shown themselves unable to carry this burden of public trust. As a result, political ethics is regulated from a perspective of public distrust, associated with fears of political corruption. Despite my personal reservations about professional ethics models (recorded here by reference to recent fictional work of novelist J.M. Coetzee), I revive a trust-based perspective to make a case for a regime of self-regulation for democratic politicians, based on a democratic hope that politicians can be trusted to act as responsible professionals.

In the management of public sector ethics, codes, commissions, and cops all have their place. They are particularly useful in combating political corruption. But what works in encouraging political ethics, in sustaining a political system that values political decency? My preference is to avoid cumbersome legal prescription and rule-compliance approaches. Talk is better than chalk: what passes as political ethics is itself a political issue, best determined through political processes giving the public opportunities to weigh contending views about the prudence and good sense of questionable political conduct. Open deliberative processes can allow politicians to account for and justify the public value of suspect conduct, before other politicians and before the public. Prudence is more valuable than prescription, although prescribed structures of public deliberation can bring prudence to the fore – if used responsibly by politicians. Ultimately, that is a question for the public to judge.

Does this sound like a very soft version of a regulatory system? If so, this is because I am sketching a regulative ideal rather than a regulatory mechanism. The ideal trusts politicians to reward decent and honorable conduct and to punish unethical conduct. How they do that is best for them to judge, according to the constitutional conventions of each political system. My preference for deliberative structures is consistent with many of the checks and balances common to liberal constitutionalism, and even if the regulative ideal is never matched in political practice it at least gives politicians a fair sense of the standards of political ethics that a democratic political community might want of them.

THE ISSUE OF RESPONSIBILITIES

My argument is in two parts. The first reduces the prominence of 'professional' in the style of professional ethics we might expect of politicians. The aim here is to clear a space for what I am tempted to call real ethics by reducing the domination of professional or role ethics. The second part builds on this by widening the scope of the political in political ethics to include recognition of, and even encouragement for, decent political ethics to balance the prevailing focus on indecent or corrupt political ethics. What might encourage ethical political decency? Drawing on principles of deliberative democracy, including those examined in my *Deliberative Democracy in Australia* (Uhr, 1998a), my answer is that public political deliberation can encourage political decency. How can public deliberation strengthen political decency? By allowing all parties to governance relationships to have their say on the state of their official responsibilities, thereby providing the public, should it be in a position to listen, with opportunities to review standards of political responsibility.

Much turns on these two concepts of responsibility and relationship, clarified below. The two parts of my argument work together to support my contention that democracy has more to gain by trusting politicians to take greater (but not by any means total) responsibility for regulating their own ethics than by distrusting politicians and subjecting them to regulation primarily through external anti-corruption commissions. The term *politicians* covers a diverse class of public actors. My scheme presumes that this very diversity can encourage a pro-active system of checks and balances where nonexecutive politicians (e.g., legislators, backbenchers, the opposition) use the publicity of deliberative processes to keep those with greater political power (e.g., heads of government, cabinet ministers) responsible in the conduct of their official relationships (e.g., ministers with civil servants). The hope is that structures of public deliberation can provide politicians with professional capacities to be trusted to regulate much of their own public conduct.

I acknowledge that the odds are against me. The case against professional ethics faces two prominent claims, among many others. Most basically, there is the theoretical claim that the full nature of ethical conduct cannot be reduced to the forms appropriate to professional conduct, despite the welcome public benefits of properly managed professional conduct. Ever since Bradley (1927, pp. 160–213) explored the ethic of 'my station and its duties,' the ethics of office or role have won at best only qualified praise – even from Bradley himself, although this reservation escaped the attention of his early critics like Sidgwick (1967, pp. 284–287). Second, there is the practical claim that forms of self-regulation typical of professional ethics are plagued by practical defects deriving from the capture of the regulatory system by the professions. Contaminating private interests too often weakens the promised public benefits. Taking these two claims into account, political occupations provide one of the hardest test cases for advocates of professional ethics, who face considerable odds in persuading critics that either or both of these two counterclaims can be overcome.

While I acknowledge the force of the general case against professional ethics, I want to sketch principles to construct a version of professional self-regulation suitable to democratic politics. One test of professionalism is the capacity for self-regulation of official conduct. I favor models of political ethics that include opportunities for politicians to take greater responsibility to regulate their own conduct. This preference is unrelated to any political professionalism. The reverse is more likely: politics being a public rather than simply a professional activity, decisions about what constitutes appropriate political conduct are matters for public debate. Politicians can help or hinder that process, but they should not be excluded from it because of any fears about conflicts of interest. Conflicts of interest can and do arise, and abuse of office has to be regulated. But there can also be conflicts of responsibility as well as conflicts of interest, where competing ethics of political responsibility clash.

The most dramatic example from recent Australian experience comes from President Bush's 2003 visit to the Australian Parliament, where his address was interrupted by two Greens senators who then refused to vacate the chamber when so directed by the presiding officer. The government successfully moved to exclude the two Greens senators from the next day's joint session with the Chinese president. Both incidents, the senators conduct in interrupting President Bush and the government's exclusion of them from the subsequent parliamentary meeting with the Chinese president, ignited considerable public debate over who should have the political power to determine how elected representatives conduct themselves when engaged in parliamentary business. One extreme supported the right of every elected representative to make their own decision on when and where to speak out on issues of public concern including, if they are prepared to stand by their judgment, interrupting an address to the national Parliament by the U.S. president. The other extreme supported the decision of the Howard government that this conduct was irresponsible and should not be repeated – particularly at a time when Australia was about to sign a huge energy contract with China.

These extremes reflect contrasting norms of political responsibility, with no hint that either is tainted by suspicion of illegality or corruption. But the lively community debate over these contrasting ethical postures tells us much about the neglected end of political ethics: democratic communities are surprisingly keen to talk through the political ethics of self-government when confronted with contrasting examples of responsible ethical judgment by politicians. My point is not to award ethical points for exemplary decency to either position but to call attention to the larger issue of process: democratic political ethics are tested through public deliberation over the responsibilities of debatable political conduct. This deliberation occurs in relation to contrasting models of political decency no less than in relation to models of corruption. Frequently this involves no issue of self-interested abuse of office, but rather a clash of ethical expectations about the proper use of political office or about standards of political decency. Debate over failures by politicians to do the right thing (e.g., failure to listen in silence to the visiting head of government, or failure to allow elected representatives their right to join other parliamentarians in a meeting with a visiting head of government) can be just as central to public life as debate over alleged criminal misconduct by politicians.

ETHICS OR CORRUPTION?

My point of departure is that it is misleading to treat political ethics solely with the analytical tools used to deal with political corruption. Large parts of the ethics in political ethics go uninvestigated when the methods of corruption analysis dominate the scene. To exaggerate for effect, ethics itself is corrupted when the focus is on the negative effects of corrupt conduct with little or no interest in the positive effects of ethical conduct. For those who like big concepts, this analytical corruption limits our access to the phenomenology, or full range of characteristic conduct, captured by the category of political ethics. Missing from most accounts are the phenomena at the ethical end of political ethics. One useful example of neglected practice is the investigation of types of exemplary public conduct published in Terry Cooper and Dale Wright's (1992) reader, *Exemplary Public Administrators*.

Importing a distinction I defend at greater length in my book *Terms of Trust* (Uhr, 2005), I distinguish studies of political ethics from studies of political corruption by reference to the public conduct they seek to explain. Put crudely, corruption analysis explains how different forms of external accountability (i.e., external to the politicians concerned) impede political corruption, and ethics analysis explains how different forms of internal responsibility (i.e., internal to the politicians concerned) promote political ethics. Those familiar with the old Friedrich–Finer debate in U.S. public administration will recognize this as derivative from that influential exchange over the contest of the two values of accountability and responsibility – values that are distinguishable even if in practice they are inseparable.

The topic of political ethics covers two poles of conduct: the unethical pole with the tension between corruption and its detection through public accountability, and the ethical pole with the tension between ethics and its discovery through personal responsibility. Here, I want to distinguish the study of political ethics from the study of political corruption, usually understood as a form of criminal misconduct best regulated by nonpoliticians. Investigation of political ethics gets at other forms of abuse of office – conduct that is not illegal but not necessarily right or decent. I argue that democratic standards of ethical political conduct are matters for political debate and determination, ideally (nice word!) managed politically through processes of political argument and public deliberation.

THE ISSUE OF RELATIONSHIPS

My take on professional political ethics will focus on the ethics of official relationships. Ethical responsible conduct by democratic politicians is largely about their management of official relationships. Other approaches deal with conflicts of interest or with outright corruption. My worry is that many aspects of what we might term constitutional morality go unnoticed in these approaches. Of particular concern to me is the lack of scholarly attention to the ethical responsibility politicians have for managing relationships among the various institutions of government. To the extent that politicians have professional duties, I think these duties derive from their share in the collective or shared responsibility for the appropriate public use of political power. As I describe a little later, different political offices will have different types of responsibilities depending on the specific powers at their disposal (legislative, executive, head of government, member of cabinet, senior advisor, civil service, military service, etc.). As responsibilities change, so too do the specific institutional relationships so necessary to give effect to the public powers in question. The ethics of institutional relationships might be less tidy than the ethics of personal power, but they are the building blocks of any profession of public responsibility suitable to a democratic society.

To simplify, ethical responsibility is tested in judgments about the management of political relationships. My suggested distinction between political ethics and ethical politics can help keep the focus on ethical relationships. By political ethics, I am referring to the political conventions for managing disputes over ethical conduct through rules and regulations over the fine lines between private interest and public duty. This is what is usually meant by ethical regulation of political conduct, the aim being to reduce the incidence of private use of public office. The conventional approach moves along a path of distrust, based on assumptions that politicians generally cannot be trusted with the responsibility of regulating their own ethical conduct. Relevant policy prescriptions include peer investigation but increasingly focus on external regulation of political conduct by ethics or integrity commissions and the like. In contrast, ethical politics builds on trust rather than distrust, conferring a kind of professional autonomy on politicians to manage their own power relationships with considerable self-regulation. Here the aim is not the negative one of reducing the incidence of the vices associated with the private use of public office, but the more positive one of stimulating the virtues associated with praiseworthy political management of official relationships of power.

I concede that politicians cannot be expected not to be political. It therefore makes good policy sense to take precautions against unethical forms of political conduct. The path of distrust leads to greater and greater public accountability of politicians, with many external accountability agencies holding the line against formal breaches of ethical rules and expectations. But it also makes good policy sense to try to promote higher forms of ethical political conduct than simply compliance with the rules. This alternative path of trust opens up possibilities for more substantial ethical responsibility, in the quite traditional sense represented by the political virtue of prudence as the driver of ethical responsibility in public life. In its most expansive sense, for politicians being ethical means acting prudently – taking prudence to mean the political virtue of practical wisdom so necessary for the sound management of official relationships. Actions speak louder than words, and political actions that build relationships can be more effective in promoting ethical politics than any number of fine words in a formal code of conduct.

I admit that it stretches belief to suggest that the use and abuse of political prudence lends itself to professional self-regulation. Prudence, thus understood, is not only the exercise of judgment but it is the exercise of political judgment in managing official relationships. Matters of judgment attract debate over the use and abuse of discretion, and matters of political judgment attract debate over the use and abuse of political deliberation by parties to the decisions in dispute. But this very recognition of prudential deliberation through open political debate highlights the nature of the professional standard invoked when speaking of professional ethics for democratic politicians. The model of professionalism here is not that of the single provider responsible for professional services, but that of an assembly sharing responsibility for the provision of professional services. That, at least, is the ideal.

BUT IS POLITICS A PROFESSION?

Does the ideal match our realities? The case for treating politicians as professionals deserving the public trust associated with self-regulatory professional responsibilities seems, at least initially, farfetched. Across the democratic world, politicians universally lack the public confidence of professional occupations like health professionals, legal professionals, teachers, many police forces, and the military. This lack of public confidence reflects widespread suspicion that politicians lack the capacity for responsible self-regulation of their professional conduct.

This suspicion might be well founded. After all, politics is an occupation open to all comers, with no easily discernable professional training that might qualify would-be politicians for political practice. The best-known case for treating politics as a vocation – that presented by Max Weber (1994) – certainly had an ethical theme, and related writings by Weber highlight the importance of supervised experience and career training in the development of political leaders. But remember the nature of this ethical theme: politics can be treated as a vocation because of the distinctive calling seen in the practice of truly great political leaders who are prepared to live for and not simply off politics. These exceptional public figures not only break the rules but also break the mold of conventional political ethics. They take personal responsibility for their own political conduct and are prepared to be judged by the consequences of their own decisions. By taking responsibility they are not simply taking charge but, in democratic systems, preparing themselves to face a wider public reckoning of their political ethics.

Weber's approach is less an argument for professionalism and more for exceptionalism: political ethics are exceptions to the normal ethical rules. This is one of the most influential arguments in favor of a kind of ethical autonomy for politics. But it is an argument that seems to concede too much autonomy, sheltering irresponsible schemers beneath the scaffolding intended for responsible leaders. Weber's ethic is compatible with the dirty-hands ethic, which, certainly in the time since Weber, has been reformulated to justify everything from the grand exceptionalism of a (capital M) Machiavellian leader to the corrupt conduct of many (small m) machiavellian schemers. What holds for leaders does not necessarily hold for schemers. This schemer stealth is a classic example of what gives professional ethics a bad name. Norms of appropriateness devised to apply to distinct and distinguished practitioners are seized on by indistinct and undistinguished competitors. The danger is that any public benefit accruing to professional claims of ethical exceptionalism will be jeopardized by the private benefits of the professional pretenders. Most professional associations granted self-regulatory powers strive to justify their due diligence in policing their own professional ethics. Once again, politics is exceptional, in that there are so few examples to reassure a suspicious public that politicians deserve to be granted authority to regulate their own affairs.

Periodic stories of corruption are enough to drive out the high hopes for ethically responsible politics.

The dismal record of political self-regulation is one important practical count against political professionalism. Another is the deeper theoretical reservation about the ethical integrity of professional or role ethics. One of the most striking examples of the critique of professional ethics in public life comes from the recent novel *Elizabeth Costello* by the 2003 Nobel Prize winner for literature, J. M. Coetzee. South African author Coetzee now lives in Australia where he is based at the University of Adelaide – when he is not associated with the Committee on Social Thought at the University of Chicago. His novel contains a dramatic illustration of the merits and pitfalls of professional or role ethics. Within limits, I support a professional approach to the regulation of politicians' ethical conduct, one which confers considerable responsibility on elected or representative politicians to take the initiative in managing the resolution of conflict over alleged breaches of appropriate standards of ethical conduct. The relevance of Coetzee's novel is that it helps clarify what I mean by within limits.

The novel draws attention to the limits of attempts to reduce ethics to role compliance, and implicitly to the dangers of professions' claims of ethical exceptionalism. At the end of the day, being ethical means doing the right thing regardless of what one's profession deems to be right according to the professional role. In the case of politicians, this means that being ethical is more than simply not breaching the rules of official conduct or even obtaining formal clearance from an ethics committee of one's peers. Weber, to his credit, knew this and made the test of ethical responsibility a demanding version of consequentialism: having the courage to stand firm, taking personal responsibility for noncompliance with the unconditional obligations of conventional orthodoxies, and being prepared to justify the public benefits of one's deviation from traditional norms.

RETHINKING THE ETHICAL IN PROFESSIONAL ETHICS

The novel *Elizabeth Costello* is subtitled *Eight Lessons*, with the eight substantive chapters each tackling a particular lesson. The topic of professional ethics appears in the last lesson, entitled "At the Gate," when the chief character is called on to account for her moral beliefs (Coetzee, 2003, pp. 193–225). This character is an imaginary Australian writer, Elizabeth

Costello, who in her older years becomes the invited celebrity at many literary and academic conferences. She knows that her celebrity reflects her early work, not her present writing, and she knows that these invitations cannot last. In some ways, the end of these invitations would be a blessed relief as she would be released from the obligation of having to explain herself and her work, a task which she finds increasingly difficult as she ages and rethinks the merits of her earlier work and becomes increasingly aware of the better work that she has never completed. Much of the novel deals with this tension between the public persona of the author and the private character of the writer who is increasingly detached from her prominent role as celebrity author. Tired of making public statements, Elizabeth Costello retreats into a private world where she permits greater honesty about herself and her talents as a writer and as a person.

Lesson eight deals with Elizabeth Costello's final lesson as she imagines what her final act of public scrutiny at the gate of heaven might look like. Think of this as her imaginary anticipation of her most important public justification of her use of her time down below. This is what she envisions. Arriving at the gates by bus (we are not alone even in this, the final journey), Elizabeth asks permission to pass through the closed gate separating heaven from the world of the still-restless souls. But, before she can enter, she is told by the authorities (the guardians, as they are called) that she must make a statement. "Will this posturing never end?" she thinks, "Why can't I simply pass through the gate and put paid to my earthly debt?" Handed a blank piece of paper, Elizabeth is told that the required statement is to be a statement of what she believes. As the burden of this trial begins to dawn on her, Elizabeth realizes that before she will be found good she must do what she can to provide evidence of her goodness in her beliefs.

Can her beliefs carry this burden? Elizabeth protests that, as a writer, "It is not my profession to believe, just to write. Not my business. I do imitations, as Aristotle would have said." Then she begins a slippery process of plea bargaining: "I can do imitation of belief, if you like." She gets no encouragement. She later regrets this tendency to flare up, which reflects her conviction that she is typically misunderstood and that she deserves better. She is a true professional and wants to be appreciated as a model of a professional writer. Generally, she resists inquiries into her inner world of personal interest and deflects attention back to the external world of her professional capacity.

Now taking an even more radical turn, Elizabeth writes a statement of belief to challenge the rule about statements of belief. Understanding herself as a writer who trades in fictions, she records that she maintains beliefs only provisionally: "Fixed beliefs will stand in my way." So on these grounds, which she calls professional or vocational, Elizabeth requests exemption from a rule requiring every petitioner to hold one or more beliefs. Her strategy is unsuccessful. The guardian tries to encourage her with an incentive. He allows her a brief glimpse of the brilliant light through the open gate, and then in a surprisingly personal gesture he acts out of keeping with his own professional role and pats her on the arm, inviting her to try harder. Forgetting herself or her place, Elizabeth tries to behave smarter rather than harder. She begins to joke with the guard, but to no avail. Humor works no better than serious pleas for exemption, so she accepts that she had better return to the task and prepare the required statement of beliefs.

Elizabeth takes stock of her situation and returns to this, the most difficult act of writing she has ever attempted. Eventually, she completes the statement to her satisfaction and her day in court arrives. Elizabeth is called before the court of nine elderly male judges to present her statement. She begins reading her statement, explaining why writers have no beliefs. Her thesis is simple: "My calling: dictation secretary." Later she identifies this as a secretary's way of life, their special vocation being to record but not to judge the worth of what they hear. Claiming that as a writer it is not her role to interrogate or to judge the beliefs of those about whom she writes, Elizabeth says that what she writes is what she hears, not what people might want to hear. As a good secretary, the writer should have no beliefs. It is inappropriate to the function. Her rather compelling argument is that personal beliefs act as obstacles to writers, impeding their capacity to hear properly what others say and believe.

The response is not long coming. Says one judge: "Without beliefs we are not human." Elizabeth's response is that her sense of duty follows her function, with the result that "I have beliefs but I do not believe in them." The next response is quick and acute: "What effect," the judge asks, "does this lack of belief have on your humanity?" Elizabeth protests that her own humanity is of no consequence, claiming that her own emptiness is outweighed by her contribution as a writer to the humanity of her readers. For professional reasons, Elizabeth cannot afford to believe: she cannot afford to take herself too seriously. She begins to appreciate that this must sound as though she is treating the court proceedings with contempt.

At this point a judicial voice asks: "And what of the Tasmanians?" What might appear an obtuse aside is, in fact, a confronting move intended to tease out whether this Australian writer really has no beliefs to guide her in thinking about the miserable fate of the indigenous Tasmanians – exterminated, Elizabeth now recognizes to herself, by her countrymen, her ancestors. A judge asks why Elizabeth presents herself "not in your own person but as a special case, a special destiny, a writer ... ?" Forcefully, the judge asks if being a professional secretary means that one makes no judgments and is therefore bankrupt of conscience. Elizabeth now knows that she is cornered, beaten down by what appears to be a contest of rhetoric rather than a real interrogation into truth. Weighed under by too many heady abstractions, Elizabeth departs the hearing with a severe headache, knowing that she has lost her case.

Eventually she gets a second chance. She is now aware that her problem is that she cannot afford to believe, because in her line of work one has to suspend belief. Despite this, Elizabeth gets her second hearing, this time before a new panel of judges, smaller than the first and now including a female judge. She takes advice from another petitioner and presents a case illustrating her passion rather than her beliefs. It is a riveting performance, an exemplary apologia of her life history, presented not as a writer but "as an old woman ... telling you what I remember" – a remarkable presentation about her memories of her childhood in rural Victoria and her relish for the natural environment. The judges are confused. Is Elizabeth replacing her former plea with its absence of beliefs with a new one based on explicit beliefs? Or, are her recollections of her passionate life evidence of a very human belief in life? Elizabeth's desperately truthful answers to their many questions are attempts to defend the integrity of both her two formal statements of belief. This is of little avail, finally provoking the judges to howl with laughter at this picture of strained personal integrity. Elizabeth recognizes that the special fidelities of her vocation will not allow her to win this final rite of passage.

Coetzee does not allow us to see any further into Elizabeth Costello's imagined final saga. The lesson ends where it began, with Elizabeth restlessly wondering just what it takes to get through the gates to the peace on the other side. Elizabeth ponders her new knowledge of the cost of her own loyalties to her vocation, appreciating that fidelity is the word on which all hinges. At least she has learned that pride in her professionalism does not count for much in the eyes of her gatekeepers. The advice to try the path of passion is useful because it brings out more of her own personal beliefs, even if Elizabeth is ill prepared to explain their meaning. Her tendency to slip back into her professional mode of nonevaluative recording probably shows that the early passion has faded, at a cost only now beginning to be appreciated in the afterlife of this gifted writer.

Where does this leave us? Elizabeth Costello presents herself very much as an individual but for our limited purposes, which do less than justice to

Coetzee's own purposes, she can stand as an example of a professional type. Professions differ, and not all have the same degree of impersonality that the writer Costello thinks appropriate to her calling. Nevertheless, this studious impersonality, with its restraints on partiality of judgment in the business of storytelling, causes us to wonder about the parallels with other professions. In general, ethics of professionalism are variations on this theme of impersonality. Professional ethics tell practitioners to carry out their duties informed by their professional as distinct from their personal judgment about a responsible course of conduct. This highlights rather than minimizes the role of discretionary judgment in professional practice, but according to a demanding model of discretion with little or no place for personal value judgment. For good reasons, practice is never as tidy as this impersonal model: the best professionals tend to be good human beings as well as good professional practitioners. In the context of his novel, Coetzee invites us to ask if the judges are so blind that they cannot see that Elizabeth Costello is a good person as well as a good writer. Perhaps they are the models of professional limitation, so blinded by their adherence to form that they fail to give Elizabeth her due justice.

RETHINKING THE POLITICAL IN POLITICAL ETHICS

I move now from reorienting ethics to reorienting politics. The first reorientation attempted to widen the scope of appropriate ethical conduct to include the positive pole of the decent as well as the negative pole of the dishonest. Of course, broadening the category of researchable conduct does nothing to increase the incidence of decent conduct. Broadening the category simply opens up the possibility of fresh research into debates over decency to balance the prevailing preoccupation with debates over dishonesty. Decency typically begins with compliance with the rules, but there is plenty of scope for debate over the supralegal expectations of appropriate political conduct. To my mind, this is as much a political as an ethical question: in fact, it is an ethico-political question.

The second reorientation reinforces the turn from political ethics generally to ethical politics more specifically. If democracy is the basic political norm under consideration, then the study of ethical politics is going to involve investigation of a democratic ethic of shared responsibility for self-government. What orientation to the political would be compatible with this new research impetus? My suggestion is one drawn from theories of deliberative democracy because of their attention to the importance of norms of responsible political argument in structuring democratic politics. To say that decency or ethical responsibility among politicians is an ethico-political question is to say that standards of appropriate conduct are, in a democracy, ideally determined through responsible public deliberation over the forms and substance of ethical politics. This allows for considerable contribution by politicians through open and accountable systems of self-regulation of suspect or debated instances of political conduct. While the standards of appropriate conduct might be thought to belong to the democracy itself, responsibility for detailed management of claims and counterclaims over suspect conduct rests with serving politicians, in keeping with their public responsibilities as representatives of the political community.

What institutional implications flow? To me, the most important principle is that professional political ethics only makes sense if we recognize the collective character of political professionalism. Think of this as a version of the many hands thesis: political responsibility is shared responsibility – between electors and the elected, between executive and legislative officials, between political branches and the judiciary, between cabinet ministers and the bureaucracy, between insiders and outsiders, and so on. In keeping with the many hands thesis, politicians can evade ethical responsibility by claiming that others took a greater role in instances of debatable conduct.

There is another dimension to this collective arrangement sometimes neglected in the many hands literature. This is the other side of the evasion story: political ethics is not so much about individual conduct as about shared responsibility for the conduct of relationships. If we put to one side the conventional approach to criminal misconduct through abuse of office, there is still plenty to investigate in the legal but questionable conduct by politicians in the use and abuse of relationships of public power.

Westminster-derived parliamentary systems provide many examples: in the ways that prime ministers dominate relationships with cabinets; ministers dominate relationships with civil servants; ministerial consultants dominate relationships with both ministers and civil servants; and higher civil servants dominate relationships with lower civil servants, who in turn dominate service providers who dominate consumers of public services. I emphasize domination to bring out the incompatibility of these sorts of power relationships with democratic norms. This recital of dominating relationships is a caricature but it conveys the message: political ethics is about many things, not least the conduct of those official relationships among public institutions that constitute the political and policy process. The study of political ethics deals with the state of relationships among the many political offices sharing political power, including the basic organizing offices of citizen and government. Thus, political ethics includes the study of the norms that constitute democracy as evident in the political management of governance relationships.

A final institutional consequence to note here is that political relationships are relationships of mutuality. Political ethics cannot be gauged solely through investigation of one party to the relationship. Indeed, whole webs of relationships influence the political conduct of individual political actors. The institutional implication is that political ethics should include the study of the conduct of public processes and not just the study of the conduct of individual actors. To give but one illustration, parliamentary systems typically have codes of ministerial conduct, occasionally even including independent advisors on ethics and integrity. Within limits, these codes of conduct can help clarify expected standards of official conduct by ministers. But in almost all instances, the codes are creatures of the political executive, illustrating a very circumscribed relationship between the holders of executive power. When push comes to shove, professed standards of high responsibility are overridden by operational norms of executive convenience.

The Australian story is one of prime ministerial discretion to interpret ministerial conduct in the light of the political interests of the serving government. The relationship does not include the wider body of elected representatives, despite the constitutional rhetoric of responsible parliamentary government. Elsewhere I have argued that Parliament has only itself to blame because it has failed to deal itself in by establishing or instituting a relationship with ministers whereby they agree to honor parliamentary as distinct from ministerial standards of public conduct (Uhr, 2001a). This failure also means that Parliament has failed in its relationship with electors by not living up to its responsibilities as an accountability agency protecting the public interest in open and honest government.

ETHICS BY EXAMPLE

I bring this together with an Australian example, the so-called *children overboard affair* in the lead up to the 2001 national election. This example balances my earlier use of Coetzee's novel with an account of Australian lapses in political decency that reads all too much like a novel. If only the events described were fictional.

There is a growing academic literature on the political and administrative ethics surrounding these events, most of which suggests that the reelection of the Howard government came at the price of unprecedented damage to the government's reputation for public integrity. The government won the election and, not surprisingly, defends its integrity in terms of having earned the public mandate to retain the responsibilities of executive power. The government has defended its ethical credentials by pointing to the balance between its right to use the responsibilities of governmental power as it sees fit (acknowledging that this right is subject to the limits of the law) and its proven public accountability as evidenced by its electoral victory. From the government's point of view, no law was broken during its tenure in office and the people have spoken, giving fresh legitimacy to the governing coalition. In this simplified account, the government's take on ethics in government is a classic attempt to justify the government's discretionary use of its powers by reference to the renewal of public trust in the government granted by electors.

Mandates are tricky things, and the same election also returned a solid nongovernment majority in the Senate, which contests the right of any government to claim a mandate to govern. The Senate select committee that inquired into a certain maritime incident reported adversely on the government's ethical performance. A subsequent Senate committee built on this initial inquiry and reported the need for new legislation to bring greater accountability to bear on government's use and abuse of the hidden power of ministerial staff (Select Committee on a Certain Maritime Incident, 2002; Finance and Public Administration References Committee, 2003). Both reports contain detailed examinations of suspect conduct of government ministers in abusing their powers over the public service and abusing responsibilities stipulated in the ministerial code of conduct not to deceive the public and their obligation to correct any misleading public information, even in cases where there has been no deliberate intention to deceive.

The best investigative account of the children overboard affair and related incidents is Marr and Wilkinson's (2003) *Dark Victory* (see also Weller, 2002). This book is a war story of sorts, detailing the armed resistance marshaled by the Australian government against the perceived threat posed by boat people to the security of Australian sovereignty in the months leading up to a general election. It is also a political thriller, documenting the struggle within the government over deployment of military forces and the daring risk management of the government's most astute political advisers, who won out against traditional caution, and risk-averseness of the professional military, particularly the Navy, committed as much to due process as to results.

The authors suggest that the 2001 electoral victory is stained, marking the Howard government's deceit of the public through manipulation of the truth about the significance of the increase in asylum seekers (boat people) during 2001, culminating in the contortions of the children overboard affair which helped consolidate electoral support for the government. The attack became an election theme: the undocumented aliens were not only unwelcome queue jumpers but were untrustworthy and uncivilized manipulators of Australian assistance, even to the point of throwing children overboard to get Australian compliance with their demands for rescue and access to Australian care and custody. Or so the government claimed, attributing the intelligence to Navy officials when it originally seemed correct, but failing to mention subsequent contrary doubts or uncertainties when the story wore thin.

CONCLUSION

The above example illustrates my focus on professional relationships. It also illustrates my interest in political conduct that is, paradoxically, as corrupting as it is legal. Although this Australian practice is broadly consistent with current regulatory expectations, it falls far short of the regulative ideal I began with. The story is significant because it highlights the suspect ethical quality of so many political relationships in Australian government – including the relationships of accountability. I have no magic box of regulatory mechanisms that can transform Australian or similar systems. Intent on bringing politicians closer to the task of self-regulation, I have contrasted prevailing tendencies with a regulative ideal. For all practical purposes, the prevailing tendencies are winning.

The children overboard story does not turn on mundane conflicts of interest but on conflicts of constitutional responsibility, taking constitutional to refer not to the black letter of the law but to the norms of the different political offices constituting a democracy. It is a classic example of the contestability of political ethics, testing in unprecedented ways the decency of many political relationships by politicians whose personal decency is not the question. It is a good example because it shows how political corruption advances under the cover of many disguises, including the disguise of politics as usual (Uhr, 2001b, pp. 723–726). Putting Australian developments to one side, I conclude with some general lessons arising from this attempt to apply a professional ethics framework to democratic political ethics.

Most forms of professional or role ethics apply group norms to recognized individual practitioners of the profession in question. Politics is different, not only because the professional skill is unrelated to any specialized training and any associated professional academy, but also because the practice in question is fundamentally shared or collective. This is so particularly in democratic regimes, which quite properly pride themselves on participative public decision making and typically privilege the constitutional power of an elected assembly, even to the point of protecting the participation rights of nongovernment or opposition members. The collective nature of political professionalism extends beyond power sharing within the ranks of elected representatives to include relationships between politicians and related professionals in public administration.

In this approach, professional political ethics refers to the widely distributed responsibility for determining appropriate standards relevant to these relationships of shared power and, in addition, to the collective resolution of disputed instances of unethical conduct. Particulars of responsible ethical conduct vary according to the nature of the political office under discussion, the precise ethical responsibilities varying with the power relationships managed by different political offices. This range of official responsibilities is itself subject to any formal constitutional constraints – a matter for the collective determination of the assembled professional politicians, subject to public oversight (Uhr, 1998b, pp. 11–23).

Thus, professional political ethics as used here refers to the collective determination of appropriate political conduct, which will be more ethically responsible when structured around due processes of fair and open political deliberation in place of politics as usual. Most existing systems of political ethics try to overcome the defects of politics as usual by conferring special power on small groups of politicians comprising dedicated ethics or privileges committees with responsibility for investigating and adjudicating ethics infringements, judged against the rules or codes of official conduct. My idealized model differs because it is relationship-centered rather than a rule-centered approach. My approach is inevitably more uncertain and unpredictable than narrower forms of professionalism based on compliance with the rules. But this very openness reflects the true nature of political ethics as a matter of political judgment, with disputes managed through collective political deliberation over appropriate relationships of power – representatives relating to their own offices and relating to other public offices sharing public power.

The implications of this focus on collective professionalism are considerable, including, not least, a surprising role for the public as the court of ultimate appeal. Democratic politics rests on the relationship between the professionals and the people, and the ethical quality of democratic politics depends in no small part on the ethics of the relationship between the people and their political representatives. Democracy can be thought to hold the people in some sort of professional regard, in that they have the responsibility (the final say) over the system of self-regulation we call democratic self-government.

REFERENCES

Bradley, F. H. (1927). *Ethical studies* (2nd ed.). Oxford, UK: Clarendon Press.
Coetzee, J. M. (2003). *Elizabeth Costello*. Sydney: Random House Australia.
Cooper, T. L., & Wright, N. D. (Eds) (1992). *Exemplary public administrators: Character and leadership in government*. San Francisco: Jossey-Bass.
Finance and Public Administration References Committee. (2003). *Staff employed under the Members of Parliament (Staff) Act 1984*. Canberra: The Australian Senate.
Marr, D., & Wilkinson, M. (2003). *Dark victory*. Sydney: Allen and Unwin.
Select Committee on a Certain Maritime Incident. (2002). *Report*. Canberra: The Australian Senate.
Sidgwick, H. (1967). *History of ethics*. London: Macmillan.
Uhr, J. (1998a). *Deliberative democracy in Australia: The changing place of parliament*. Melbourne: Cambridge University Press.
Uhr, J. (1998b). Democracy and the ethics of representation. In: N. Preston, & C. Sampford, with C.-A. Bois (Eds), *Ethics and political practice* (pp. 11–23). London: Routledge.
Uhr, J. (2001a). Moderating ministerial ethics. In: J. Fleming & I. Holland (Eds), *Motivating inisters to morality* (pp. 187–200). Aldershot, UK: Ashgate.
Uhr, J. (2001b). Public service ethics in Australia. In: T. L. Cooper (Ed.), *Handbook of administrative ethics*, (2nd ed.) (pp. 719–740). New York: Marcel Dekker.
Uhr, J. (2005). *Terms of trust: Arguments over ethics in Australian government*. Sydney: University of New South Wales Press.
Weber, M. (1994). The profession and vocation of politics. In: P. Lassman & R. Speirs (Eds), *Political writings*. Cambridge, UK: Cambridge University Press.
Weller, P. (2002). *Don't tell the Prime Minister*. Melbourne: Scribe Publications.

ETHICAL POLITICAL CONDUCT AND FIDELITY TO THE DEMOCRATIC ETHOS

Colin M. Macleod

ABSTRACT

Ethical conduct by politicians involves more than respect for the law and adherence to rules governing conflicts of interest. It displays fidelity to a democratic ethos. In this chapter, I provide a characterization of the democratic ethos and sketch its connection to recent work in democratic theory. Second, I describe the sort of fidelity to the democratic ethos that is a condition of ethical conduct by politicians. Third, I suggest a mechanism through which greater adherence to a suitable version of the democratic ethos might be achieved.

My point of departure is a set of observations about the state of democratic practice that poses a challenge to democratic legitimacy, the most important of which is that citizens are disaffected from democratic politics. Many feel that elected officials inadequately represent their views and interests. Citizens generally view professional politicians with suspicion and disdain.

They have grown accustomed to political scandal and many believe that corruption pervades the political arena.

Similarly, the exercise of political power seems to reflect a triumph of partisanship over a commitment to serve the public interest. Photo opportunities are staged; policy announcements are timed to maximize coverage of popular measures and minimize attention to unpopular measures. Contemporary political campaigns seem to be dominated by powerful special interests who try to orchestrate electoral outcomes by employing sophisticated techniques – spin doctors, focus groups, elaborate polling, hot-button issues, etc. – designed to manipulate the electorate.

In general, strategy has displaced substance in democratic discourse. There is little reflective discussion and examination of substantive policy issues or political principles in the mass media. News coverage focuses on who can win and what strategies are likely to be successful. There is, unfortunately, much truth to James Fishkin's characterization of democratic practice as dominated by "sleazeball tactics and shrinking sound bites."[1]

Public cynicism about politics is disturbing in its own right, but the malaise infecting democratic practice seems even worse once we recognize that the cynicism is paired with political apathy and ignorance. Participation in democratic politics is low and dropping. The public is alarmingly ill-informed about many important issues.

How might this malaise constitute a threat to democratic legitimacy? The precise nature of democratic legitimacy is, of course, a contested matter, but I assume that even a modest or minimalist conception of legitimacy has at least two basic dimensions. First, there must be fair political procedures that are suitably reflective of and responsive to the will of the people. Second, there must be reasonably broad and meaningful public engagement with these procedures. Fair democratic procedures that are not accessed by most citizens or accessed by citizens who are ill-informed and unreflective about the choices facing them cannot reliably generate outcomes that reflect the will of the people.[2]

In a democracy, the legitimate exercise of political power must somehow be authorized by the collective decisions of the governed, and this sort of authorization arguably rests on the actual involvement of citizens in the authorization process.[3] So even if we concede, for the sake of argument, that existing democratic processes satisfy the first criterion of legitimacy adequately, current levels of public cynicism, apathy, and ignorance should give us pause about whether the second criterion of legitimacy is adequately met. Meaningful public engagement with democratic processes is dangerously poor (Ackerman & Fishkin, 2004).

Many factors undoubtedly contribute to the malaise of democratic practice. One might point to defects in the design of basic democratic institutions, to failures of civic education, to the dulling effects of a shallow consumerist culture, or to the failure of the mass media to provide responsible coverage of politics. In this chapter, however, my focus is quite narrow. I want to explore some ways in which we might understand and begin to address obstacles to meaningful engagement in democratic processes that are rooted in the conduct of politicians. For ease of exposition I shall refer to politicians, but I shall use this term to refer both to public office holders and to public office seekers, including those who do not succeed in attaining public office. My hunch is that unethical political conduct is an obstacle to meaningful engagement, but I also suspect that common construals of the scope and nature of democratic ethics are too narrow. I shall sketch the contours of a broader and, I hope, attractive conception of ethical conduct.

The general claim I make is that ethical conduct by politicians consists, at least in large part, in conduct that displays fidelity to a democratic ethos. In other words, an account of democratic ethics should be grounded in our understanding of democratic values.[4] In light of this, I shall argue that ethical conduct by politicians involves more than respect of the law and adherence to rules governing conflicts of interest. I shall also make a proposal about a strategy for improving the ethical conduct of politicians, but in order to set the stage for this I need to make some remarks about how we might identify and interpret standards for evaluating the conduct of politicians. The rest of the chapter is organized in the following way. First, I provide a brief characterization of the democratic ethos and sketch its connection to recent work in democratic theory. Second, I consider different interpretations of what sort of fidelity to the democratic ethos should be considered a condition of ethical conduct by politicians. Third, I suggest a mechanism through which greater adherence to a suitable version of the democratic ethos might be achieved.

THE DEMOCRATIC ETHOS

A democratic ethos can be understood as a set of values and commitments embraced by members of a community who are committed to a flourishing, and not merely functioning, democracy. Some of the basic features of a defensible democratic ethos seem fairly straightforward. Democrats are committed, for instance, to nonviolent means of resolving political disagreements, and the procedures they adopt are predicated on an ideal of the basic political equality of citizens. In representative forms of democracy, we expect candidates to abide by the articulated rules of fair democratic procedure both in the pursuit of power and in the exercise of power that comes with elected office. We expect politicians to be responsive to the concerns of citizens and constituents but also to be sensitive to the public good. As I implicitly suggested above, democracy also has a deliberative component. Democrats value informed, reflective, open, and honest discourse about political matters in which reasoned justifications for policies and positions are presented and considered by politicians and citizens alike. Meaningful engagement with democratic institutions by the public can be hampered if political actors – e.g., citizens, the media, public servants, special interests, or politicians – behave in ways that betray these ideals.

I think the idea of a democratic ethos provides a fruitful way of thinking about contour and content of democratic ethics. The suggestion is that we consider what kind of conduct by political actors is required by fidelity to the democratic ethos. I take it as obvious, for example, that efforts by politicians to buy votes, rig voting lists, or otherwise subvert the fair functioning of basic democratic procedures are betrayals of the democratic ethos. They are, as such, unethical and they can diminish public engagement with democratic institutions. Diminished engagement can be caused both directly and indirectly. It occurs directly when political conduct blocks or reduces access of some citizens to normal opportunities for democratic participation. It occurs indirectly when awareness of unethical political conduct alienates the public from the normal democratic process.

Of course, noting that fidelity to the democratic ethos requires conduct that displays respect for democratic procedures is hardly controversial. The question is what more is required of an ethical politician. In this context, the issue I want to broach concerns what might be called the deliberative responsibilities of politicians. These are the responsibilities of politicians to conduct themselves in ways that contribute to reflective discussion and consideration of matters of importance. To what degree, if any, does fidelity to the democratic ethos impose constraints and requirements on how politicians should discharge their deliberative responsibilities? I shall briefly consider three ways of answering this question, each of which is linked to a different understanding of democratic legitimacy.

PLURALISM AND DEMOCRATIC LEGITIMACY

Many recent discussions of democratic theory treat the problem of legitimacy as centrally concerned with the task of devising an appropriate response to the pluralism characteristic of modern societies. Pluralism has different dimensions. One dimension concerns social, cultural, regional, national, ethnic, and linguistic diversity. There are, in short, salient sociological differences in societies that for various historical, economic, and logistical reasons have some claim to political recognition. A different, but to some degree related, dimension of pluralism concerns moral pluralism that gives rise to political disagreement.[5] Citizens of the same political community hold different and divergent religious, philosophical, and moral views that affect their opinions on political matters. (This is roughly what Rawls refers to as the fact of reasonable pluralism.) Legitimate democratic institutions arguably should be responsive to both these dimensions of pluralism by: (a) giving suitable recognition in political structures and processes to the diverse make-up of the political community, and (b) providing a "morally justifiable way of making binding collective decisions in the face of continuing moral conflict" (Gutmann & Thompson, 2000, p. 161).

Simplifying matters somewhat, there are two main kinds of responses to the challenge of devising a suitable response to moral pluralism.[6] First, proceduralist accounts treat legitimacy as sufficiently secured by the existence of fair procedures for the aggregation of the interests. The exercise of political power is justified if it is sanctioned by a fair political process – e.g., majority rule – that gives equal consideration to the interests of citizens. For my purposes, what matters is that on proceduralist views democracy legitimacy is detached from any substantive requirement that democratic processes be sensitive to the character of the reasons that ground citizens' political preferences. This does not imply that proceduralist accounts necessarily reject a distinction between better and worse forms of political reasoning or justification. But such a distinction is not crucial to assessments of the smooth operation of democracy. Democracy can flourish even if political discourse is unreflective and shallow and public reasoning is demonstrably poor.

Proceduralism has its adherents, but many theorists now argue that it offers an impoverished account of legitimacy that does not take seriously enough the ideal of political equality at the heart of democracy. Recognizing the equal political standing of citizens involves more than assigning citizens equal formal weight as inputs in a fair aggregative process. Instead, political equality entails a form of mutual respect that requires contestants in political competitions to grapple publicly with the reasons for rival positions. The acceptability of an outcome determined by a fair process is partly a function of there being a genuine commitment by participants in the process to engage in reason giving and reason taking.

A second way of responding to pluralism is provided by deliberative conceptions of democracy. These accounts view democratic legitimacy as rooted in a conception of public justification that is expressly sensitive to the character of reasons that figure in democratic discourse. They do not eschew procedural mechanisms for generating authoritative collective decisions, but they insist that the institutional arrangements relied upon to generate decisions should foster reasoned discussion and reflection on public issues. For purposes of this discussion, we can distinguish stronger and weaker versions of deliberative democracy. Robust forms of deliberative democracy of the sort associated with Cohen (1989, 2003) and Gutmann and Thompson (1995, 1996, 2000) treat the process of collective decision making as ideally regulated by a special conception of mutual justification. Legitimate exercises of political power are ones grounded in reasons that "citizens who are motivated to find fair terms of cooperation can reasonably accept" (Gutmann & Thompson, 2000, p. 161). These theories revolve around the development of a substantive conception of public reason that forms the basis for achieving consensus among citizens with divergent comprehensive moral or religious views. Less ambitious conceptions of deliberative democracy place emphasis on more generic and formal features of good deliberation. Public discourse should display sensitivity to relevant empirical facts, reasoned justifications for public policy stances should be publicly available, and citizens should have opportunities to reflect carefully upon and discuss political proposals, etc. Unlike robust forms of deliberative democracy, moderate forms are not regulated by a special ideal of public reason. For example, Ackerman and Fishkin (2004) point to three features of good democratic deliberation: (a) it reflects acknowledgement of uncontroversial facts; (b) it displays normative completeness – an awareness and understanding of arguments offered in support of rival views; and (c) it is grounded in receptiveness to entertaining the views of others seriously. A moderate conception of deliberative democracy aims at collective decision making that reflects mutual understanding and the informed reflection of the citizens with whom authority ultimately resides. Unlike the robust conception, successful deliberation in the face of moral disagreement does not require, even as an ideal, the provision and acceptance of reasons for positions that are "persuasive to all" (Cohen, 1989, p. 23).

CHARACTERIZING DELIBERATIVE RESPONSIBILITIES

I have offered this thumbnail sketch of approaches to democratic legitimacy because I think our conception of what fidelity to the democratic ethos entails by way of deliberative responsibilities will be influenced by our conception of democratic legitimacy.

Minimalism

Proceduralism, for instance, suggests a fairly minimalist conception of democratic ethics in general, and the deliberative responsibilities of politicians in particular. On this approach, fidelity to the democratic ethos by politicians principally consists of conduct that is commensurate with maintaining the integrity of the expressly articulated rules that govern the operation of fair democratic procedures. Ethical conduct consists in respecting the law and faithfully abiding by regulations concerning conflict of interest, campaign finance, and political interference with operation of the public service. In terms of deliberative responsibilities, politicians have duties to respect the rights of citizens, to express their views publicly, and to gain access to information about government activity. Politicians should faithfully reflect, in accordance with fair procedures for doing so, the preferences of the electorate. And presumably, politicians should not misrepresent the public record – e.g., by distorting the state of public finances – or engage in other forms of deliberate deception. However, fidelity to democratic procedures per se does not require proactive efforts to stimulate and enrich public deliberation about political matters. Thus, decisions on whether to debate political opponents, to present arguments in support of positions, to emphasize image over substance on the campaign trail, or to meet with the press regularly all fall outside the purview of a democratic ethics tied to proceduralism. Instead, such matters are considered discretionary, and are appropriately decided by appeal to strategic political considerations.

In my view, the minimalist conception of democratic ethics is as unattractive as the proceduralism from which it flows. Nonetheless, I think it is quite consistent with popular understandings of scope and content of ethical standards for the regulation of political conduct. With the odd exception of sexual indiscretions in a politician's personal life, unethical conduct by politicians is viewed mainly as conduct that involves a conflict of interest or the abuse of power that contravenes procedural rules.

Robust Deliberative Responsibilities

Proceduralist accounts of legitimacy yield too narrow a view of the deliberative responsibilities of politicians. Now let us consider how interpreting the democratic ethos through the lens of deliberative democracy affects our understanding of the deliberative responsibilities of politicians. Given the distinction between robust and moderate conceptions of deliberative democracy, there are two corresponding accounts of deliberative responsibilities.

Fidelity to a robust conception yields a very demanding, though not unattractive, account of politicians' deliberative responsibilities.[7] In conducting themselves ethically, politicians would have duties to engage in thoughtful and mutually respectful political discourse and to refrain from pursuing shallow and manipulative political strategies that derail rather than facilitate reflective deliberation. Moreover, they would have a duty to restrict the reasons they invoke in political discussion to those compatible with a special conception of public reason. There is controversy as to how the relevant conception of public reason is best understood (and different deliberative democrats favor different construals). But a general worry here is that the category of eligible reasons, insofar as it predicated on substantive distinctions between reasons, is unfeasibly and unacceptably restrictive. It is difficult to imagine, for instance, how politicians could be reasonably expected to restrict their public political discourse to reasons persuasive to all. But something like this restriction would seem to be entailed by Cohen's model of deliberative democracy. Fidelity to a democratic ethos that included a rarefied notion of public reason would be too demanding and would set the bar for ethical conduct unreasonably high. Even the requirement that politicians refrain from appeals to sectarian or controversial religious or philosophical doctrines when offering justifications of their political platforms seems contentious and problematic. Robust deliberative democrats might reply that, properly understood, the substantive constraints entailed by an ideal of public justification are weaker and hence less restrictive than I have suggested. If this turns out to be case, then the contrast between robust and moderate forms of deliberative democracy will be less clear than I have provisionally assumed.

Rather than pursuing this issue further, I will turn to consideration of the deliberative responsibilities entailed by a moderate conception of deliberative democracy that does not impose substantive filters on acceptable forms of political discourse. Robust conceptions of deliberative democracy can be viewed as ways of supplementing and enriching moderate conceptions. So the contours of the deliberative responsibilities of a moderate conception will be relevant, I think, to a robust conception of deliberative responsibilities. In this respect, I hope the discussion of the moderate conception may be of interest even to robust deliberative democrats.

Moderate Deliberative Responsibilities

In a moderate conception of deliberative democracy there are no substantive filters on what counts as an admissible public reason. Instead, the idea is to identify various generic or broadly formal features of reasoned discourse about political matters and to assess the conduct of political actors in relation to an ideologically neutral[8] conception of public reason. In other words, we place a general ideal of mutually respectful and reasoned discourse at the heart of the democratic ethos. The precise parameters of such a conception can be made more precise in various ways, but here are at least some implications of what fidelity to a moderate deliberative ethos would have for understanding the deliberative responsibilities of politicians. First, on the positive side, there would be requirements that politicians provide clear, accurate, full, and accessible information about their political views and policy positions. Second, politicians would have a duty to present, explain, and defend their views and policy proposals in a wide range of public fora (e.g., radio and television appearances, formal debates, etc.). Third, politicians would have a duty to offer justifications for their positions and to engage the views of their rivals. In order to discharge such duties in a meaningful fashion, politicians would also have duties to refrain from conduct of a sort that has become all too familiar. Thus, politicians would have a duty to answer pertinent questions from the public, media, or opponents in a direct and non-evasive fashion. Similarly, they would have duties not to avoid questions (e.g., from the media or the public) or reasonable challenges (e.g., to debate or to respond to criticism) from rivals. There would be a duty to represent the views of political opponents fairly and accurately and to avoid distorting or misleading characterizations of rivals' positions. More generally, politicians would have a duty to eschew political tactics involving misdirection and emotional manipulation of the public.

I hope that this sort of characterization of deliberative responsibilities is attractive, at least as an ideal to which politicians might aspire. I want to suggest, however, that if we accept the idea that ethical conduct is guided by fidelity to the democratic ethos, and if we accept a moderate ideal of deliberative democracy as animating the democratic ethos (at least in part), then we should view violation of deliberative responsibilities by politicians not as a regrettable failure to live up to a laudable but optional ideal. Rather, we should view and label such conduct as unethical. This conceptualization of the scope of democratic ethics is broader than is typical and hence may seem controversial. However, if we find the underlying idea of deliberative democracy attractive, then I think we have a reason to favor a broader construal of democratic ethics. After all, it is plausible to suppose that realization of deliberative democracy depends crucially on the actual conduct of politicians (along with their handlers and advisors). We can hope both to drive home the importance of conduct conducive to genuine deliberation and to secure some commitment to deliberative ideals by treating departures from relevant democratic values as unethical. In effect, the broader conceptualization of political ethics opens the door to moral suasion in the service of democratic ideals. Amy Gutmann (2003) notes that

> when the pressure of moral suasion is justified, it can be welcomed as a way of socializing people to think about how they should live their lives and whether or not they should contribute to just causes. Public life in democracies includes practices of moral suasion. Moral suasion can change how people lead their lives. It also distributes praise and blame in ways that affect people's reputations. (p. 139)

We can adapt and develop Gutmann's observation by envisioning ways in which fidelity to a deliberative democratic ethos could assume greater importance in the public conduct of politicians than it currently does.

SECURING ADHERENCE TO MODERATE DELIBERATIVE NORMS

There are different and sometimes complementary social mechanisms through which adherence to justified social norms can be achieved. In the context of politics, civic education plays a role in developing an understanding of and commitment to the democratic ethos. We teach new citizens and children about democratic procedures and often seek to encourage certain kinds of conduct – e.g., participation in the political process, respect for the law, and tolerance. It might well be a good thing for politicians to be educated in democratic theory, but I assume here, however, that a formal program of civic education alone is not sufficient to secure adherence by politicians to deliberative norms. Instead, I want to briefly examine three other norm-reliant mechanisms for influencing conduct.

First, conduct can be directed and guided by *formal norms*. These are norms that are explicitly, publicly, and authoritatively articulated in the form of official regulations or laws.[9] Those who engage in conduct prohibited by such rules are subject to serious penalties ranging from imprisonment, to fines, or to dismissal. It seems appropriate for there to be formal norms prohibiting political corruption and abuse of power. Similarly, there are good reasons to formalize conflict of interest rules and to punish violators of these rules. The existence of formal norms is typically accompanied by formal processes through which charges of wrongdoing can be made official and which provide those accused of wrongdoing with an opportunity to defend themselves against allegations. I assume that it would not be feasible or appropriate for deliberative responsibilities of the sort I have outlined to be regulated via the establishment of formal norms. We cannot fine a politician who refuses to answer questions directly or to meet with the press regularly.

The link I made between deliberative responsibilities and moral suasion suggests a second way of influencing conduct; namely, by reliance on what I shall label *informal norms*. Informal norms are standards of conduct that are widely known and accepted but are not explicitly or authoritatively articulated. They do not have standing as official laws or rules. The sanction that accompanies violation of them is public disapproval and disapprobation. In the political realm, there are some informal norms that play a significant role in securing democratic legitimacy and the smooth functioning of democratic processes. For example, there are informal norms of civility and cordiality that are often observed in politics. When a well-known politician dies or retires from public office after a long career, it is common for even longstanding political opponents to acknowledge the politician's public service and contributions to the community. Another example is the practice of losers of political contests conceding defeat and congratulating the winners graciously. There is no official rule requiring this kind of conduct and no formal penalty for failing to act appropriately, but I think it is reasonable to say that losers who do not acknowledge defeat appropriately betray the democratic ethos – they seem, at best, grudgingly prepared to abide by the outcome of fair democratic processes.

To some degree, the deliberative responsibilities of politicians are loosely regulated by informal norms. There is a general expectation that politicians will debate their opponents and articulate platforms, and failure to do so occasions public disapprobation to some degree. However, it is arguable that informal norms, at least given the current malaise of democratic practice, are not sufficient to secure strong adherence to deliberative norms. The competitive nature of politics puts pressure on politicians to pursue winning strategies, and if the best winning strategies are ones that diminish the quality of deliberation then it is likely that a commitment to contribute to fulsome democratic deliberation will give way to the desire to win. This will be especially true when other politicians have adopted what are thought to be successful but deliberatively dubious political strategies. Informal deliberative norms have too weak a grip on politicians to prevent the race to the bottom, and we end up with 'sleazeball tactics and shrinking sound bites.'

There is, however, a third (and to my knowledge, underexplored and underutilized) way of influencing conduct that lies between reliance on formal and informal norms. Conduct can be guided by what I shall call *semiformal norms*. These are public standards of conduct that are explicitly and authoritatively articulated, but violation of them carries no official sanction. They provide more express guidance than informal norms and they provide an explicit public affirmation of values relevant, in this context, to ethically responsible conduct by politicians. In this way, they facilitate a form of moral suasion that is arguably more direct and less open to contestation than that provided by informal norms.

Semiformal norms have some parallel with mission statements that include an articulation of the values that are officially embraced by an institution or organization. A common limitation with these mission statements is that, even when they reflect the sincere intentions of those who created them, they can function mainly as public relations devices that provide only a veneer of ethical legitimacy. This occurs, in part, because it is common for ethical standards articulated in mission statements to be vague and platitudinous. (We've all read the standard statements of the form that 'this institution is committed to upholding the highest standards of ethical conduct....') A second problem is that there is seldom any meaningful monitoring of the degree to which the values articulated in a mission statement have been honored by the institution in general or by specific actors in the institution whose conduct is supposed to reflect fidelity to the values.

The scheme of semiformal norms I have in mind for influencing the conduct of politicians in meeting their deliberative responsibilities seeks to avoid the limitations of mission statement style ethics in two ways. First, insofar as possible, the description of the deliberative responsibilities of politicians should be fairly specific. For instance, rather than a platitudinous statement about commitment of politicians to the core values of democracy, there would be a statement of distinct duties. The challenge would be to specify the duties in a way that would permit monitoring of the degree to which the relevant standards had been met. Of course, even with a reasonably determinate description of deliberative responsibilities, there will be room for interpretation about what constitutes appropriate conduct. However, it should be possible to devise standards that will permit identification of obvious and egregious failures to discharge moderate deliberative responsibilities. Second, adherence to the semiformal deliberative norms should be monitored by a politically neutral and independent body, with the authority to issue reports on the degree to which politicians have successfully discharged their deliberative responsibilities. I have in mind here something like a domestic version of what Thomas Pogge (2002, pp. 156–157) has called a *democracy panel*. This is an impartial panel composed of jurists and other experts on democratic procedures who are charged with the task of monitoring the degree to which political communities function democratically. Pogge's democracy panel is intended to assist fledgling democracies in the development and maintenance of basic democratic procedures. It does not focus on monitoring the quality of democratic deliberation. The domestic version of the democracy panel I am suggesting would be focused on deliberative responsibilities.[10] The monitoring of adherence to deliberative norms by such a panel could take two complementary forms. First, there could be a complaint-based form of monitoring – members of the public could lodge complaints with the panel about the conduct of politicians, and the panel could undertake to investigate such complaints. Second, there could be more general oversight of the conduct of politicians with respect to the degree to which deliberative responsibilities are met. The panel might issue an annual report that provides an evaluation of the conduct of politicians and the overall caliber of democratic discourse. The point of the monitoring would not be to subject the conduct of politicians to intrusive and constant scrutiny, but rather to focus attention on the more obvious and egregious failures to discharge deliberative responsibilities. One would expect that public disapprobation would be directed at politicians (or political parties) who were identified as flouting their deliberative responsibilities. In the account of deliberative responsibilities I have offered, such conduct is appropriately labeled as unethical. Presumably, most politicians would seek to avoid being identified as acting unethically even when it would carry no official penalty. So, the creation of semiformal norms along with a suitable monitoring body might well put pressure on politicians to improve their deliberative conduct.

The foregoing is, of course, only the barest sketch of how a scheme of semiformal norms might help to facilitate a more deliberative style of politics. I am sure that various objections could be mounted to the proposal. For instance, one might wonder whether a domestic democracy panel is institutionally feasible or whether it could operate in a suitably impartial and effective manner. Similarly, there might be worries about the appropriateness of an official bureaucratic body monitoring and passing judgement on, even in a generic way, the deliberative conduct of politicians. Such objections, or others, might turn out to be decisive against the current proposal or variants of it. Nonetheless, I think the idea of harnessing semiformal norms in the service of a moderate conception of deliberative democracy is worth further consideration.

CONCLUSION

Gutmann and Thompson claim (1995) that

> the point of a deliberative conception of democracy is not to elevate one institutional form of democracy above the others, but rather to find ways of making each form more deliberative. The practical task of deliberative democrats is to consider how each political institution can be designed to facilitate deliberation. (p. 110)

In this chapter, I have tried to contribute to this practical task in three ways. First, I have argued that the conduct of politicians vis-à-vis deliberative ideals is an appropriate focus of democratic ethics. Second, I have outlined an account of the deliberative responsibilities of politicians that is animated by a moderate conception of deliberative democracy. These first two ideas are linked to the general idea that ethical conduct by politicians should be understood as involving fidelity to a democratic ethos. Finally, I have sketched a scheme of semiformal norms that might be harnessed to encourage politicians to discharge their deliberative responsibilities more fully and meaningfully. The analysis presented does not, of course, provide the basis of a full remedy for the malaise of democratic practice that I noted at the outset. But perhaps it is a start toward a partial remedy.

NOTES

1. Fishkin coined this phrase during a lecture to the Victoria Colloquium in Political, Social, and Legal Theory at the University of Victoria on April 2, 2004. It resonated deeply with the audience.

2. Some elite and social choice theories of democracy may reject the requirement of meaningful public engagement with fair democratic procedures. However, for the purposes of this discussion, I shall assume without argument that a broadly participatory model of democracy is sound and feasible (Pateman, 1970; Barber, 1984). Contemporary theories of deliberative democracy also endorse this aspect of legitimacy, although they tend to set the standards of citizen reasoning quite high (see Freeman, 2000 and Chambers, 2003 for useful reviews of developments in deliberative theory that bear on this point). For my purposes, meaningful public engagement in democratic politics does not require all citizens to acquire technical expertise about complex policy issues or to engage in sophisticated debates in political philosophy. But citizens should be conversant with the principal issues facing them in a way that does not reflect gross ignorance of relevant facts. There is evidence that even this modest standard is not met. For example, "in the run-up to the war with Iraq and in the post-war period, a significant portion of the American public has held a number of misperceptions relevant to the rationales for going to war with Iraq" (Kull, Ramsay, & Lewis, 2003, p. 571). In the summer of 2003, 45–52% of Americans falsely believed that the U.S. had discovered clear evidence of a link between Saddam Hussien and al Qaeda (Kull et al., 2003, p. 572).

3. The authorization process need not involve direct involvement by citizens in decision making through a form of direct democracy. Various forms of representative democracy can provide suitable processes of authorization.

4. This may sound true by definition, but I think many popular construals of the ethical conduct of politicians treat, at least implicitly, ethical conduct as detached from democratic values. Ethical conduct is characterized in terms of generic moral virtues such as honesty, courage, and loyalty without much attention to how manifestation of these virtues bears upon the realization of democratic values. For instance, the fact that a politician has a successful marriage or deeply loves his or her spouse is often seen as a political virtue even though there is no obvious connection between this fact and successful or virtuous discharge of the duties of public office.

5. What I have called salient sociological pluralism often issues in moral pluralism, but it need not. For instance, ethnically or linguistically different groups need not disagree on matters of political policy. There may, nonetheless, be reason to give recognition to sociological diversity even when it does not track political disagreement.

6. I only briefly sketch the contrast between proceduralist and deliberative accounts of democracy. There are various formulations of each of these views. In addition, a third view – constitutional democracy – is sometimes distinguished from either of these approaches. See Gutmann and Thompson (1995, pp. 99–105) for a discussion of the contrast between deliberative democracy and constitutional democracy.

7. I assume that the deliberative responsibilities of deliberative conceptions of democracy include those entailed by a proceduralist conception. The key difference is that the former conceptions impose additional demands on ethical conduct.

8. Perhaps complete neutrality is impossible, since even attention to formal features of reasoned discourse may have substantive implications.

9. By authoritatively articulated, I mean roughly created by an elected body that has the legal authority to prescribe enforceable standards of conduct.

10. The domestic democracy panel might operate under the auspices of a government ethics commissioner. The chief role of the recently created ethics commissioner for the Canadian House of Commons is to administer a code of conduct concerning conflict of interest. (That the role of the ethics commissioner is understood solely in terms of conflict of interest reflects the minimalist approach to ethics that is widespread.) In principle, the role of the ethics commissioner could be expanded to include the administration of a deliberative code of conduct.

REFERENCES

Ackerman, B., & Fishkin, J. S. (2004). *Deliberation day*. New Haven, CT: Yale University Press.

Barber, B. (1984). *Strong democracy: Participatory politics for a new age*. Berkeley: University of California Press.

Chambers, S. (2003). Deliberative democratic theory. *Annual Review of Political Science, 6*, 307–326.

Cohen, J. (1989). Deliberation and democratic legitimacy. In: A. Hamlin & P. Petit (Eds), *The good polity: Normative analysis of the state* (pp. 17–34). Oxford, UK: Basil Blackwell.

Cohen, J. (2003). Procedure and substance in deliberative democracy. In: T. Christiano (Ed.), *Philosophy and democracy: An anthology* (pp. 17–38). Oxford, UK: Oxford University Press.

Freeman, S. (2000). Deliberative democracy: A sympathetic comment. *Philosophy and Public Affairs, 29*, 371–418.

Gutmann, A. (2003). *Identity in democracy*. Princeton, NJ: Princeton University Press.

Gutmann, A., & Thompson, D. (1995). Moral disagreement in a democracy. *Social Philosophy and Policy, 12*, 87–110.

Gutmann, A., & Thompson, D. (1996). *Democracy and disagreement*. Cambridge, MA: Harvard University Press.

Gutmann, A., & Thompson, D. (2000). Why democracy is different. *Social Philosophy and Policy, 17*, 161–180.

Kull, S., Ramsay, C., & Lewis, E. (2003). Misperceptions, the media, and the Iraq war. *Political Science Quarterly, 118*, 569–599.

Pateman, C. (1970). *Participation and democratic theory*. Cambridge, UK: Cambridge University Press.

Pogge, T. (2002). *World poverty and human rights*. Cambridge, UK: Polity Press.

GOVERNING PLURALISM

Andrew Sabl

ABSTRACT

This chapter treats the ethical consequences of the diffusion of political power and authority from state to nonstate actors. It claims that with the increased power of civil society or NGOs come more stringent political responsibilities. The sources of these responsibilities resemble those of classic political duties – ordinary moral obligations, Weber's ethic of responsibility, and responsibilities attaching to democratic relationships – but their form differs across roles, tracking the different forms of politician–citizen relationships. NGO politicians should adopt, and be held to, a stringent role ethic as the least bad substitute for the accountability mechanisms of classic, state-based politics.

The topic of this chapter is political pluralism and democratic ethics. Pluralism can mean many things (mostly things I favor). But this chapter is not about interest group pluralism, cultural pluralism, or moral pluralism. It is about what I call *governing pluralism*, a concept I touched on briefly in my book *Ruling Passions* (Sabl, 2002, pp. 2, 15, 315–316, 321–325) but did not flesh out. I welcome the opportunity to say more here. With luck, it will be either consistent with my previous treatment or an improvement.

As a political phenomenon, governing pluralism refers to the diffusion of political power and public legitimacy from classic, state-based politics and politicians to nonstate actors: preachers, organizers, the heads of social movements, and NGOs. Such diffusion has always been the norm in the U.S. (so diffusion is not really the right word there); it is increasingly the norm elsewhere. As an ethical claim, governing pluralism means the moral consequences of that. With the increased power of nonstate actors comes increased responsibility. Governing pluralism is about what this responsibility looks like and how politicians who uphold it, or do not, should be judged.

My claim is that nonstate actors face the same sources of political obligation as classic governmental politicians, but that these similar starting points are consistent with, in fact entail, great substantive differences in the nature of these obligations across different roles. There are differences of obligation between state and nonstate politics, and differences among different kinds of nonstate politics as well. This, in turn, implies that very different sorts of people are likely to fulfill these obligations well and reliably: governing pluralism means that different kinds of politicians require different qualities of character to help them face their respective normative demands.

POLITICAL ETHICS, WITHIN STATES AND WITHOUT

To explain how this works, it is still best to start with politicians who are part of the state – the formal governing structure – since we are used to them as models. Such politicians have obligations arising from three sources. First, their ordinary moral obligations as persons, which politicians continue to be (though both they and their critics may forget this). Second, something like Weber's ethic of responsibility. Commanding resources that ordinary people do not have access to, and may be helpless in the face of, means having a greater obligation than those who lack power to "give an account of the foreseeable results of one's action" (Weber 1946, p. 120).[1] This entails both an affirmative duty to devote oneself strenuously to one's political duties, and a negative requirement not to stand punctiliously on one's personal moral beliefs if too many citizens, who may not share those beliefs, will demonstrably suffer as a result.[2]

The third source of obligation is that stemming from democratic relationships between particular kinds of politicians and the groups of citizens to which each claims to be a responsible servant. In a democracy, ordinary people are supposed to get more or less the politicians that they want, and are entitled to expect their politicians to further their constituents' or followers' interests (at the same time as they pursue their own fame). This is, I would argue, the most crucial source of obligation in a democracy, and it gives rise to most of the interesting questions of political ethics.[3]

Democratic relationship duties suggest, in particular, that moral autonomy is a luxury not allowed to democratic politicians – who are supposed to be acting in ways that their constituents can rely on over time, rather than constantly revising their positions as new arguments strike them. While moral theory commonly portrays the conscientious agent as making choices independently of others' unjustified opinions and sentiments, democratic politicians are supposed to pursue their constituents' interests, or their wishes, or both, rather than merely freelancing.[4] Of course, this pursuit ought to take place with moral side constraints and in the context of a duty also to pay attention to the interests of others who are not constituents or direct supporters. But to lose sight of democratic relationships altogether is to elide the difference between a democracy and an aristocracy of self-proclaimed moral heroes. Absent a sense of relationships and responsibility, even a strict and noble professional ethos tends to be less a tool for furthering democratic control or refining its operation than an elaborate excuse for avoiding such control out of contempt for ordinary people whom one comes to regard as lacking professional *gravitas* (see Finer, 1941). Below I shall defend such an ethos as the least bad alternative when other checks are absent, but we should remember that it is always a second choice.

Most codes of political ethics, both popular and scholarly, follow one of these three royal roads to political duties. Scholars tend to stress the first two. Ordinary citizens, who worry about the demonstrated fidelity of their agents rather than the state of their consciences, often stress the last. It is not often noted, however, that these sources of duty translate to the less formal offices of civil society, third sector, or social movement politics as well. This is, of course, true of ordinary morality. It is also easy to see how it is true of democratic relationship obligations. In fact, it may be less controversial to attribute such duties to nongovernmental politicians than to legislative or executive leaders. Speaking for a neglected or powerless group is, for civil society politicians, their whole reason and justification for being. It is possible (though I would say mistaken) to argue that a legislator in the U.S. Senate or British House of Commons should represent neither a partisan nor a constituency position, but solely the national interest. It is harder to claim that the head of the National Association for the Advancement of Colored People may not concentrate on the particular interests of African-Americans. (I shall say more about this later.)

It is harder to see, but no less true, that informal politicians have obligations of responsibility. Despite Weber's Prussian obsession with the state, the logic of much of his argument applies just as well to nonstate actors. Two aspects of responsibility in particular come to mind. The first is what Weber called "trained relentlessness in viewing the realities of life" (1946, p. 127): politicians who intend to accomplish something must see human nature as it is. They must resist the temptation to engage in wishful thinking and to assert that human nature will transform itself comprehensively and durably if only we state moral demands with sufficient force or insistently demand greater and greater rationality, reciprocity, civic virtue, or what have you. Second, responsibility "for what may become of [one]self" – for the fact that movements and organizations over time tend to become less charismatic and exciting, more routine, and subject to petty motives and careerism. A politician in any role must be able to live with routinization (Weber, 1946, pp. 125–126).[5]

These attitudes or orientations, or if one likes, virtues, are hard to internalize. (That is why Weber says relentlessness must be trained, and stresses that not everyone who thinks he has a political vocation in fact does.) They are hard, in particular, for what I have in my work called *moral activists*.

Such activists – on behalf of racial or indigenous rights, women's equality, the environment, and so on – believe in standing on principle, and tend to self-select on the basis of a taste for expressive over instrumental rationality. This is sometimes as salutary as it seems. The purpose of such activists is to remind us of the core principles that are not merely matters of interest and bargaining but call for, or remind us of, a framework of political and social values that sets the boundaries within which bargaining and everyday argument take place. Absent attention to these values, everyday politics – which does not necessarily involve a consensus on principle, and is mostly based on interest, broadly understood – would exclude too many legitimate voices, and would lack stability, legitimacy, and moral worth. At the same time, moral activism must guard against a powerful antipolitical impulse, a desire to chastise politicians for being responsive to the constituencies that elect them and for favoring the overall responsibilities of their role over the single-issue commitment that only an activist has a right to pursue.

OFFICE DIVERSITY

The sources of politicians' obligations mentioned above apply to different political roles or offices to different degrees and in different ways. But some things are the same. The usual range of ordinary moral obligations applies to governmental and nongovernmental politicians alike, though we have all studied situations in which extreme necessity might override them.[6] So does the special ethos of trained relentlessness, or what I have called *democratic constancy* – not the kind of virtue that makes them perfect human beings, but the kind that makes them reliable politicians, steady in their aims and loyal to core followers even in the face of necessary compromise.[7]

Different roles, however, also differ in their duties, in the substantive content of how constancy plays out, what it actually demands of those who hold those roles. This allows what I have called a "division of moral responsibility" (Sabl, 2002, pp. 44–45, 48–49) that lets certain democratic values or goals be pursued by specialists in the kinds of politics that best further them – allowing others to specialize in something else. Bob Dole could not be trusted to lead a civil rights march, nor Martin Luther King to balance a budget. But neither needed to do the other's job. It makes no sense to wish for politicians who can successfully take on, in turn or simultaneously, every conceivable political role or task. A division of moral responsibility is good for ordinary citizens, who benefit from the specialization. It is also good for the vocation of those who want to make politics their profession: it allows for a variety of people to have a calling for politics in ways Weber never imagined. Women's rights advocates can legitimately mix an absolutist ethic of ultimate ends with an ethic of responsibility in ways that are appropriate for them but would not be for a general (and vice versa).

Responsibility also has many shapes. Weber's focus on the responsible use of force applies most strongly to the political roles most familiar to him – executive leaders and violent revolutionaries. It is less salient for legislators, and even less so for informal politicians in civil society to the degree that they refrain from certain means. As soon as informal political actors resort to violence, they of course face much the same questions of the legitimate and responsible use of force that state actors incur (whether or not they see themselves as challenging the state). Other means, coercive but not violent, entail lesser degrees of responsibility, on a descending scale: threats of violence with no intention of carrying them out; the creation of barriers and physical coercion short of violence; economic boycotts and strikes, with economic but no physical consequences; and, finally, ostracism and reputational penalties, which often, though not always, entail no loss of livelihood.[8] Any form of effective political or social power comes with its own form of proper responsibility. Activists can legitimately reject the ethic of responsibility completely, pursuing a pure ethic of ultimate ends, only if they plan to remain absolutely powerless. (Even the power to persuade through argument entails responsibility – which is why many a youthful communist, for instance, feels not just an urge but a moral responsibility to become a vocal anticommunist later to mend the cultural damage once caused.)

What vary across political offices, systematically and profoundly, are the obligations stemming from relationships. Governing pluralism is clearest here. What people need from civil rights activists is very different from what they need from their senators. The qualities they expect community organizers to have as they try to defuse a tense racial situation in a neighborhood are very different from those they expect transport ministers to have.

In the best case, the variation of responsibility across different roles closely tracks differences in the implicit and explicit promises that politicians make to their formal constituents or less formal followers. Legislators implicitly promise, or should be expected to promise, good legislative results along with democratic responsiveness to constituent wishes. The compromises they are required to strike, and the detailed attention to legislation they are required to display, would be not so much immoral as beside the point for moral activists. Their job is to mobilize a group of purist supporters while translating a moral message for a larger society that (almost by definition) is not disposed to think the message valid or the messenger particularly legitimate. Finally, the neighborhood organizer just mentioned is not expected to deal primarily in either legislative detail or moral witness, but rather in a certain talent in getting people to recognize their own enlightened interests and to build relationships with their close neighbors that are grounded in engagement and sympathy, overcoming hostile stereotypes and habits of separation. An ethic of responsibility looks different for different political actors because the consequences each is responsible for are different. And an ethic of fidelity to democratic relationships varies in shape according to the relationship. I expect Supreme Court justices to judge impartially; I would be understandably incensed if the head of my favorite political party did the same.

THE DIVISION OF MORAL LABOR IN INTERNATIONAL CONTEXT

In my book (Sabl, 2002), I portrayed my analysis as widely applicable but was inspired specifically by the U.S. experience. We southern North Americans, descendants of rebels, have never much liked the idea of sovereignty.

We display both an irreverence toward the (so-called) state and, as Tocqueville (2000, pp. 233–235) noted, a willingness to let citizen-level, nonstate actors do many things that elsewhere either states or elites would do (and do better). Some of the roles I talked about, in fact, do not export well. U.S. senators, for instance, play a distinct role in American politics that has little analog elsewhere, probably because in few other countries (Australia being the most prominent exception) are upper houses both directly elected and legislatively equal with lower parliamentary assemblies.[9]

The politics of civil society, however, is infectious. NGOs, of course, are both burgeoning and popular; few Europeans under 40 seem to doubt that they have much more legitimacy and serve much more important purposes than governments. And the politics of international human rights promises (or threatens) to bring the moral jeremiad, once a U.S. specialty, onto the world stage. NGOs do, famously, a great deal to further the interests and rights of the helpless. Even from the perspective of citizens in rich countries – who need them less – these groups embody a new vocation: they harness the energies of many public-spirited people who do not find compelling the old-fashioned political ethics of parliamentary ambition or faithful state service. Where politics is corrupt or states are authoritarian, or failed, this might seem the only kind of political vocation worth having.

This is not just good for politicians but good for citizens, as nonstate actors have a prerogative, indeed a duty, to do things that the government authorities have a duty not to do. For a Czech president to say that resident Roma should seek success in Czech society by putting aside cultural and social habits (e.g., disrespect for education) that stand in the way of such success would border on racism. For a Roma leader to say the same would be quite different. Motives matter, and so does the signaling effect of an official message, which can be completely different from that of an unofficial one.

This is a matter of symbol (though symbols matter). A division of moral responsibility can, however, also allay more tangible fears. For Doctors Without Borders to offer to provide medical services in war-torn regions of the Congo is one thing; for the U.S. Army to do so – even if its intentions were very similar – would be another. Governing pluralism often works precisely by severing (bits of) governmental capacity from the claim to possess legitimate command over violence in a territory. Recent outrage at American officials' statements that NGOs receiving U.S. aid are "a force multiplier ... an important part of our combat team" (U.S. Department of State, 2001), "an arm of the U.S. government" (InterAction, 2003), has been slightly overblown, and slights what I would consider a duty of quiet gratitude toward a huge source of relief funds.[10] But it reflects the essentially correct judgment that only a division of moral responsibility lets nonstate actors fulfill their rightful mission. Doctors Without Borders is allowed leeway to do its job because it is also without tanks.

But the fragmentation of political responsibility also has costs. The increased prominence of nonstate politics has given rise to questions of legitimacy. Environmental, peace, and human rights activists clearly believe their devotion to unselfish ideals makes them more legitimate than craven, compromising politicians. Critics, including Dennis Thompson (1999, esp. pp. 116–118), have rightly countered with suggestions that the democratic legitimacy of actors who are, after all, self-appointed may not stand up to that of governments.

From the perspective of political ethics, however, the problem is not so much illegitimacy as irresponsibility. NGO politicians often fail to recognize the extent to which they face all the requirements of an ethic of responsibility – and generally fail them. The more successful nonstate actors are in affecting political outcomes, the more responsibility they should be asked to take for those outcomes. Peace activists must, but rarely do, propose practical, stable, and peaceful resolutions to the conflicts they oppose – and should (but rarely do) present themselves for judgment by the victims if pacifist agitation causes policy changes that result in aggression or genocide.[11] If Doctors Without Borders becomes, by its voluntary efforts, de facto the only medical service in Congo, it must adopt de facto the same moral burdens of triage, public health ethics, and so forth that a national health service would incur. It might be said that requirements like this would discourage idealistic people from pursuing creative nonstate solutions to international conflicts and humanitarian crises. In response: anyone not willing to take seriously the burdens that certain kinds of political actions have always placed on state actors – who willingly accept these burdens and steadily reflect on them – should leave types of action that effectively amount to politics to those actors.

But attention to the third source of political ethics, democratic relationships, would do the most to clarify the duties of nonstate politicians and to demystify extravagant moral claims on their behalf. For one thing, it would draw attention to the fact that moral spokespeople are not automatically democratic at all: they are responsible to no antecedently defined set of elites, let alone the masses. Elected politicians are constantly reminded of their relationship to the constituents whose interest they are supposed to serve: a politician who ignores constituents' wishes and interests, or denies their relevance, will be removed. But activists, who are not thus accountable, are capable of forgetting issues of responsibility altogether – or worse, misdefining them as a matter of responsibility to donors rather than to those affected by their money, influence, and power. It is not democratic for "Californians whose idea of an electricity crisis is a handful of summer blackouts" to determine dam-building policy in Uganda, and not on its face democratically responsible for NGO activists to help them do so (Mallaby, 2004, p. 52; compare Bond, 2000). When *The Economist*'s foreign editor called NGOs "the sometimes admirable, sometimes maddening, always self-appointed, often unaccountable, ubiquitous practitioners of all political arts except that of contesting and winning elections" (Grimond, 2001, p. 18), the tone was snide, but the content hardly deniable. Moral activists, *because* they practice political arts without contesting elections, need a more self-conscious political ethos than they have, as the best (because only) check on what they do.[12] The rest of us must hold them to that ethos, as defined by them or, with luck, by a fair number of people in the places they operate.

Idealism will not be a sufficient content for such an ethos. Absent democratic accountability, activists characteristically rely for legitimacy on the claim that their principles are more moral than those of the forces they oppose. But given that two of the central purposes of democracy are to adjudicate disputes among people and groups, each of whom considers its moral judgments superior to those of others, and to balance the relative priority of moral ends when not all can be maximally pursued at the same time, this is more question-begging than international rights activists tend to admit. Moral activists must ask themselves, internationally no less than domestically: For whom do I speak? Why might others disagree? How can I deal respectfully with those who have no reason to grant me legitimate authority but whom I still hope to influence?

CONCLUSION

To ask these questions is to give up the dream of an international moral consensus. But if activists come to recognize that they command allegiance among some of the world's citizens, and at most respectful disagreement from others, this could lead to a more real, and more genuinely consensual, legitimacy. Moral activists' legitimacy – not automatically present anywhere, contingently possible everywhere – is an indispensable supplement to that of formal politicians, which is the other way around. Heads of government command legitimate authority over a set of citizens, but their very particularistic duties to those citizens inhibit their ability to speak for moral reform issues outside their countries. When they claim to have cosmopolitan allegiances, they are quite rightly treated as the hypocrites they are.

Thus, the fact that moral activists are formally responsible to nobody in particular, gives them a claim to speak for, and have special importance to, a general, possibly worldwide audience of all who believe what they say and think they are good at saying it. Since moral activists characteristically claim to speak for oppressed people or permanent minorities who cannot be heard through formal political channels, the democratic relationship between activists and their followers perfects the democratic ideal of equal political influence among all citizens. Thus, moral activists help plug the moral gaps that formal political systems, even democratic ones, necessarily leave.

So responsible freelancing, within proper limits, has its distinct virtues and fulfills crucial moral purposes. I have treated a single case but intend a general lesson: by acknowledging governing pluralism, each type of politician – acting in full knowledge of its own others' particular but potentially complementary roles – can come to live its own vocation while respecting the benefits gained by others' leading different ones.

NOTES

1. Weber was, of course, concerned specifically with the responsibility of those who commanded violence, but the text expands his notion to those who command influential or coercive political resources generally. This reflects the scope of the inquiry: Weber was lecturing during a time of war, revolution, and counterrevolution, whereas our current concern is with normal, mostly peaceful politics.

2. An extension of this, logically clear but often psychologically hard to recognize, is that political actors are also responsible for the consequences of any inaction that they bring about when action would otherwise have been taken. If, as is often claimed, anarchist antiglobalization protestors in Seattle prevented the lowering of rich countries' trade barriers on poor countries' goods and agricultural products (I have not studied this closely and cannot claim to know for sure), they must morally answer for the consequences for people in Nigeria and Bolivia who have gone hungry as a result. Anarchism, when enforced on others, is potentially the most irresponsible of political positions, for it undercuts all others' attempts to coordinate action in the service of one another and third parties. I thank Pat Dobel for discussion on this point.

3. This includes conflict-of-interest questions so ably canvassed and analyzed by Stark (2000). In the U.S., at any rate, ordinary citizens see the problems of corruption and conflict of interest as interfering not with the public good or discussion of issues on the merits, but with the ability of politicians to understand and identify with ordinary people, their opinions and interests. For empirical evidence of this see Hibbing and Theiss-Morse (2002). Stark (2000, p. 121) notes one excellent reason why scholars might endorse this perspective as well: the public good is so hard to

discern that it is also hard to make a standard against which ethical violations are measured. Another reason, more alluded to than fleshed out – since Stark's concern is overwhelmingly with administrative officials – is that few political roles involve, as administrative ones do, an exclusive fiduciary responsibility to the whole public as opposed to parts of it (2000, p. 89). At least, that is the construction that I would endorse. I should note in passing that the focus on democratic relationships distinguishes my use of Weber from the neo-Machiavellian one rightly opposed by John Uhr in his chapter in this volume – and, possibly, from an orthodox reading of Weber himself.

4. Pitkin (1967) focuses much of her discussion of representation on the question of what to do if interests and wishes do not coincide (and the questions of what this would look like and how often it happens). But much contemporary political ethics seems to counsel democratic politicians to ignore both their constituents' wishes and their interests in the name of deliberative rationality.

5. While the stress on the responsible use of force is the part of Weber's essay that gets the most attention, the lengthy section of the essay that deals with the rise of machine-like political parties deserves more emphasis (1946, pp. 99–114). Weber deplores such parties in some ways but finds them, in tragic mode, inevitable and something that politicians must get used to and find ways to reconcile with ethical and responsible independent action. Many contemporary commentators on both politics and ethics, in contrast, retain a romantic view of politics: they display a distinct impatience with the fact that politicians in a mass democracy must keep party and movement activists on board and must use simplified messages to win over a public with diverse (mostly nonpolitical) interests and limited political attention.

6. There are also certain exceptions having to do with role expectations: everyone expects a union leader beginning a round of collective bargaining to lie about the lowest wage for which his members will work. Statements about the details of military plans in the middle of a declared and just war (as opposed to the policy deliberations concerning whether to wage war!) should be viewed in the same way: caveat auditor.

7. To simplify a very long treatment from Sabl (2002): Constancy is a minimal requirement for all democratic politicians, who must show a group of followers that they can be trusted to perform, fairly predictably, the political actions that people lack the time, taste, and skill to perform for themselves. Constancy is the virtue of democratic politicians because ordinary citizens cannot themselves pay constant attention to political events and because political accountability is (rightly) episodic rather than continual.

8. This insight is not new. Some of the classic examples of *dirty hands*, and indeed the phrase itself, come from stories about terrorists and revolutionaries, not governors (Walzer, 1973; Sartre, 1989). Nor is the literature on civil disobedience lacking. We could, however, use more work on the ethics of strikes, lockouts, boycotts, blacklists, anti-scab campaigns, and the like – many of which are in the U.S. generally legal, even in extreme cases (*NAACP v. Claiborne Hardware Co.*, 1982), but not always moral. In general, I suspect that an ethos of confrontation that was originally adopted for extreme cases – nonviolent coercion is justified when oppression is so egregious that violent coercion would be justified, or nearly so – is subject to inflation: its habitual practitioners take its legitimacy for granted when the issues

at stake are not extreme enough to justify such actions. Some of these themes are covered in Sabl (2001).

9. Current agitation over the future shape, power, and electoral responsibility of the British House of Lords might change this, and provide a fascinating comparative case – though it does not seem likely that any option will give the Lords equal power of legislation, as the Senate enjoys in Australia and the U.S.

10. For the outrage, see among others Burnett (2004) and Klein (2003). The first two text quotations are from the then Secretary of State Colin Powell (U.S. Department of State, 2001; in wider context the remarks seem somewhat less sinister) and the last is a summary of remarks, of which the full text is unfortunately unavailable, from U.S. Agency for International Development head Andrew Natsios (InterAction, 2003).

11. If this sounds harsh, consider by analogy the usual requirement that those engaging in civil disobedience be willing to suffer punishment. The consequences of international disobedience often being greater than those of civil disobedience – lives and the defense of countries are at stake – the willingness to suffer should, it seems, be greater as well.

12. I would claim that international NGOs, who are less likely than domestic activist groups to have overlap between their members and donors and their intended beneficiaries, have an even greater need for such an ethos. The Red Cross' code of conduct for NGOs engaged in disaster relief (International Federation of Red Cross and Red Crescent Societies, n.d.) proclaims its signers (currently 307 groups) "accountable to both those we seek to assist and those from whom we accept resources." While the sentiment is admirable, this seems to place two forms of accountability, of very different kinds and importance, on a par. Donors are likely in practice to have more influence over NGOs' actions than are aid recipients, for the obvious reason that the former have more power – but ethics would suggest that the opposite should be the case. Nor has this code in practice prevented scrambles for preeminence in relief efforts at the cost of efficiency and service (Sins of the Secular Missionaries, 2000). Finally, disaster relief is in some ways an easy case, as the interests of local people are relatively clear. NGOs active in preventing development or preserving indigenous ways of life face more acute questions of local accountability.

ACKNOWLEDGMENTS

This chapter is a revised version of a paper delivered before The Governance of Ethics in Politics workshop, University of Montreal, May 14–15, 2004.

I would like to thank the many participants at the conference, and in particular Patrick Dobel, John Uhr, and Dennis Thompson, for their comments.

REFERENCES

Bond, M. (2000). The backlash against NGOs. *Prospect, 51*, 52–55.
Burnett, J. S. (2004, August 4). In the line of fire. *The New York Times*, p. 17.

Finer, H. (1941). Administrative responsibility in democratic government. *Public Administration Review, 1*, 335–350.
Grimond, J. (2001). Civil society. In: D. Fishburn (Ed.), *The world in 2002* (p. 18). London: RAC Publishing.
Hibbing, J. R., & Theiss-Morse, E. (2002). *Stealth democracy: Americans' beliefs about how government should work*. Cambridge, UK: Cambridge University Press.
InterAction. (2003). *Natsios: NGOs must show results; promote ties to U.S. or we will "find new partners."* Synopsis of panel from InterAction Forum 2003, May 19–21, Washington DC. Retrieved August 4, 2004, from http://www.interaction.org/forum2003/panels.html
International Federation of Red Cross and Red Crescent Societies. (n.d.). *The code of conduct for The International Red Cross and Red Crescent movement and NGOs in disaster relief*. Retrieved February 17, 2005, from http://www.ifrc.org/publicat/conduct/index.asp
Klein, N. (2003, June 20). Bush to NGOs: Watch your mouths. *The globe and mail*, p. A15. Reprint: The war against NGOs, June 23. Retrieved August 4, 2004, from http://www.tompaine.com/feature2.cfm/ID/8180
Mallaby, S. (2004). NGOs: Fighting poverty, hurting the poor. *Foreign Policy, 144*, 50–58.
NAACP v. Claiborne Hardware Co. (1982). 458 U.S. 886.
Pitkin, H. F. (1967). *The concept of representation*. Berkeley: University of California Press.
Sabl, A. (2001). Looking forward to justice: Rawlsian civil disobedience and its non-Rawlsian lessons. *Journal of Political Philosophy, 9*, 307–330.
Sabl, A. (2002). *Ruling passions: Political offices and democratic ethics*. Princeton, NJ: Princeton University Press.
Sartre, J. -P. (1989). Dirty hands. In: I. Abel (Trans.), *No exit and three other plays* (pp. 125–241). New York: Vintage International.
Sins of the Secular Missionaries. (2000, January 29). *Economist*, pp. 25–27.
Stark, A. (2000). *Conflict of interest in American public life*. Cambridge, MA: Harvard University Press.
Thompson, D. (1999). Democratic theory and global society. *Journal of Political Philosophy, 7*, 111–125.
Tocqueville, A. (2000). In: H. C. Mansfield & D. Winthrop (Trans.), *Democracy in America*. Chicago: University of Chicago Press.
U.S. Department of State. (2001). *Remarks by secretary of state Colin L. Powell to the national foreign policy conference for leaders of nongovernmental organizations (NGO* [sic]*)*. October 26. Retrieved August 4, 2004, from http://japan.usembassy.gov/e/p/tp-se0577.html
Walzer, M. (1973). Political action: The problem of dirty hands. *Philosophy and Public Affairs, 2*, 165–166.
Weber, M. (1946). Politics as a vocation. In: H. H. Gerth & C. W. Mills (Trans. and Eds), *From Max Weber: Essays in sociology* (pp. 77–128). New York: Oxford University Press.

ETHICAL REASONING, EPISTEMOLOGY, AND ADMINISTRATIVE INQUIRY

James W. Myers and Fred Thompson

ABSTRACT

Theories of knowledge are critical to practical reasoning. Nevertheless, most students of management pay little or no attention to the disciplines that deal most directly with questions about knowledge, its origins, and its nature: epistemology primarily, but the philosophy of science and other related disciplines as well. Even where underlying philosophical assumptions influence their thinking and writing, students of practical reasoning often fail to acknowledge these influences. That is a great pity. By looking to epistemology, a richer and more coherent development of practical reasoning and its contribution to administrative inquiry as a field of intellectual endeavor may be possible. Moreover, the relationship between our understanding of knowledge and our understanding of practical reasoning is potentially reciprocal. A fuller exploration of this relationship may help us better understand social epistemology as well as promote conceptual development in the fields of practical reasoning and administrative inquiry.

Administrative inquiry and argumentation is inherently ethical inquiry. Its focus is on taking good actions and avoiding bad ones. Of course, the process of crafting appropriate and effective responses to administrative situations also implies concern about their workability, practicality, and freedom from greater evils. However, to identify the best available alternative, it is first necessary to comprehend social value, the desirability of ends sought. Lacking this knowledge, we cannot engage with others in effective argumentative exchange about the shape and content of administrative interventions or make sense of our intellectual performances retrospectively and, thereby, mature into genuinely reflective practitioners. Ethical reasoning is, therefore, eminently practical.

One conclusion we reach from this line of reasoning is that part of the educational process in management should include straightforward discussion of the intellectual performances involved in ethical reasoning. We must provide our students with the tools needed to engage in effective argumentative exchange: shared cognitive models of practical reasoning and communication (Gaskins, 1992; Walton, 1994; Simons, 2001) and of social mechanisms and processes (Hedstrom & Swedberg, 1996; Tilly, 2000).

The other, perhaps more controversial, conclusion we reach is that administrative argumentation/learning/knowledge creation is a social process and that administrative inquiry ought to be firmly grounded in an appropriate social epistemology. The purpose of this essay is the exploration of this conclusion. What we find is a fundamental, unresolved tension at the heart of all theories of social inquiry. While this approach still seems far more useful for understanding and advancing a collectivity's capacity to create value by doing things cooperatively than traditional moral reasoning, with its emphasis on individual decisions, it too is ultimately inconclusive.

Creating, sustaining, and using knowledge to create value – what we call administrative inquiry – is the gist of managing the 21st century organization. This simple claim raises a rather basic question, however: What is knowledge? It is easy to define the term: Knowledge is justified true belief, individual and social, tacit and explicit, drawn from experience and information, dialog and debate. But, defining the term does not really answer the question. To do that, we must say what we can know and how we know what we know. These are hard questions, which have long preoccupied philosophers. They have no definitive, indisputable answers to these questions and we will offer none here. Nevertheless, philosophers have sharpened various approaches to resolving them, thereby providing us with a set of well-reasoned, logically appealing, internally coherent answers to the fundamental problems of knowing.[1] At a minimum, this should help us understand what people who write about administrative inquiry are trying to say, and save us time and energy in evaluating their conclusions.

Moreover, we know where to look for critiques of most theories of knowledge (e.g., coherence theories are criticized by other idealists, and at another level by both correspondence theorists and consequentialists). Finally, if writers about administrative inquiry made their underlying theories of knowledge explicit, we believe they could explain their beliefs and the evidentiary basis for those beliefs more clearly and coherently.

Fortunately, we need not investigate every epistemology to figure out what philosophers can teach us about organizational inquiry. It follows from our topic that we are concerned only with practical or instrumental knowledge, which simplifies our task considerably. We may dispense with epistemologies of pure reason as well as those that deny human agency. Given our topic, it follows also that our main concern is social knowledge, which suggests that we should start with epistemological formulations that have social construction as a feature. We may ignore consideration of purely individual philosophies (existentialism, say). Instead, we will discuss briefly three theories of knowledge that emphasize practical, social reasoning, one from each of the main approaches to warranting truth – coherence, correspondence, and consequence:

- Absolute idealism, which understands the world of man to be a creation of man – in effect, a creation of the human mind, that can be made or unmade through acts of will;
- Zen Buddhism, which presumes that reality is a flow and knowledge a socially mediated harmony with the world; and
- Pragmatism, which presumes that knowing is a social process and creativity a flow.

COMPETING FOR THE FUTURE

In philosophy, idealism is any theory positing the primacy of spirit, mind, or language. German or absolute idealism was a philosophical movement of the late 18th and early 19th centuries, which developed out of the work of Immanuel Kant and had affinities to romanticism and revolutionary politics. Its champions were Johann Gottlieb Fichte (1762–1814), Friedrich Schelling, and Georg Wilhelm Friedrich Hegel.

According to Fichte,[2] German idealism stresses the ability of the perceiver to remake the world. People are free agents with self-determining activity as their primary and supreme characteristic.

> The ego, or will, for Fichte, is the source, the creator of the world we know. Man can understand only that which he has created. (Frost, 1962, p. 168).

Fichte believed that our very existence is predicated upon the principle of freedom, and that this principle allows us to transcend causal necessity. This means that neither human actions nor the consequences of those actions are predetermined. Hence, each individual has the potential to fulfill his highest nature – making the world over in his own image.

As S. E. Frost explains:

> Fundamental to Fichte's point of view [is] the belief in freedom, the idea that the will, or as he called it "the ego" (meaning the "I"), is not a link in the scientific chain of cause and effect, but is free, self-determining activity. This will is, for him, the only real thing in the universe. The ego, being pure activity, creates the world that it knows. My world is not something given to me from the outside, but is a creation of the pure, active, free ego, of which I am a part. (Frost, 1962, p. 148)

Individual freedom sets the stage for the recreation of the world, therefore, – if leaders can free themselves of preconceived methodologies and world views, allowing new perspectives to develop and flourish.

Fichte further argued that the mind, or ego, is everything. Even the material world is a creation of mind. According to Frost (1962, pp. 242–243), the material world is a projection into space of objects that exist only in the mind. It is emphatically not made up of dead things, arranged in a spatial-temporal causal order; freedom means that causal relationships are products of human consciousness. Consequently, for Fichte, reality is what one makes of it. The only reason for positing anything as real beyond immediate impressions is a practical one. According to Henry Aiken, one must go beyond immediate impressions in order to set goals and to move toward those goals:

> Properly understood, all thought is an anticipation of experience, the 'correctness' of which is finally established by its capacity to serve our needs. The highest achievement of the intellect, therefore, is not 'contemplation' but practical problem solving. The 'real,' so to say, is not an object contemplated, but that which we finally accept as the satisfactory solution to our problems. (Aiken, 1984, p. 59)

For all his egoism, Fichte is profoundly aware of the social and even institutional character of all human activity:

> We don't think of ourselves, in practice, as working alone, nor do we regard our standards as peculiar to ourselves. In short, any enterprise in which we engage whether it be something we call moral action or scientific inquiry, we think of ourselves as bound by 'objective' or interpersonal criteria, to which others, like ourselves, are also committed. If we did not presuppose that others, like ourselves, exist, there would be no point in talking about objective criteria at all. And if we did not presuppose that there is a community of beings like ourselves who are willing to live by them there would be no point to the claim that any rational being ought to acknowledge them. (Fichte, 1869, p. 43)

The social problem for the creative ego is that of raising the mass of ordinary humans to his or her level (Fichte, 1889, (*I*),214–217). Unfortunately, "most of the rank and file cannot embrace freedom ... to make anew the world" (p. 214). Fichte (p. 216) emphasizes that the best way to transmit reality-altering ideas to rational beings is by means of Platonic discussion and dialog – "strenuous intellectual communion and intimate personal intercourse." Nevertheless, he wistfully concludes, "The inertia of mankind in the mass has never in fact been overcome by the exclusive use of the Platonic method." To draw the inert majority along in the creative minority's train, it is necessary to reinforce the preferred method of debate and dialog with the expedient method of social drill – "the realization of human potentialities requires leaders who will take command and issue new orders."[3]

Ultimately, Fichte (1869) concludes; "There is nothing, finally, but the seriousness of our own commitments and our loyalty to our own ends to guarantee any procedure or rule as a standard of validity or justification" (p. 343). Or, as he elsewhere explains:

> Just as no moral law can bind me unless I myself elect to be bound by it, so no supposedly impersonal laws of the human understanding can legislate how I must play the game of knowledge unless I am prepared to make those laws my own. Any 'reason' to which I am to be held responsible must be my reason. (Tsanoff, 1967, pp. 194–195)

Gary Hamel and C. K. Prahalad echo Fichte's metaphysics in their highly successful book about administrative inquiry, *Competing for the Future* (Hamel & Prahalad, 1994). Hamel and Prahalad take the position that visionary leadership at the top of the organization is the key to organizational success. They insist that administrative inquiry is not about foreseeing the future, but creating it. The visionary leader's "goal is not to predict the future, but to imagine a future made possssible by changes in technology, life style, work style, regulation, global geopolitics, and the like" (p. 11). "In business, as in art, what distinguishes leaders from laggards, and greatness from mediocrity, is the ability to uniquely imagine what could be" (p. 27). Without a belief in "the opportunity for change – for revolution – a company is more likely to forfeit the future than own it" (p. 26). Hence, Hamel and Prahalad's purpose in writing *Competing for the Future* is to "help managers imagine the future and, having imagined it, create it" (ibid.). They conclude that "only those who can imagine and preemptively create the future will be around to enjoy it" (p. 12).

In other words, Hamel and Prahalad see the world as pliable and market success as the ultimate organizational goal. Knowledge is the mechanism through which the organization's leaders direct the organization to obtain this goal. Hamel and Prahalad further argue that "anybody who really believes 'that's the way it is,' anybody who is too lazy to ask, 'why couldn't it be different?' will never see the future" (1994, p. 97). "Nothing," they say, "is more liberating than becoming the author of one's own destiny" (p. 12). To paraphrase Fichte, if managers will not embrace freedom, they will fail to make the world anew. To Hamel and Prahalad the future is there for the making, and the way to get there is via force of will exerted by leaders striving to accomplish their vision of the future.

It is important to note that we are not saying that Hamel and Prahalad are idealists. While they express strong opinions about knowing and the knowable, how organizations create knowledge is not the primary focus of *Competing for the Future*. Rather, Hamel and Prahalad are mainly concerned with knowledge use. Their key contribution lies in the notion of core competencies – knowledge assets – and the contribution core competencies make to the growth of the organization – how those assets are sustained, diffused, and transformed. Nevertheless, so far as they go, Hamel and Prahalad's epistemological premises appear to have much in common with idealism. It seems reasonable, therefore, that management theorists could use idealism's set of well-reasoned, internally coherent answers to the fundamental problems of knowing and the knowable to gain a deeper understanding of Hamel and Prahalad's position. Moreover, because philosophers have thoroughly evaluated idealism, management theorists could avail themselves of these evaluations to assess critically Hamel and Prahalad's conclusions, as well.

For example, analytic epistemologists insist that genuine knowledge must be true. As Aarons explains:

> Something cannot be knowledge without it having some strong connection with the real facts of the world. How can you genuinely know something without that knowledge being true and accurate? You can't know that aliens live amongst us if there are in fact no aliens. (Aarons, 2004, p. 8)

Hamel and Prahalad's conception of knowledge seems to lack this specific connection with the idea of truth. Indeed, what they describe sounds more like belief than knowledge. Of course, beliefs matter. The relationship between circumstances or situations and beliefs is almost necessarily reciprocal. Situations shape beliefs and beliefs shape situations. Even so, Aarons argues persuasively that:

> Knowledge must be grounded in real world properties and processes, even though our conceptions of these may be socially constructed in some sense ... The reason that an appeal to realism and truth is compatible with a social conception of knowledge is that it

does not deny the fact that social factors are real... There is a sense in which money is purely a social construct – the concept only acquires its significance through social convention and agreement. There is no money in nature. Yet money is also quite real, and all our talk of interest rates, budgets, financial markets, etc. is clearly about real entities as opposed to purely fictional entities ... The overall point here is that there need not be any conflict between social constructivism and knowledge as truth – indeed, a connection to the truth seems an essential part of even a social account of knowledge. (Aarons, 2004, p. 8)[4]

THE KNOWLEDGE-CREATING COMPANY

Western students of epistemology usually ignore Zen Buddhism. This is probably the case, at least in part, because Buddhist thought is relentlessly practical – focused upon human beings, their needs, and their actions. It largely ignores the abstruse metaphysical matters that preoccupy Western epistemologists. According to Nakamura, "metaphysical speculation concerning problems not related to human activities and the attainment of Enlightenment is discouraged – e.g., problems such as whether the world is infinite or finite, whether the soul and the body are identical with, or different from, each other" (1973, p. 250). This is one of the main contrasts between Buddhism and most formal Western epistemological systems.

Given our topic, practicality is a virtue, of course. But that virtue would have been insufficient to capture our attention, had not two of the most insightful students of administrative inquiry, Ikujiro Nonaka and Hirotaka Takeuchi, declared in *The Knowledge Creating Company* (1996) that their conclusions reflected the epistemological premises of Zen Buddhism.[5]

Zen Buddhism is a philosophical system premised on the postulate of organic unity and the pertinence of sound reasoning as a guide to human action. Like Fichte, Zen Buddhists presume human agency. They also presume that thought and action are purposeful and practical, but where idealists worship reason, Buddhists seek harmony. This difference follows from the Buddhist understanding of the nature of reality, which is a process or flow rather than a state or even a sequence of evolutionary, revolutionary, or emergent states. Given that they understand reality as flow and construe reality as an almost infinitely complex set of currents and eddies, it is somewhat remarkable that Buddhists are also, in the main, materialists. Most Western philosophers who have made use of this trope have been idealists of one stripe or another. Buddhists' philosophical materialism seems even more remarkable from a Western perspective (popular as well as philosophical) when one takes account of their mysticism, their adherence to the Hegelian view[6] that opposites are relational and, therefore, fundamentally harmonious, and their efforts to liberate themselves from their own material drives, desires, and wants.

Alan Watts explains their philosophical materialism, noting that "Taoism, Confucianism, and Zen are expressions of a mentality which feels completely at home in the universe, and which sees man as an integral part of this environment" (1957, p. 170). This sense of fitness does not just happen; it results from individual struggles to understand the nature of the universe and the self. Buddhism, or, perhaps, more correctly, the Buddhist experience, is a means of self-liberation. Self-liberation comes through wisdom and insight. As Hajime Nakamura explains:

> Buddhism has asserted the following: life is suffering; the struggle to maintain individuality is painful. It asks: Why do we suffer? The answer is, because of the transience, the impermanence of human existence. There is no substance that abides forever. Suffering is caused by desire, since what we desire is impermanent, changing, and perishing. These desires are caused by ignorance. We are ignorant concerning our true nature and the nature of the universe in which we live. And we may be freed from our ignorance by following the Path. Through the wisdom, which comes from reflection on the transitoriness of life, by following the Path taught by the Buddha, everyone can attain Enlightenment, which characterizes Nirvana, the ideal state. (Nakamura, 1973, p. 250)

Preoccupation with individual spiritual enlightenment often promotes a kind of insensitivity to worldly considerations. Buddhist notions about the good life, together with Zen's concrete, matter-of-fact perspective, offset this propensity somewhat. "The way of the Buddha is called the Middle Path because it avoids the extremes of the pursuit of worldly desires or the practice of several asceticisms" (Nakamura, 1973, p. 252). The ideal person or organization, presumably, is one whose actions reflect wisdom in understanding not only the oneness of humanity and nature and the oneness of mind and body, but also the oneness of self and others. The emphasis on living with others in harmonious unity is reflected in Zen Buddhism's fundamental virtues: (1) generosity, (2) benevolence, (3) cooperation, and (4) service. Courtesy, sympathy, and honesty, etc., are also encouraged.

Furthermore, according to Nakamura:

> Buddhism presupposes universal laws called *dharma*s, which govern human existence and may be known by reason. ... Personal relations should be brought into harmony with the universal norms, the universal laws that apply to all existence, regardless of time and space. (Nakamura, 1973, p. 249)

In other words, there is a reality out there; it is a flow; it comprehends our social relationships; and, to bring ourselves into harmony with it, we must (and by reason may) understand it. Buddhists in general, and Zen Buddhists

Ethical Reasoning, Epistemology, and Administrative Inquiry

in particular, tend to believe that reality can be truly appreciated or understood only through experience – participating in the process, learning by doing, going with the flow. Experience, then, is the source of real knowledge and, through enlightenment (which requires acts of will), wisdom.

Any information that abstracts from experience, that codifies it, unavoidably distorts the nature of reality. This, too, turns Western conventions upside down. We tend to rank codified knowledge over mere experience. As Watts explains:

> The reason Taoism and Zen present, at first sight, such a puzzle to the Western mind is that we have taken a restricted view of human knowledge. For us, almost all knowledge is what the Taoist would call conventional knowledge, because we do not feel that we really know anything unless we can represent it to ourselves in words, or in some other system of conventional signs such as the notions of mathematics or music. Such knowledge is called conventional because it is a matter of social agreement as to the codes of communication. Just as people speaking the same language have tacit agreements as to what words shall stand for what things, so the members of every society and every culture are united by bonds of communication resting upon all kinds of agreement as to the classification and valuation of actions and things. (Watts, 1957, p. 18)

Watts illustrates the distinction between experiential and conventional knowledge with the following analogy:

> We have two types of vision – central and peripheral, not unlike the spotlight and the floodlight. Central vision is used for accurate work like reading, in which our eyes are focused on one small area after another like spotlights. Peripheral vision is less conscious, less bright than the intense ray of the spotlight. We use it for seeing at night, and for taking 'subconscious' notice of objects and movements not in the direct line of central vision. Unlike the spotlight, it can take in very many things at a time. (Watts, 1957, p. 21)

Watts further asserts that:

> By far the greater part of our important decisions depend upon 'hunch' – in other words upon our 'peripheral vision' of the mind. The reliability of our decisions rests ultimately upon our ability to 'see' the situation, upon the degree to which this 'peripheral vision' has been developed. (Watts, 1957, p. 27)

As Nonaka and Takeuchi explain: "This orientation has provided a basis for valuing personal and physical experience over indirect, intellectual abstraction" (1996, p. 29). Nonaka and Takeuchi refer to experiential knowledge as tacit knowledge and conventional or codified knowledge as explicit knowledge. In their view, tacit knowledge has two dimensions: a technical dimension that "encompasses the kind of informal and hard-to-pin-down skills of crafts captured in the term 'know-how' [and a cognitive dimension that] reflects our image of reality (what is) and our vision for the future (what ought to be)" (Nonaka & Takeuchi, 1996, p. 8). In contrast, explicit knowledge is systematic:

> Explicit knowledge can be expressed in words and numbers, and easily communicated and shared in the form of hard data, scientific formula, codified procedures, or universal principles. Thus, knowledge is viewed synonymously with a computer code, a chemical formula, codified procedures, or a set of general rules. (ibid.)

Nonaka and Takeuchi conclude that understanding the two types of knowledge and bringing them into harmony with each other is what administrative inquiry is all about. Knowledge managers are orderly brokers who bring internal and external harmony to organizations. Nonaka and Takeuchi believe that knowledge and innovation exist naturally in organizations, as a necessary consequence of experience, and will manifest themselves where virtuous relationships can be established and maintained. To be fully productive, however, these virtuous relationships must include all the members of an organization – executives, middle managers, and workers – working in harmony with its goals and possibilities. If the members of the organization are in harmony, everything else will fall into place for the organization to be successful.

The concept of duality brought into unity also runs throughout their text. Administrative inquiry is primarily concerned with communication between individuals. In this process, middle managers play a vital mediating role in turning tacit into explicit knowledge, much like Zen masters or teachers: (a) expressing the figurative and symbolic, (b) communicating personal knowledge with others, and (c) allowing new understanding to develop from initial ambiguity through repeated conversation (Nonaka & Takeuchi, 1996, pp. 13–14).

> The recognition of tacit knowledge and its importance has a number of crucially relevant implications. First, it gives rise to a whole different view of the organization – not as a machine for processing information but as a living organism. Within this context, sharing an understanding of what the company stands for, where it is going, what kind of a world it wants to live in, and how to make that world a reality becomes much more crucial than processing objective information. (Nonaka & Takeuchi, 1996, p. 9)

In understanding the importance of tacit knowledge in the context of the organization and its affect on individual action, they note:

> Once the importance of tacit knowledge is realized, then one begins to think about innovation in a whole new way. It is not just about putting together diverse bits of data and information. It is a highly individual process of personal and organizational renewal. The personal commitment of the employees and their identity with the company and its mission become indispensable. ... To create new knowledge means quite literally to re-create the company and everyone in it in an ongoing process of personal and

organizational self-renewal. It is not the responsibility of the selected few – specialists in research and development, strategic planning, or marketing – but that of everyone in the organization. (Nonaka & Takeuchi, 1996, p. 10)

This Zen Buddhist perspective rejects the notion that knowledge creation is either the result of top-down initiative from the leadership in the organization or a bottom-up initiative from the workers, and substitutes in its place a harmonious vision of the organization. Human potential in this setting is understood as the perfection of a system of knowledge exchange. By joining a team and by understanding and internalizing the goals and world view of the organization, its members reach their full potential.

This philosophy plays itself out by seeing the world as one both inside and outside the organization. The search for knowledge reflects a search for truth and harmony. The knowledge capability within the organization results from (1) moving from idea to reality, (2) moving from personal knowledge to organizational knowledge, and (3) moving from uncertainty to depth in knowledge. These are all movements from disharmony to harmony.

Clearly, Zen Buddhism provided Nonaka and Takeuchi with a set of internally coherent answers to the fundamental problems of knowing and the knowable, which helped them formulate and explain their position. Unfortunately, as we noted at the outset, Western philosophers have largely ignored Zen Buddhism. Consequently, they have not subjected its epistemology to the kind of thorough critique that would allow us to assess critically Nonaka and Takeuchi's conclusions. As will be seen in the next section, however, many of the criticisms of pragmatism hold a fortiori where Zen Buddhism is concerned.[7]

WELLSPRINGS OF KNOWLEDGE

The brainchild of Charles Sanders Peirce (1839–1914), William James (1842–1910) and John Dewey (1859–1952), pragmatism is basically a theory of knowledge.[8] Pragmatists substitute an experimental, methodological conception of truth for the materialist/idealist and subject/object conundrums of traditional epistemology: Experience is the ultimate warrant of truth; knowledge is merely a predicate of effective action; and meaning is understood in terms of consequences. Indeed, Dewey prefers to talk about intelligence rather than knowledge or truth: "The function of intelligence is ... not that of copying the objects of the environment, but rather of taking account of the way in which more effective and more profitable relations with these objects may be established in the future" ([1925] 1984, p. 17).

Organized inquiry or experiment strengthens and deepens intelligence. Four presumptions are central to most versions of pragmatic inquiry:

- Consequentialism – beliefs are warranted by their practical consequences.
- Fallibilism – all warranties are limited; intelligence is always open to criticism and revision, so that nothing is ever finally or absolutely true (indeed, confidence in a belief is reflected in the readiness to put it to the test).
- Anti-skepticism – complete doubt, treating all beliefs as equally likely, is impossible, a mere philosophical pretension.
- Creative flow – problematic situations drive inquiry. Situations give inquiry focus and gauge the transformations that accompany it (learning). Problematic situations are not static, however. Experience gives rise to an endless sequence of problematic situations, which continuous, disciplined inquiry transforms, through virtuous spirals, into a creative flow of intelligence.

To these basic presumptions, Dewey adds several ideas about science and democracy. For our purposes, the most important of these is democratic social constructivism – pragmatism is an integrated process of social inquiry that is democratic to its core. This has the effect of converting pragmatism from a theory of knowledge to a theory of social inquiry. Of course, social knowledge is necessarily socially constructed. Dewey explains:

> To represent things as they are is to represent them in ways that tend to maintain a common understanding; to misrepresent them is to injure – whether willfully or no – the conditions of common understanding. An understanding is an agreement; a misunderstanding a disagreement, and understanding is a social necessity because it is a prerequisite of all community of action. It is no accident that the terms communication and community lie so near together; or that intercourse means equally speech and any mode of associated life. ([6]Dewey, [1911] 1978; p. 67).

However, the notion that democracy is a necessary part of a pragmatic theory of social inquiry is by no means obvious, and needs explication.

Dewey believed that social intelligence is practical and forward looking, aimed at helping people deal with real "tensions, needs, and troubles," and that to be useful, in this sense, it is necessary to make "the widening and buttressing of knowledge a business" (1916, p. 76). This implies that, as a methodology or mode of inquiry, pragmatism is almost necessarily a social or collective enterprise, which in turn implies a community of inquirers.

But, why conflate pragmatism with democracy, especially an all-inclusive participatory democracy? The facile claim that face-to-face problem-solving conversation, the heart of pragmatic inquiry, is inherently egalitarian that just does not cut it. Face-to-face conversation is as much honored in hierarchies as in democracies (Schudson, 1997). Dewey's answer to this question is multifaceted. He begins with the pragmatist's presumption that "intelligence is present most distinctively ... in the work a day practicality of the masses" (MacGilvray, 1999, p. 551). Next, he provides a model for a cooperative, problem-solving community, the scientific community,[9] which is democratic with respect to membership and open to the participation of all. Science also provides Dewey with a set of conversational norms – open-mindedness, honesty, impartiality, and regard for empirical consequences – that communities of inquirers ought to use to design experiments and to communicate, interpret, and evaluate their results. The adherence to these norms allows for an all-inclusive collective search for shared meaning.

However, Dewey's approach to practical reasoning stressed democratic accountability as much as democratic conversation. He argued that a community of inquirers must be inclusive because, if the consequences of conjoint activity are to be understood, they must not only be freely communicated to all the members of the community, but they must also be interpreted by all those who experience them. This, Dewey argued, required

> (1) positive control of the resources necessary to carry purposes into effect ... and (2) mental equipment with the trained powers of initiative and reflection requisite for free preference and for circumspect and far-seeing desires. ... No government by experts in which the masses do not have the chance to inform the experts as to their needs can be anything but an oligarchy managed in the interests of a few. (Dewey, [1927] 1984, p. 364)

Finally, Dewey stressed the potential force of collective intelligence. He believed that direct participation in decision-making would foster a talent for thoughtful deliberation in ordinary people. "We lie in the lap of an immense intelligence," Dewey said ([1927] 1984, p. 17). The difficulty is to unleash this intelligence, which remains dormant until "it possesses [a] ... community as its medium" (ibid.). In *The Public and its Problems*, he outlined an elaborate program of truly participatory democracy, one built around face-to-face conversations in neighborly communities. In other words, Dewey argued not only that ordinary people can always better understand and appreciate their own circumstances and interests than can experts, they are collectively smarter, at least potentially.[10] What ordinary people need to achieve their potential is training in collective inquiry and the motivation to participate in decision-making. As he explained, democracy, rightly conceived, is a process. In Dewey's words, it is

> a wider and fuller idea than can be exemplified in the state even at its best. To be realized it must affect all modes of human association, the family, the school, industry, religion ... Democracy is not an alternative to other principles of associated life. It is the idea of community life itself. (Dewey, [1927] 1984, p. 148).

One further point: despite his emphasis on participative and deliberative norms, Dewey reserved an important place for leaders in his communities of inquiry. Of course, Dewey's leaders are not Hamel and Prahalad's. Dewey defined leadership in terms of its functions, not as an attribute of office.[11] Consequently, his leaders are more like teachers or guides than principals or bosses. Their aim is the development of human potential. Their job is preparing ordinary people to share effectively in social life, especially as members of communities of inquirers. This means structuring experience and activities so that people learn by doing and by publicly reflecting upon what they have done.

As we have seen, both Hamel and Prahalad, and Nonaka and Takeuchi ground their lines of reasoning on a theory of knowledge. Indeed, Nonaka and Takeuchi take explicit account of formal epistemological theories and premises. In contrast, Dorothy Leonard, in the *Wellsprings of Knowledge* (1998), pays almost no attention to these concerns; she does not ask how we know or what we can know; she does not even make a logical case for a particular approach to knowing. Instead, her purpose is relentlessly empirical. She describes the attributes and processes of successful knowledge-based organizations and compares them to conventional organizations. Nevertheless, her knowledge-based organizations sound remarkably like Dewey's communities of inquirers; her knowledge managers are Dewey's guides or teachers.

Consider her governing metaphors: managers are nurturing farmers; they grow abilities within the fertile confines of the organization. By planting the seeds of knowledge, and nurturing them, the organization acquires increased capabilities, which can be harvested in the marketplace. Leonard's leaders are like Dewey's in that they recognize that they must

> respect and encourage the accumulation of knowledge as a legitimate undertaking and one for which they are responsible... [S]uch leaders [try] to foster an atmosphere in which a thousand flowers could bloom" (Leonard, 1998, p. 116).

They further understand that

> people who are knowingly engaged in building core technological capabilities are *curious*: they are information seekers... The only fundamentally important skill is the ability to learn ... [T]echnologically talented employees could create whole new businesses for corporations, starting with an experimental project or process. (Leonard, 1998, pp. 261–262)

Experimenting and prototyping provide the energy behind a continuous creative flow (Leonard, 1998, p. 30). As she explains:

> Despite the Greek Myth about goddess of wisdom, Athena, who burst full-grown from Zeus's forehead, knowledge does not appear all at once. Rather, knowledge accumulates slowly, over time, is shaped and channeled into certain directions through the nudging of

hundreds of daily managerial decisions. Nor does knowledge occur only one time; it is constantly aborning. ... Knowledge reservoirs in organizations are not static pools but wellsprings, constantly replenished with streams of new ideas and constituting an ever-flowing source of corporate renewal. Therefore, the development of core capabilities is inextricably linked to learning; knowledge is both raw material and finished goods in today's corporations. (Leonard, 1998, p. 3)

The Wellsprings of Knowledge metaphor reflects Leonard's concept of knowledge as a flow and its practical application to the problems of the collectivity. She describes wellsprings as

constant, reliable, and their waters pure ... (Their) flows ... feed the biological systems around them, so in the same way, flows of appropriate knowledge into and within companies enable them to develop competitively advantageous capabilities. (Leonard, 1998, p. 13).

Learning is the product of an ongoing flow of events that includes ideas, claims, observations, processes and their measurement and experimental testing: "experimentation creates what has been termed 'requisite variety' in products and processes – i.e., a diverse portfolio of technological options" (Leonard, 1998, p. 14).

In other words, knowledge flows from the lowest level of the organization and grows to perfection, evolving over time by nourishing itself via interaction between its parts. These include: (a) people's skills; (b) knowledge embodied in physical systems; (c) managerial systems that support and reinforce knowledge growth; and (d) values that support the accumulation of knowledge, which necessarily involves teamwork and shared problem solving at the lowest level. Organizations that focus on nurturing capabilities at the lowest level and growing them properly, succeed. Experimentation is essential to building and sustaining this process or flow. Knowledge capability develops and ultimately manifests itself in the relationships between people in the organization, the activities they perform, and their consequences. Workers catch sight of innovations, become conscious of them, and internalize them through experiment, use, and practice; at the same time, current practices and yesterday's innovations fade from individual memory and the operating procedures of the organization. To paraphrase Leonard, this evolving flow reflects a view of human potential as improvement over time – the gradual socialization of new knowledge, which grows from the seeds of innovation, planted in the fertile ground of the organization and is fed by its wellsprings.

Leonard also cautions against allowing the dead ideas of the past – set patterns, fixed outlooks, or notions about how things ought to be done – to constrain the ability of the organization to learn and innovate. "Decisions and events from the past intrude on the present and shape the future" (Leonard, 1998, p. 35), resulting in solidified organizational outlooks and routines. They interfere with learning because "experimentation is limited when knowledge extension flows along well-worn paths rather than creating new options" (Leonard, 1998, p. 39). Indeed, much of what Leonard has to say about knowledge creation is concerned with overcoming obstacles to collective learning – core rigidities and their ubiquitous companions, knowledge-inhibiting activities.

Physical plant and equipment and its layout, managerial systems, skill sets, and organizational culture and values are all potential sources of core rigidities. Physical and structural rigidities are relatively easy to fix. Social and intellectual rigidities – working relationships, communications patterns, skill sets, and culture and values – are hard to change. Leonard observes that reducing social and intellectual rigidities requires the active participation and engagement of nearly the whole organization, which in turn means empowering workers to apply what they have learned to the problems at hand. The key to successful organizational growth is,

> continuous learning and knowledge accumulation [that] depend on the sense of ownership derived from special educational systems, on values embedded in policies and managerial practices, as well as on specific technical skills ... If all employees conceive of their organization as a knowledge institution and care about nurturing it, they will continuously contribute to the capabilities that sustain it. (Leonard, 1998, pp. 266–267)

To Leonard, knowledge creation is not great leaps forward or startling innovations that sweep the industry: it is participation in a community of learners; it is collective intelligence; and it is excellence contributed by everyone in the organization. Consequently, the sources of a knowledge-based organization's competitive advantage will be practically invisible to the outsider. The example Leonard cites of such an organization is Chaparral Steel, whose CEO brags that competitors can tour Chaparral's plant with impunity because its competitive advantage lies in the skills of its employees and the face-to-face relationships they have with one another, and not on any technological innovation outside of the workers themselves. This reflects Leonard's vision of innovation as knowledge development and growth taken down to the lowest level of the organization, and of the manager as the wellspring of support for this process.

Reductio ad absurdum, or reduction to self-contradiction, is one of the more widely used tools of traditional philosophy. In the case of pragmatism, reduction to self-contradiction means rebutting its epistemological claims on consequentialist grounds, i.e., showing that they are neither useful nor practical. Dewey's claims about the social processes through which knowledge is broadened and strengthened, especially his conflation of pragmatism with democracy, have often been dismissed as utopian (in the negative sense of the term).

In fact, Dewey's version of participatory democracy does seem to fly in the face of what we know about the limits of political engagement and participation, which undermines the credibility of pragmatism as a philosophical system and not merely as a political doctrine. Moreover, Dewey acknowledges the problem: citizens have only a casual interest in the doings of the polity. Most citizens do not see government as central to their lives and, because participation in decision making is costly, they largely opt out of the process. According to Robert Westbrook (1992), however, Dewey's conclusions about all-inclusive communities of inquiry were shaped, not by his ruminations on the polity (although that was the subject of *The Public and its Problems*, where he laid out his notions of democracy as a process integral to pragmatism as a mode of inquiry), but on organizations, especially the conflict between labor and management. Westbrook claims that Dewey's aim was inspired by a vision of organizations as cooperative commonwealths – industrial democracies that would be more harmonious, more productive, and more creative than the organizations he knew:

> Plato defined a slave as one who accepts from another the purposes which control his conduct. This condition obtains even where there is no slavery in the legal sense. It is found wherever men are engaged in activity which is socially serviceable, but whose service they do not understand and have no personal interest in. ... The chief opportunity for science is the discovery of the relations of a man to his work – including his relations to others who take part – which will enlist his intelligent interest in what he is doing. Efficiency in production often demands division of labor. But it is reduced to a mechanical routine unless workers see the technical, intellectual, and social relationships involved in what they do, and engage in their work because of the motivation furnished by such perceptions. (Dewey, 1916, p. 85)

Work is central to people's lives. Nowhere, outside of the home, are the consequences flowing from shared activities and institutions more exigent or absorbing than at work. Because job-related decisions do impinge upon their vital interests, ordinary people want to participate in making them, when given the opportunity to do so. One of the most interesting things about Leonard's work, at least from the perspective of a pragmatist, is that it puts paid to the claim that Dewey's ideas about democratic communities of inquiry are entirely useless or impractical – you can get there from here.

This raises a second question: How do we get from here to there? Nonaka and Takeuchi do not answer that question. They simply assume a community of interests and values. But, if you must first have a community to get a community of inquirers, you have only answered part of the question, arguably the easiest part. Leonard goes further. Like Nonaka and Takeuchi she seems to presume that, if management will just get out of the way, communities of interest will emerge spontaneously within the organization, although she also argues that leaders are needed to shape the conversations that take place within organizations to make them productive.

Dewey never satisfactorily answers the question, maybe because he was aiming too high, or maybe because he had no conclusive answer to it. Instead, he made the best bet he could: he put his money down on education. His basic notions about education for democracy and learning by doing are practically ubiquitous in American (and Japanese) schools of education; they have shaped the content and the pedagogy of public education in both countries to a remarkable degree. It is possible that the kind of organizational arrangements, processes, and mechanisms Leonard describes are now feasible at least in part because of groundwork laid in the public schools: that participation in a community of inquirers is a matter of readiness and, after decades of exposure to the tenets of progressive education, workers are ready to participate fully in knowledge-based organizations. Of course, this answer presumes a certain kind of leadership. Interestingly, given Leonard's implicit claim that managers are the main hindrance to knowledge creation (see also Brown & Duguid, 1991; Weick, 1991), professional schools are one place where Dewey's ideas about education for democracy[12] have seldom been influential (Shields, 1998, 2003).

Our point is that social harmony cannot simply be assumed. Dewey's pragmatism understates the pervasiveness of conflict, a problem it shares with approaches to administrative inquiry like Nonaka and Takeuchi's and Leonard's, which presume voluntary communities of interest. Of course, Dewey acknowledges that cooperative collective problem solving requires a great deal of the participants. At a minimum, they need the means to engage with others in reflective argumentative exchange – shared cognitive models of practical reasoning and communication – as well as shared conversational norms. Even when these conditions are met, however, some conflicts still have to be resolved, which implies a further need for mediating processes and arbitrating mechanisms.

Evans and Wurster (1997, pp. 70–71), for example, argue that, in the future, all knowledge-based productive relationships will be designed around fluid, team-based collaborative communities, either within organizations (deconstructed value chains), or collaborative alliances like the "amorphous and permeable corporate boundaries characteristic of companies in the Silicon Valley" (deconstructed supply chains). They assert that, in these relationships "everyone communicates richly with everyone else on the basis of shared standards" and that, like the Internet itself, the architectures of object-oriented software programming, and packet switching in telecommunications, they will eliminate the need to channel information, thereby eliminating the tradeoff between information bandwidth (richness) and connectivity (reach). "The possibility (or the threat) of random access and information symmetry," they conclude, will destroy all hierarchies, whether of logic or power. Maybe. But, how exactly, will these relationships be governed?[13]

Value-creating collective interactions often give rise to substantial public or collective goods (in the technical sense of those terms) and thereby to myriad potential conflicts of interest – with customers, suppliers, shareholders and lenders, between employees and managers, departments, and functions – both in organizations and alliances. Sound governance mechanisms and institutions permit value-creating cooperation; bad ones lead to the exploitation of some by others (win/lose) or, worse, the exploitation of all by all (lose/lose). The design of governance mechanisms is something about which management theorists know all too little. Arguably, political scientists and political philosophers understand collective choice mechanisms and their pitfalls better than do others. Alas, even they do not understand them well. Until design solutions are found to collective-choice problems that work better than either hierarchy or nose counting, the usefulness of Dewey's pragmatism remains open to question.

Finally, comparing, Hamel and Prahalad, Nonaka and Takeuchi, and Leonard makes us think that people in different parts of the organization at different times might, perhaps, need different theories of knowledge. Certainly, Hamel and Prahalad, Nonaka and Takeuchi, and Leonard put us in mind of the Zen koan about the three blind sages and the elephant (it's a rope/tail; it's a fan/ear; it's a tree/leg). Nevertheless, all three are talking about the same elephant – large multiproduct, multifunctioned organizations.

SUMMING UP

Creating knowledge requires inquiry, and inquiry necessarily implies a standard for warranting beliefs. An epistemology is merely a set of standards that people use (or should use) to justify their beliefs. Where organizational knowledge is concerned, it is a set of standards the people in an organization use (or should use) to justify shared beliefs (which, in turn, provides the basis for a collectivity's capacity to create value by doing things cooperatively). The standards that should guide administrative inquiry may ultimately derive from coherence, correspondence, or consequence claims.

Unfortunately, where practical, social reasoning is concerned, these different approaches to warranting truth all seem to raise a fundamental problem of practical reasoning: the mismatch between processes of inquiry and governance mechanisms. Fichte regretfully truncates the process of inquiry to solve the governance problem by deferring to the strongest will. Buddhists rely on generosity, benevolence, cooperation, service, courtesy, sympathy, and honesty to guide social inquiry along virtuous paths and finesse the problem of governance by assuming harmonious unity. Pragmatists offer a fully fledged theory of social inquiry that people in an organization could use to justify shared beliefs. However, pragmatists acknowledge, often implicitly, that they do not have a solution to governance problems. That is, they cannot identify a set of governance mechanisms or institutions that would make their approach to administrative inquiry feasible.

That does not mean that there are no such mechanisms. Indeed, from this perspective, the relationship between epistemology and administrative inquiry may very well be reciprocal. Aarons makes this point clearly and elegantly:

> Philosophers are still largely ... obsessed with understanding the origins and justification of knowledge rather than the dynamics of knowledge as a process. Here we can actually turn things around and look to [administrative inquiry] to provide some inspiration for philosophy ... This will involve extending the accounts of collaborative knowledge production, as provided by philosophy, to broader accounts of collaborative knowledge use. This is where the practical dimension of [administrative inquiry] can actually help to enrich our philosophical understanding of the nature of knowledge, and thereby lead to stronger approaches to [administrative inquiry] grounded in coherent and sound philosophical theory. (Aarons, 2004, p. 11)

It is reasonable to assume that students of administrative inquiry would:

- provide an account of who determines what information counts as evidence and of who determines what is sufficiently justified to count as knowledge, and
- enumerate the ways in which people classify things, conditions, problems, and opportunities, and the ways in which people in organizations come to classify their bodies of knowledge.

Understanding these relationships could help to identify the feasible set of processes or mechanisms for creating and sustaining knowledge – those that are thinkable, available or likely to be adopted in a particular situation – or say how organizational characteristics and configurations should be transformed to exploit the most effective processes and mechanisms of administrative inquiry and argumentation. This could be very useful knowledge; it might even be critical to understanding social inquiry in general. We know that in many if not most organizations senior managers determine what information counts as evidence and what beliefs are sufficiently warranted to count as knowledge. Much the same set of observations applies to functional staff specialists and middle managers. It stands to reason that some approaches to administrative inquiry may be wholly incompatible with particular organizational arrangements. Changing these organizational characteristics and configurations is almost certainly one of the keys to the success of administrative inquiry efforts. Consequently, a reasonable person ought to endorse the proposition that a good organizational sociology of inquiry would be very useful. It might actually help to enrich our philosophical understanding of the nature of knowledge itself.

NOTES

1. Obviously – we got 70,000 hits when we Googled < knowledge-management (KM) and epistemology>. See, for example, Aarons (2004), Allix (2003), and Gourlay (2000). Nevertheless, Aarons is right on target when he observes:

> It is almost impossible to read an introduction to Knowledge-Management (KM) without some mention of philosophy. Indeed, the KM literature is literally riddled with references to philosophers and philosophies. Yet surprisingly, despite the consistent mention of philosophical theory, it is rare to see any detailed connections made between the theory of knowledge *qua* philosophy and the practice of administrative inquiry. (Aarons, 2004, p. 1)

2. Hegel is, of course, the most prominent of the German idealists. One might expect that we would feature his ideas here. However, Hegel was much more concerned with understanding the world than with changing it. For that reason and given our purposes, Fichte, with his emphasis on moralaf0 reasoning and human agency, is better. Besides, he writes more clearly.

3. Nevertheless, Fichte (1846) asserted that reason would ultimately triumph over human instinct, in the full noontide of spiritual human fulfillment that would follow an age in which rational policies would be gradually recognized and adopted by society.

4. Frankly, although we have tried to present these ideas fairly and honestly, idealism seems like a strange, even exotic, growth to us – more like a carbuncle than a blossom. We simply cannot take hold of the notion that the material world is a creation of the mind. On the other hand, we can see why this view could be extremely appealing to readers of the *Harvard Business Review*. The heroic picture it paints of top management is flattering, if not now entirely credible. It reminds us of another

German idealist, Karl von Clausewitz, who described Napoleon as a genius who could grasp the situation at a glance and whose iron will pulverized obstacles into dust.

5. Nonaka and Takeuchi (1996) also include an extended discussion of the history of Western philosophy. Even so, Aarons is largely correct in his claim that Nonaka and Takeuchi make almost no connections between the philosophical ideas of Plato, Aristotle, Descartes and Locke, Kant, Hegel and Marx, Husserl, Heidegger, Sartre, Merleau-Ponty, Wittgenstein, James and Dewey, which they discuss in chapter two, and "their practical discussion on how one goes about the business of knowledge-management" (2004, p. 4). One could argue that Nonaka and Takeuchi's discussion of epistemology helps to explain why some of its premises are relevant to administrative inquiry and others are not, but they don't explicitly make that argument, as Aarons does, for example.

6. Hence, conflict is always comparatively superficial, for there can be no ultimate conflict where opposites are mutually interdependent. Like Hegel, Zen Buddhists reject subject/predicate/object distinctions. Watts (1957, p. 19) attributes these distinctions to language. In English, things and actions are distinguished from each other as nouns and verbs. In languages that use Chinese characters, words can be both nouns and verbs, which results in an ability to see things as events and entities as processes. In this respect, German seems closer to Japanese than to English. In any case, we should not be surprised to learn that Zen Buddhists do not distinguish the dancer from the dance.

7. We are struck by the many points of similarity between Nonaka and Takeuchi's thinking and the ideas of Mary Parker Follett (1965), as elaborated in *The New State*, originally published in 1918, "Community Is a Process" in *Philosophical Review* in Follet (1919), and *Creative Experience* in Follet (1930) (and described by Keith Snider [1998]). Follett was a self-declared follower of both James and Dewey. That declaration led us to look into her work for this article. Indubitably, William James'(1981) psychology (the stream of consciousness) and John Dewey's democratic experimentalism influenced her thinking. However, her pursuit of harmony premised upon an organic social unity seems more important to us than her pragmatism. As Follett explained (all references are to *The New State* as cited by Snider [1998]), people relate psychically in such a way that their consciousnesses interpenetrate. Organizational consciousness emerges out of the encounter between individual consciousnesses. Each new activity and experience adds to the experience of the group. Further, the degree to which interpenetration occurs in an organization depends upon the genuineness and authenticity of the relations among its members. That is, interpenetration harmonizes differences. Members achieve this by recognizing the objective demands of the situation and the needs and powers of their fellows. For Follett, reality is relating.

> The only reality is the relating of one to the other which creates both. Our sundering is as artificial ... an act as the sundering of consciousness into subject and object. The only reality is the interpenetrating of the two into experience. (1998, p. 61).

Facts emerge in relation, purposes emerge in relation, and relations create both personal and group identities.

> I learn my duty to my friends not by reading essays on friendship, but by living my life with my friends and learning by experience the obligations friendship demands.... Ideas

unfold *within* human experience, not by their own momentum apart from experience. (1998, pp. 192–193)

Further, we know only in a tentative way because situations and relations are always interweaving, constantly creating new facts and purposes (1998, p. 210). Finally, "Life is the true revealer: I can never understand the whole by reason, only when the heartbeat of the whole throbs through me as the pulse of my own being" (1998, p. 265).

8. We base most of our claims on the writings of Dewey (1929, 1930, 1938, 1978, 1997). While several pragmatists – Peirce (1955a, b, c), Josiah Royce, and George Herbert Mead – made contributions to our understanding of how people order and maintain social relations based on language and our capacity to understand and respond to others, only Dewey built a formal theory of social knowledge. Unfortunately, Dewey's meaning is often as obscure as Hegel's.

9. In a very similar vein, Aarons (2004, pp. 10–11) argues that the philosophy of science would be a rewarding place to look for knowledge management insights. He claims that philosophers of science are now less concerned with developing general accounts of what science is (e.g., Karl Popper and Thomas Kuhn) than they are with building a picture of knowledge creation in a group context, what he calls "looking more closely at the fine detail of science." These fine details have to do with how scientists work, reason, experiment, collaborate, etc., although he cautions,

> current approaches in the philosophy of science ... are still somewhat lacking ... [T]hey provide a detailed account of knowledge *production*, but little or no account of knowledge *use*. ... [T]hey have little to say about the pragmatics of knowledge storage, knowledge sharing, and knowledge dispersal, all essential aspects of knowledge management projects.

10. Economists who accept the strong version of (financial) market efficiency go even further than Dewey does: they argue that collective intelligence always exceeds individual intelligence. James Surowiecki (2003) takes an intermediate position: he argues on empirical grounds that, if four basic conditions are met, collective intelligence will consistently outperform experts. He claims that the evidence supports his position even when members of the collectivity do not know all the facts or choose, individually, to act irrationally. The necessary and sufficient conditions identified by Surowiecki are (1) diversity of opinion, (2) independence of opinion, (3) decentralization to those with an interest (not necessarily a selfish interest) in the outcome, and (4) a good method for aggregating opinions. Diversity brings in different information; independence keeps people from being swayed by a single opinion leader; people's errors balance each other out; and including all opinions guarantees that the results are smarter than if a single expert had been in charge.

11. Although, to be honest, that distinction is open to interpretation – it is not always clear when Dewey is talking about known institutions or organizations, democracy as a process, or migration paths from where we are to his ideal community of inquirers. The comments that follow reflect our reading of *Democracy and Education* (1916), probably Dewey's best-known work.

12. Total quality management (TQM) is an exception to this generalization. Many schools of engineering, management, and public affairs teach TQM. There is evidence that Shewhart, Deming, and Juran were influenced by Dewey's preoccupation with method and argument. How much is a matter of speculation, certainly, Deming, with his distaste for authoritarian, command-and-control hierarchies, often sounds

like Dewey. However, most of the evidence for pragmatism's influence on quality management is circumstantial, e.g., TQM's and pragmatism's procedural and methodological affinities – the plan, do, check, act cycle, for instance.

13. Note that we are not saying that they cannot be governed, or that self-organization is infeasible, merely that voluntary collaborative relationships imply far worse collective goods problems than are encountered in organizations designed to carry out repetitive processes. Given that we lack the codified knowledge needed to master collective goods problems in traditional organizations (although in practice they are, nevertheless, frequently surmounted through some combination of social solidarity, personal charm, and organizational craftsmanship), it is not obvious that we will soon figure out how to govern voluntary collaborations – which suggests a surprising inference about management training and research. If the purpose of organizational scholarship is answering important questions and not merely codifying existing knowledge, political study and analysis are much more crucial to our efforts than has hitherto been recognized.

ACKNOWLEDGMENTS

We wish to express our gratitude to Perri 6, Cindy Bond, Ruth Crowley, and Patricia Shields for their comments and suggestions for correcting earlier versions of this article. Of course, the errors remaining are entirely our own.

REFERENCES

Aarons, J. (2004). From philosophy to knowledge management and back again. Victoria, Australia: Monash University, *School of Information Management and Systems*. Retrieved September 24, 2005, from http://home.iprimus.com.au/jpaarons/papers/ISD2003Aarons.pdf.

Aiken, H. D. (1984). *The age of ideology*. New York: New American Library.

Allix, N. M. (2003). Epistemology and knowledge management concepts and practices. *Journal of Knowledge Management Practice, 4*. Retrieved May 27, 2005, from http://www.tlainc.com/.

Brown, J. S., & Duguid, P. (1991). Organizational learning and communities-of-practice: Toward a unified view of working, learning, and innovation. *Organization Science, 2*, 40–57.

Dewey, J. (1916). *Democracy and education*. New York: Macmillan.

Dewey, J. ([1927]1984). *The public and its problems*. Athens: Ohio University Press.

Dewey, J. (1929). *Experience and nature* (2nd ed.). LaSalle, IL: Open Court Press.

Dewey, J. (1930). *The quest for certainty*. London: Kegan Paul.

Dewey, J. (1938). *Logic: The theory of inquiry*. New York: Holt, Rinehart & Winston.

Dewey, J. (1978). The problem of truth. In: J. A. Boydston (Ed.), *The middle works of John Dewey*, (Vol. 6, pp. 12–68). Carbondale: Southern Illinois University Press (Original work published 1911).

Dewey, J. (1997). The influence of Darwin on philosophy. In: J. Dewey (Ed.), *The influence of Darwin on philosophy and other essays* (pp. 3–14). Amherst, NY: Prometheus (Original work published 1910).

Evans, P. B. and Wurster, T. S. (1997). Strategy and the new economics of information. *Harvard Business Review (Sept.–Oct.)*, 71–82.

Fichte, J. G. (1869). The science of rights (trans.), *Grundlage des Naturalrechts*. Philadelphia: originally published 1796.

Fichte, J. G. (1889). Popular Works (various works translated by William Smith, 1848–1849). London.

Follett, M. P. (1919). Community is a process. *The Philosophical Review*, *28*(November), 576–588.

Follett, M. P. (1930). *Creative experience*. New York: Longmans, Green.

Follett, M. P. (1965). *The new state*. Gloucester, MA: Peter Smith.

Frost, S. E., Jr. (1962). *Basic teachings of the great philosophers*. Garden City, NY: Dolphin Books.

Gaskins, R. H. (1992). *Burdens of proof in modern discourse*. New Haven: Yale University Press.

Gourlay, S. (2000, February). Frameworks for knowledge: A contribution towards conceptual clarity for knowledge management. Paper presented at Knowledge Management: Concepts and Controversies Conference, BPRC, University of Warwick, Coventry, UK.

Hamel, G., & Prahalad, C. K. (1994). *Competing for the future*. Boston: Harvard Business School Press.

Hedstrom, P., & Swedberg, R. (Eds) (1996). *Social mechanisms: An analytical approach to social theory*. Cambridge, UK: Cambridge University Press.

James, W. (1981). *Pragmatism*. Indianapolis, IN: Hacket Publishing Co.

Leonard, D. (1998). *Wellsprings of knowledge*. Boston: Harvard Business School Press.

MacGilvray, E. A. (1999). Experience as experiment: Some consequences of pragmatism for democratic theory. *American Journal of Political Science*, *43*, 542–565.

Nakamura, H. (1973). Buddhism. In: *Dictionary of the History of Ideas* (Vol. 1, pp. 248–257). New York: Charles Scribner's Sons. Retrieved September 24, 2005, from http://etext.lib.virginia.edu/cgi-local/DHI/dhi.cgi?id=dvl-34.

Nonaka, I., & Takeuchi, H. (1996). *The knowledge creating company*. New York: Oxford University Press.

Peirce, C. S. (1955a). The fixation of belief. In: J. Buchler (Ed.), *The philosophical writings of Peirce* (pp. 5–22). New York: Dover.

Peirce, C. S. (1955b). How to make our ideas clear. In: J. Buchler (Ed.), *The philosophical writings of Peirce* (pp. 23–41). New York: Dover.

Peirce, C. S. (1955c). The scientific attitude and fallibilism. In: J. Buchler (Ed.), *The philosophical writings of Peirce* (pp. 42–59). New York: Dover.

Schudson, M. (1997). Why conversation is not the soul of democracy. *Critical Studies in Mass Communication*, *14*, 297–309.

Shields, P. (1998). Pragmatism as a philosophy of science: A tool for public administration. In: J. White (Ed.), *Research in Public Administration* (Vol. 4, pp. 195–225). Stamford, CT: JAI Press.

Shields, P. (2003). The community of inquiry: Classical pragmatism and public administration. *Administration and Society*, *35*, 510–538.

Simons, H. W. (2001). *Persuasion in society*. Thousand Oaks, CA: Sage.

Snider, K. F. (1998). Living pragmatism: The case of Mary Parker Follett. *Administrative Theory and Praxis*, *20*, 274–286.

Surowiecki, J. (2003). *The wisdom of crowds: Why the many are smarter than the few and how collective wisdom shapes business, economies, societies and nations*. New York: Doubleday.

Tilly, C. (2000). Mechanisms in Political Processes. *Annual Review of Political Science 4*, 21–41. Retrieved May 27, 2005, from http://www.asu.edu/clas/polisci/cqrm/papers/Tilly/TillyMechs.pdf.

Tsanoff, R. A. (1967). Johann Gotlieb Fichte. In: *The Encyclopedia of Philosophy* (Vol. 3, pp. 192–196). New York: Macmillan.

Walton, D. (1994). *Persuasive argument in everyday conversation*. Albany: SUNY Press.

Watts, A. W. (1957). *The way of Zen*. New York: Pantheon Books.

Weick, K. (1991). The nontraditional quality of organizational learning. *Organization Science*, 2, 116–124.

Westbrook, R. B. (1992). Schools for industrial democrats: The social origins of John Dewey's pragmatism. *American Journal of Education, 100*, 401–419.

SUBJECT INDEX

accountability 3, 7, 32, 41, 43, 47–48, 52, 73, 75, 77, 83, 85, 87, 99, 101–102, 137, 179–181, 190, 198, 202–204, 211, 213, 221–223, 243, 251, 253–254, 269
activists 11, 22, 191, 246–248, 250–253
administrative inquiry 257–259, 261, 263, 265–267, 269, 271, 273–279, 281
appeals 104, 128, 234
appearance standards 45, 60
applied 2–3, 56, 60, 66, 130, 165
argumentation 3, 257–258, 277
Attorney General v. Harper 125
Australia 7, 10, 16, 18, 24, 85, 94–95, 97, 101–102, 104–106, 208, 210, 215, 249, 254

Bill C-4 7, 19, 24, 73, 98
Bill Clinton 38, 124, 147
Bill of Rights 9, 94, 131–132
Bouchery Commission 58
bribery 49–50, 60, 94–95, 114, 135, 137, 140, 175
Britain 6–10, 16, 18–19, 22–24, 35, 39, 41, 79, 85, 110, 112
British Civil Service 32, 59
Buddhism 259, 263–264, 267

Cabinet 52, 72–82, 84–85, 87, 101, 110–112, 114–118, 121–124, 132, 209, 212, 220
campaign finance 109–110, 123–125, 129, 132, 138, 140, 148, 151–152, 164–165, 233
Canada 2, 4, 6, 8–10, 15–16, 18–19, 22–24, 44, 67, 71–74, 76–77, 81, 84–86, 89, 94–95, 98–99, 101–102, 104–105, 109–115, 117–133
capacity 3, 10, 44, 96, 110, 112, 125, 133, 143, 188, 196, 198, 200, 203–204, 209, 214, 216–217, 249, 258, 260, 275, 279
careerism 246
Charles Keating 151
checks and balances 10, 84, 86, 208–209
civic education 229, 236–237
co-regulation 7, 22
code 2, 7, 13–14, 24–25, 30, 33, 43–66, 72–73, 75, 87–88, 95–97, 100–102, 105–106, 111, 115–118, 122, 132, 140, 143, 155, 168, 171, 180, 207, 213, 221–222, 224, 242, 245, 254, 265–266
codes deontologiques 51, 65
codes of conduct 2, 7, 43–49, 51, 55–58, 62, 65–66, 97, 105–106, 221
coherence 259, 276
Commission 7, 10, 22, 44, 57–58, 62–63, 88, 96–99, 101, 103, 105–106, 136, 138–139, 141, 146, 149, 152, 156, 158–160, 162, 164, 168, 170–171, 207, 209, 212
Committee on Standards in Public Life 7, 9, 12, 19, 50, 52–53, 55, 60, 93, 96, 101–102, 106
committees 30, 37, 81, 84, 96–98, 101–102, 107, 136, 141, 149, 152, 158–160, 164, 168, 170, 224
Common Cause 15, 20, 136, 142
compliance 31, 46, 156, 159, 171, 213, 215, 219, 223–224

283

conditionality 31–32, 40
conduct 6–9, 11–15, 20, 22, 24–25,
    30–39, 41, 46–47, 49–51, 53–54, 57–59,
    61–64, 66, 72–73, 88, 93–98, 100–102,
    104, 106, 132, 137–139, 142, 150–151,
    156, 159–164, 167–168, 171, 175,
    207–215, 219–224, 227, 229–231,
    233–242, 254, 273
confidence 2, 5–7, 15, 17, 20, 34, 39, 41,
    43, 52–53, 78, 87, 106, 137, 155, 166,
    168–169, 214, 268
conflict-of-interest 1, 13, 44, 114–115,
    117–118, 120, 122–123, 170, 252
consequence 3, 31, 39, 47, 57, 61, 76,
    78, 89, 105, 109, 135–136, 144, 146,
    159, 161, 163, 181–182, 184–186, 190,
    195, 197–198, 214, 217, 221, 243–244,
    247–248, 252, 254, 259–260, 266–269,
    271, 273, 276
contracting 1, 44, 57–58
conversational norms 269, 274
correspondence 259, 276
corruption 1–2, 11, 13, 32, 39, 44–46,
    49–50, 52–53, 55, 57–62, 65–66, 72,
    95, 98, 102, 136, 138, 140, 147–152,
    155, 162–165, 169, 175–176, 180, 207,
    210–212, 215, 223, 228, 237, 252
costs 2, 16, 19–20, 22–23, 45, 99,
    135–137, 139, 141, 143–145, 147,
    149, 151, 153, 202, 250
Council of Europe 57, 60, 66
counselor 72, 98, 116, 119–122
culture 2, 38, 41, 44, 49, 56, 66, 76,
    93, 104, 138, 148–149, 155, 161, 168,
    173–175, 187, 191, 194, 196–198, 200,
    229, 265, 272

debate 44, 48, 52, 57, 60, 77, 86–87, 94,
    103, 106, 109–111, 129–131, 187, 193,
    203, 209–213, 219, 233, 235, 238, 241,
    258, 261
decency 2, 207–208, 210, 219–221, 223
decline of trust 30, 34

deliberation 81, 86, 130, 180–181, 185,
    188, 198, 208–210, 212–213, 220, 224,
    232–234, 236, 238–240, 253, 269
deliberative democracy 208, 220, 232,
    234–236, 240–241
democracy 12–13, 15, 17, 20, 22, 32, 72,
    77–78, 81, 89, 144, 151, 169, 198, 209,
    219–221, 223, 225, 228–232, 239–242,
    244–245, 251, 253, 268–269, 273–274,
    279
Democracy Watch 15, 20, 22, 72
democratic constancy 247
design 6, 10–13, 229, 269, 275
deterrent 107, 140, 143–144, 162, 170, 172
dialogue 202
discourse 3, 39, 125, 127, 180, 228,
    230–232, 234–235, 239, 242
discretion 34, 122, 138, 141, 151,
    180–181, 203, 213, 219, 221
divestiture 120, 144

effect 2, 11–15, 17, 20, 22–23, 37, 41,
    48, 50, 54, 72, 88, 107, 111, 120–122,
    124–126, 133, 137, 141–144, 147–148,
    155, 158–162, 168–175, 186, 191, 200,
    211–212, 217, 229, 236, 249, 259–260,
    268–269
Elizabeth Filkin 103
enforcement 11, 17, 22–23, 38, 43, 45, 78,
    87, 96–97, 103–104, 106, 136, 140–141,
    152, 156, 158–160, 163, 170
ethics 1–20, 22–25, 29–41, 44–46, 53,
    56, 58–62, 66, 71–75, 77, 79, 81, 83,
    85–89, 91, 93, 95, 98–105, 107,
    109–111, 113, 115–123, 125, 127, 129,
    131–133, 135–153, 155–156, 158–176,
    203, 207–215, 219–225, 229–230, 233,
    236, 238, 240, 242–245, 249–250,
    253–254
Ethics Reform Task Force 38
ethos 3, 93, 107, 227, 229–231, 233–237,
    239–241, 245, 247, 251, 253–254
European Union 30

Subject Index

feedback 6, 8, 10–16, 18, 20, 22, 58, 184, 190, 202
financial disclosure 100, 105, 136–137, 140, 142–144, 147–148, 150, 152, 157–159, 169, 171
France 2, 44, 49–51, 55–57, 59–60, 65

Germany 2, 44, 50–51, 59–61
gifts 13, 54, 60–61, 75, 105, 116–117, 135–138, 140–142, 144, 152, 157, 159, 165, 167, 172, 174
globalization 29–30
governance 1–4, 31–33, 45, 89, 187, 208, 221, 275–276

harmony 259, 263–264, 266–267, 274, 278
historical institutionalism 8
honoraria 105, 135, 137, 140, 144, 165
House Ethics Committee 142, 145, 158
House of Commons 9, 12, 50, 72, 77–79, 81–82, 84, 93, 96, 106, 112, 242, 245

idealism 66, 251, 259, 262, 277
international Code for Public Officials 6–180
institutional 6–7, 10, 12, 16–17, 19–20, 29, 39, 66, 86–89, 109, 113, 130, 136, 148–149, 151, 155, 163, 185, 189, 194, 197–198, 212, 220–221, 232, 240, 260
institutions 2, 6, 8, 10–11, 17–18, 22–24, 29–31, 38, 41, 109, 125–127, 130–133, 169, 175–176, 179–183, 189, 194–197, 203, 212, 220, 229–231, 273, 275–276, 279
interest groups 15, 109, 124–127, 129–133, 137
Ireland 7, 80, 94–95, 97, 103
Italy 2, 32, 44, 50–51, 62–63, 65

Jean Chretien 112, 118, 123
Jim Wright 39

Johann Gottlieb Fichte 259
John Dewey 267, 278

Keating Five 151
knowledge 34, 38, 54, 74, 76, 97, 188, 191, 202–203, 218, 238, 252, 257–259, 261–263, 265–268, 270–272, 274–280

leadership 2, 39, 78, 83, 127, 133, 150–151, 164, 179, 181, 183, 186, 189–192, 194–203, 261, 267, 270, 274
legacy 179, 181–188, 193–203
legislator 2, 5–6, 12, 24, 39, 74, 109–113, 115–119, 121–122, 124, 132, 135–144, 146–148, 150–152, 155–159, 161–175, 209, 245, 247–248
legislature 2, 5–7, 9–10, 18, 22–24, 39, 51, 77, 79, 81, 86, 94–95, 97–100, 104–106, 113, 115, 132, 137, 139–140, 143–144, 147, 152, 155–171, 173, 175–176, 198
legitimacy 77, 183, 187, 222, 227–228, 230–234, 237–238, 241, 243, 246, 249–251, 253
lobbyists 123, 136–137, 139, 142, 152, 156–159, 161, 166, 170, 172–174
lock-in 16, 18, 168

management 1, 44, 50, 54–55, 58–61, 64, 66, 186, 189–190, 195, 197, 207, 212–213, 220–222, 257–258, 262, 273–275, 277, 279–280
Mary Parker Follet 278
Max Weber 190
mechanisms 2–3, 5, 11, 18–20, 25, 36, 43, 59, 63, 65, 85–86, 100–101, 106, 140–141, 159, 180, 223, 232, 236–237, 243, 258, 274–277
media 2, 13–14, 20, 33–41, 72, 87, 107, 141, 144, 147–151, 155–156, 160, 162, 166–167, 169–171, 175–176, 228–230, 235
Members' Interests Committee 7

misconduct 11, 17, 34, 36, 38, 40, 45, 56, 97–98, 100, 211, 220
monuments 185, 187, 195, 200–202
moral 2–3, 6, 12, 22, 38, 45–46, 63, 78, 85, 87, 93, 100, 127, 138, 150, 169, 175, 179–184, 198, 204, 215, 231–232, 236–238, 241, 243–253, 258, 260–261, 277

nepotism 157, 167
New Zealand 101
Newt Gingrich 39, 144
NGO 3, 243–244, 249–251, 254
Nolan Committee 103
norms 1, 6, 40, 45, 48, 78, 101, 104, 106, 109–110, 132–133, 163, 184, 191, 194, 202, 210, 214–215, 220–221, 223–224, 236–240, 264, 269–270

OECD anti-bribery convention 60, 66
organizational 45–46, 179, 181, 189, 194, 197–200, 259, 261, 266–267, 272, 274–278, 280
outsourcing 1, 44, 48

parliament 6–9, 12, 15, 24, 41, 52, 57, 62–63, 71–74, 76–82, 84–88, 94–99, 101, 103–106, 110–111, 116–117, 119, 122, 125, 131–132, 210, 221
Parliamentary Privileges Act 1987 95
parliamentary systems 9–10, 110, 114, 220–221
participation 3, 128–129, 180, 224, 228, 230, 237, 269, 272–274
partisans 83, 123, 146
partisanship 2, 33, 38–39, 71, 73–74, 78, 83, 89, 146, 228
party 10, 12, 30, 33, 38–39, 62, 71–72, 74–77, 79–84, 86–87, 89, 100, 104, 106, 110, 123–131, 133, 146, 221, 248, 253
path dependence 1, 5–6, 16, 22

Paul Martin 72, 111–112, 119, 121, 123
performance 39, 47–48, 63–64, 95, 106, 116, 133, 183, 195–197, 202–203, 218, 222, 258
personal 13, 25, 35–37, 46, 51, 53–54, 85, 110, 115, 121, 123, 128, 131, 150–151, 157, 163, 173–174, 179–182, 199, 201, 204, 207, 211–212, 214–219, 223, 234, 244, 261, 264–267, 273, 278, 280
pluralism 231–232, 241, 243–245, 247–249, 251–253, 255
policy 3, 6, 8, 10–20, 22–25, 52, 56, 62–63, 77–78, 81, 109, 114, 120–121, 137, 146, 148, 168, 183, 188–189, 191, 193, 195–197, 200, 212–213, 220, 228, 232, 235, 241, 250–251, 253
political 1–3, 5–6, 8, 10–20, 22–24, 29–41, 47–49, 51–52, 54–57, 59–60, 62–63, 66, 71–77, 79, 81–89, 91, 101, 113, 122–127, 130, 139, 141, 145–152, 156, 162–164, 168–170, 174–176, 180, 185, 187–188, 194–195, 198–199, 207–215, 219–224, 227–241, 243–253, 273, 275, 280
practical reasoning 3, 257–258, 269, 274, 276
practice 2, 9, 19, 31–32, 36, 40, 43, 45, 55, 59–60, 65, 71, 73, 105, 126, 137, 145, 156, 163, 169–170, 175, 189, 194, 196–197, 199, 208, 211, 214, 219, 223–224, 227–229, 236–238, 240, 251, 254, 260, 264, 271–272, 277, 280
pragmatism 259, 267–268, 272–275, 278, 280
press 14, 33–35, 41, 136, 141–143, 163–164, 166–167, 171–173, 176, 233, 237
prevention of Corruption Acts 46
privacy 36, 106, 139, 142, 169
procedure 2, 6, 37, 46, 52, 54, 59, 61, 63, 95–96, 98, 104, 180, 228, 230–231, 233, 236, 239, 241, 261, 266, 271

processes 3, 5, 11–12, 16–18, 20, 23–24, 29, 39, 46, 48, 63, 98, 146, 151, 168, 176, 193, 208–209, 212, 221, 224, 228–229, 231, 237, 241, 258, 262, 270–272, 274, 276–278, 280
public officials 1–2, 11–13, 20, 43–44, 46, 51, 53, 55–59, 61–62, 65, 72–73, 86, 135–136, 138–139, 142, 147–150, 168, 180, 187, 204
public sector 1, 44–45, 56, 72, 101, 106, 114, 207
public trust 1, 5–7, 17, 31, 39, 43, 75, 93, 107, 137, 147–148, 151, 168–169, 175, 180, 207, 213, 222
public–private partnerships 1
purchasing 1, 44, 57

Rechtsstaat 1, 59
recruitment 2, 99, 139, 142–144, 151, 155, 171
recusal 117, 120, 158
reform 8, 13, 17, 23–25, 29, 31, 38–39, 41, 48, 62–65, 71–73, 80, 84, 89, 96, 98, 100, 103–105, 128, 138–142, 150, 155–156, 165–169, 176, 252
regimes 2, 6, 24, 41, 50, 68, 93, 98, 101, 122, 124, 132, 207, 224
registration systems 105
regulation 1–2, 5–11, 13–20, 22–25, 39, 41, 44, 46, 50, 54, 56, 61, 66, 93–97, 100–105, 136–138, 148, 156, 162, 168–169, 171, 175, 207, 209, 212, 215, 233–234, 237, 261
regulatory agencies 1
relationships 3, 48, 52–55, 173–174, 190, 194, 208–209, 212–213, 220–221, 223–224, 243–245, 248, 250, 253, 260, 264, 266, 271–276, 280
reporting requirements 152
responsibility 3, 6, 9, 34, 48, 58–59, 63, 65, 72, 75–76, 78–79, 82, 85, 87, 101, 144, 161, 179–186, 190, 193, 203–204, 208–215, 219–221, 223–224, 243–254, 267
responsible government 71, 73, 75, 77–87, 89, 91
retention 2, 142–144, 155
revolving door 137, 156
Roman law 49–50, 59
rules 5–7, 11–17, 20, 22–25, 34, 37–38, 45–46, 52–57, 59, 75–76, 78, 87–88, 94, 97, 100–103, 106, 116, 119, 121–122, 136–137, 139, 144, 146, 148, 155, 212–215, 219, 224, 227, 229–230, 233–234, 237, 266

sanctions 7, 45–48, 56, 99, 104, 116, 152, 158
scandal 8, 13–14, 16–17, 20, 29, 32, 34, 36–41, 60, 62, 72–73, 77, 85, 88–89, 96, 100–102, 119, 123, 138–142, 148–149, 156, 162, 165, 168, 176, 228
Senate 24, 40, 73, 89, 98, 100, 102, 114, 130, 142, 151, 157–158, 161, 164, 166–167, 172, 222, 245, 254
social construction 13, 259
Spain 2, 44, 50–51, 65
stakeholders 191, 194, 197, 199
sting 38, 140, 156, 161, 163, 165
sting operations 140, 163

tangentopoli 62
term limits 113–114, 121, 132, 160–161, 173
Tom DeLay 145
training 2, 45–46, 139, 156, 171, 192, 196–197, 214, 224, 269, 280
transparency 32, 41, 44, 61, 63, 66, 105, 107, 148, 151
Transparency International 32

U.S. Congress 2, 6, 30, 84, 138, 144
U.S. inspector 121

UK 2, 44, 46, 49–51, 54–55, 57, 59–60, 65, 93–96, 100–106
United States v. Brewster 94
US 189, 205

values 2–3, 45–47, 49, 65–66, 101, 150, 171, 180, 188, 207, 211, 229, 236, 238–239, 241, 246–247, 271–273
virtue 2, 74, 87, 111, 113, 116, 118, 141, 150–151, 174, 180, 204, 213, 241, 246–247, 252–253, 263–264

vocation 214, 217–218, 246–247, 249, 252

Watergate 11, 16, 34, 38–40, 72, 136, 140, 146, 149, 155, 176
welfare state 14–15, 44
Westminster 9, 77, 79, 81, 85, 99, 106, 220
Wicks Committee 93–94, 97, 102
World Bank 31–32

Zen 259, 263–267, 275, 278

SET UP A CONTINUATION ORDER TODAY!

Did you know that you can set up a continuation order on all Elsevier-JAI series and have each new volume sent directly to you upon publication? For details on how to set up a **continuation order**, contact your nearest regional sales office listed below.

To view related series in Business & Management, please visit:

www.elsevier.com/businessandmanagement

The Americas
Customer Service Department
11830 Westline Industrial Drive
St. Louis, MO 63146
USA
US customers:
Tel: +1 800 545 2522 (Toll-free number)
Fax: +1 800 535 9935
For Customers outside US:
Tel: +1 800 460 3110 (Toll-free number).
Fax: +1 314 453 7095
usbkinfo@elsevier.com

Europe, Middle East & Africa
Customer Service Department
Linacre House
Jordan Hill
Oxford OX2 8DP
UK
Tel: +44 (0) 1865 474140
Fax: +44 (0) 1865 474141
eurobkinfo@elsevier.com

Japan
Customer Service Department
2F Higashi Azabu, 1 Chome Bldg
1-9-15 Higashi Azabu, Minato-ku
Tokyo 106-0044
Japan
Tel: +81 3 3589 6370
Fax: +81 3 3589 6371
books@elsevierjapan.com

APAC
Customer Service Department
3 Killiney Road #08-01
Winsland House I
Singapore 239519
Tel: +65 6349 0222
Fax: +65 6733 1510
asiainfo@elsevier.com

Australia & New Zealand
Customer Service Department
30-52 Smidmore Street
Marrickville, New South Wales 2204
Australia
Tel: +61 (02) 9517 8999
Fax: +61 (02) 9517 2249
service@elsevier.com.au

30% Discount for Authors on All Books!

A 30% discount is available to Elsevier book and journal contributors on all books *(except multi-volume reference works)*.

To claim your discount, full payment is required with your order, which must be sent directly to the publisher at the nearest regional sales office above.